WOMEN UNDER SAIL

WOMEN UNDER SAIL

Letters and Journals concerning eight women travelling or working in sailing vessels between 1829 and 1949

BASIL GREENHILL and
ANN GIFFARD

DAVID & CHARLES : Newton Abbot

ISBN 0 7153 4997 X

For Nancie Villiers

Set in Ten on Twelve Point Press Roman
and printed in Great Britain
by Redwood Press Limited Trowbridge Wiltshire
for David & Charles (Publishers) Limited
South Devon House Newton Abbot Devon

Contents

List of Illustrations

A WOMAN OF CHARACTER UNDER SAIL AND STEAM

THE LAST WOMAN UNDER SAIL

PART 1

The Ships they Sailed in

Commentary

Three different sets of circumstances took women to sea. There were those who were able to travel at leisure as cabin passengers, those who had a job to do as wife or daughter of the captain of a merchant vessel or who worked their passage as stewardess and there were those un-named multitudes who were classed as emigrants and whose journeys seem to us unimaginably dreadful. These last, being mostly illiterate, have left few records but a good deal is known about conditions in the steerage from letters and journals written by cabin passengers. If it was so disagreeable to travel on an emigrant ship – 'Poor as I am,' wrote Jessie Campbell, 'no consideration on earth would tempt me to trust my little family in a ship with Highland emigrants if I still had the voyage before me' – what was it like for a woman to be one of these despised souls? Lack of privacy and inadequate sanitation must always affect women more than men, add to these discomforts the care of small children under cramped conditions, particularly in bad weather, seasickness, perhaps childbirth – there were six babies born in the steerage during the *Blenheim's* passage to New Zealand – or the illness and death of children, all these things taking place in an overcrowded, smelly, noisy, sometimes violently moving vessel without heating in the cold latitudes, without proper ventilation in the tropics, and you have a miserable maritime slum.

True, there were masters who did their best, like Captain Gray in the

Blenheim, to maintain some measure of hygiene and discipline, even to promote dancing and simple games for the emigrants. True, also that many of the craftsmen, labourers and small farmers who travelled with their families under these conditions had grown up inured to hardship. If you lived on 7s 6d a week in an earth-floored, one or two-roomed cottage, cooking your food on a fire in the middle of the floor, drawing your water from a stream or a well a quarter of a mile away, relieving yourself in a privy at the bottom of the garden, the conditions on an emigrant deck seemed not very much worse. Emigrants on the North Atlantic route and travelling to Australia and New Zealand lived in temporary communal dormitories, each family allocated a bunk, or perhaps two if there were more than two children. These temporary bunks built in space normally occupied by cargo, were generally in two tiers, one above the other. Sanitation consisted of buckets, sometimes fitted with seats. There were no special washing places. Hot food was slopped out rather than served, some might not get their breakfast until supper time, some lost their dinner in a storm — 'away sailed the carrots, beef coulli and etc... and provisions once served out could not be replaced.' Shortage of water for drinking and washing was another great hardship, often it came from the river in which the vessel happened to be anchored at the time of embarkation, it smelt foul and tasted worse. Even so, except in the years of the Irish famine, the death rate amongst people who travelled under these conditions was surprisingly low.

Most women are less adventurous, more stay-at-home creatures than men, even today. For very many the wrench of leaving home must have been far greater. They accompanied their husbands and children because conditions at home gave them no alternative — it was necessity rather than choice which drove them over the oceans. Added to the discomforts, there were the fears. Even cabin passengers were prey to these as Jessie so vividly described, her nerves shattered after the death of her child, 'I sometimes fear that the man at the helm is falling asleep and not steering, then that we have too much sail up and a squall will lay her on her beam ends, next I begin to smell fire...' Amongst the emigrants in their claustrophobic conditions, rumours were rife, superstitions abounded. They often had very little idea of what it would be like to live in the country to which they were bound. There was no question of trying it out for a few years and then returning. For many there would be better times eventually, land of their own, the freedom of working for themselves, good housing and a better climate. But this was all in the future, before they could farm their land it would have to be cleared, the trees not only cut down but the stumps painfully extracted, homes would have to be built and, if they were going to North America, enough fuel and food stored before the onset of winter. Some amongst them would weep every night from homesickness for the rest of their days. The passage was a traumatic experience and it was as final as death.

For women working at sea, the prospects were different. Those who worked their passage out knew that they could work it back or marry and settle down as Anne Stanley did, in the country of their choice. For Annie Slade, the early years were the hardest, after her efforts had set the little family on its feet, she could stay home, continue to act as business manager and let her eldest son take her place as crew. It was a tough life, going to sea in a small ketch with a baby in arms, being prepared to continue at the pump or to take a turn at the wheel long after the next meal should have been cooked and eaten. But late twentieth century woman who often works alongside her husband, living with their children in places which were once considered only suitable for men, is able to comprehend this kind of existence. It assumes a partnership in married life more common today than formerly.

More difficult to completely understand is not the great length of the passages but the general attitude to the dimension of time. Could we, who regard a few hours in a Bank holiday traffic jam or a night at an airport, fogbound, as ultimate frustration, adjust ourselves to five weeks spent battering down the Channel from Gravesend to the Bay of Biscay? How could we who fly faster than sound, cram an unplanned month in Madeira, another month in Cape Town, into a business trip to India? The unpredictable date of their arrival, the ubiquitous delays were taken for granted by all the passengers in this tiny sample; this uncertainty was, of course, at least doubled for their relations at home waiting for news. Noise was a cause of great stress, then as now. For cabin passengers and steerage alike in a sailing vessel it was unremitting. Sleep for the Johnstones was impossible because of the 'awful creaking of every part of the vessel, hollering of the sailors and roaring of the sea'. During the day time was added the 'dreadful noise and riot' created by the emigrant children.

Freed from most of the acute physical discomforts and dangers of the steerage, women cabin passengers had two main concerns, one following upon the other. The first can be summed up in a quotation from a

letter of advice written in 1852 by a New Zealand immigrant to her
sister who was to follow her: 'make as little acquaintance as you can
round the ship'. This led to the second, boredom, which Rachel
Henning believed made her sister ill and of which she wrote 'The voyage
is exactly what I expected: very tiresome, but bearable, like the other
wearinesses of life'. Although she was so concerned with social position
on her first voyage, seven years later in the *Great Britain* she had
mellowed considerably and although speaking disparagingly of 'the
commercials' she showed a great deal more interest in her fellow
passengers.

No cinema, no Gala Evenings, no swimming pools, how did they
spend their time on these long, long voyages? The reader can make a list
of pastimes, not so very different from those which helped to pass long
winter evenings in the country houses of Jane Austen. Reading, writing
journals, fortune-telling, 'working a chain', chess, cribbage, watching the
emigrants dancing or playing leap-frog were some of the things open to
women when they were not sewing or washing clothes or minding their
children. For many, dinner at 4 pm was 'the great event of the day'.
Sunday was very important with its attendant dressing up and a service
taken by whoever on board was best qualified. The more intelligent and
interested could, like Thomazene Williams, Annie Slade and Anne Stanley learn a great deal about navigation and sailing, or observe the natural
phenomena which are so much closer to you in a sailing vessel than in a
luxury liner.

In sailing vessels cabins were beneath the poop, the raised deck
stretching forward from the stern, and also sometimes in houses on the
poop deck such as Mary Molesworth's round-house in the *Lady Holland*.
The most fortunate passengers had stern cabins with windows but the
airiness and comfort of these in the tropics were scarcely compensated
for by the violent motion experienced in the extreme stern of the vessel
and the danger of water coming through the plugged and barricaded
windows in bad weather. The Johnstones were at sea for a month
before their stern deadlights were taken down 'which was a great
comfort'. The food provided for cabin passengers was good by the
standards of the times. They ate with the master and mates and their
enjoyment of the voyage depended to a large extent on the personalities
of these men. This comes out clearly in all the accounts of voyages, but
particularly in those of Mary Molesworth, who thoroughly disliked
Captain Snell, and Jessie Campbell who could not say enough for the
kindness of Captain Gray.

The livestock mentioned by most of our travellers, which was shipped on deck and which in the case of the *Arab* had to be replenished at Falmouth because so many had died in the storm coming down the Channel, was for the use of cabin passengers — emigrants lived on salt beef and barrelled pork. There was sometimes another kind of animal life on board — rats — and we have vivid descriptions of this nuisance written by Hannah   , who travelled Second Class to New Zealand in the *Zealandia,* 1165 tons, Captain G. Phillips, an iron clipper ship built in Glasgow in 1869. This diary, a copy of which is now in the National Maritime Museum, was sent to us by Mrs Francois of Nelson, New Zealand. The *Zealandia* left the East India Docks on April 16, 1884, and on Friday 2 May, Hannah wrote:

...at about 4.30 I heard a gentle rustling overhead. Presently I saw the cause of it! A monster rat jumped off Ruth's bunk. I was rather scared but felt determined to bear with his company if possible without waking anybody else, and I was rewarded by seeing him walk away without nibbling anything! But not until he had made a general survey of my bunk. He came on at my feet. I could feel his little scratching nails on my bare feet, and feared every moment that he would bite, but he walked in an orderly fashion up one side of me, looking about him. On crossing my pillow he was hindered by an entanglement in my hair, at which I felt it almost impossible to keep from screaming loudly. But to my great relief he soon released himself and walked in just as orderly fashion down the other side of me and out at a hole at the foot which he had previously made. It was a struggle for me to keep quiet. The perspiration was streaming off me like rain, but I was thankful I had courage to keep quiet ... sleep is precious these days with heat *and rats* combined.

Two months later Hannah was writing:

...Aroused at 7.30 after another very stormy night, and the rats were so troublesome. They were quarrelling and splashing about in the water, [which was eight inches deep in Hannah's cabin] making a dreadful noise all night ... our jackets are hung on the saloon wall, they get in the pockets of them and nibble our handkerchiefs ... They run up and down our dresses which are hanging on the wall, and over the top of the partition.'

The vessel of the 1830s and 40s was built of wood with wooden masts and spars and rigging principally of natural fibres. Her hull was full and round. She could sit almost bolt upright on the mud of a tidal harbour, her bows were blunt and she pushed a lot of the sea in front of her as she went through it. She had a square stern into which stern windows like those of HMS *Victory* still opened. She sailed slowly and she was very bad at sailing to windward. Her rigging, her wooden spars, her ironwork, required the constant attention of the skilled craftsmen who comprised much of her crew. On long passages with emigrants, any carpenters and blacksmiths among them sometimes helped too. Each mast was in three parts and faced by bad weather the crew sent the upper parts and the attendant spars to the deck, thus reducing the wind-resistance of the complex rigging and the turning moment of the weights far aloft.

Plate 1 shows the barque *Countess of Bective,* 329 tons, built at Sunderland in 1843, lying on the mud of Swansea harbour about 1845. Against the quay wall on her starboard side is the barque *Mary Dugdale,* built in Hull in 1835. These vessels resemble those in which the two young women made their interrupted journey to India, Jessie Campbell and her family their journey to settle in New Zealand, the Johnstones their wedding journey to Australia, and, as regards rigging and construction, Thomazene Williams' *Joseph Cunard.*

These ships were safe in skilled hands providing they were in good condition and well-maintained. They tended to ride like a cork in bad weather and on the great rollers of the southern ocean on the run from Cape Town to Australasia. All passages to Australia were made east about because of the impossibility of sailing against the prevailing winds westwards from Cape Horn. These full-hulled wooden vessels shipped little water and in a severe gale they could drift to leeward without harm for days on end. But they leaked continuously and required constant pumping. This was normal, and providing it did not become excessive, worried neither crew nor passengers. Jessie Campbell relates a humorous little anecdote about it in her entry of 10 December.

The skills practised by the crews are now completely lost, indeed almost incomprehensible. When these skills were lacking, or not properly employed because of bad manning or incompetent management by master and mates, or because of drink or inadequate diet, or if the vessels were not properly maintained, then the wooden square-rigged sailing ships of the first three-quarters of the nineteenth century were very dangerous vehicles. The flimsy fabric of their masts and rigging, the continuous fight against incoming water in the leaking hulls, rendered them vulnerable to the direst consequences from incompetent handling, from the failure of any part of their fabric not promptly made good, or from fire.

Another potential cause of disaster was always present. Navigation should have been an exact science by the mid-nineteenth century. An able shipmaster should have known his position day by day to within a few miles, should have checked it almost hour by hour if necessary. Indeed Captain Westmorland was proud to inform William and Matilda Johnstone after a nineteen week passage in the *Arab* exactly when they could expect to sight land. Captain Gray of the *Blenheim* was equally accurate. But all too often from failure to use the methods tested and proved since the 1770s when Captain James Cook had established their practicability, from carelessness in observation or calculation, from over-confidence or from laziness, masters and mates did not know the position of their vessel and found it, like the officers of the *Lady Holland*, violently and disastrously when they sought to make their landfall at the end of a passage. This state of affairs continued late into the century.

Many factors worked together to change the picture of the typical merchant vessel and the conditions of her passengers in the thirty years between 1850 and 1880 when the changes at sea, even in sailing ships, were as great as they were in air transport in the thirty years up to 1970. The first regular steam service across the North Atlantic was not started until half a century after the first successful experiments with steam propulsion and in 1837, the year before the Atlantic service was established, there were still only 624 vessels with steam machinery registered at all British ports. From these uncertain beginnings the steamer developed rapidly, especially after the introduction of the compound engine in the 1860s. Before this, the simple engines of steam vessels ate up prodigious amounts of coal and so sail was used whenever possible to assist them. This was the era of steam and sail so graphically illustrated by Rachel Henning's account of her voyages to Australia in the *Calcutta* and the wonderful *Great Britain,* the world's first large sea-going screw steamship and first large iron ship, still in existence in 1970.

Under the impetus of this competition and the effects of Britain's rapidly developing industrial structure, the builders and owners of large merchant-sailing vessels took to the new materials made available by late nineteenth century technology. First large parts of the rigging, then the hulls and finally the masts and spars were made of iron and in due course hulls and masts were made of steel. The result was the great

British square-rigged sailing ships and their German and French contemporaries, the 'windjammers' as they were later called, ships like Anne Stanley's *Passat* (Plate 23). These vessels survived at sea through the strength of their steel hulls, masts, yards and wire rigging. Their upper masts were not sent down in bad weather, the sails were furled along the tops of the yards and if this could not be done in time they blew into fragments, usually long before the immensely strong rigging was in danger. But like their delicate predecessors of the first half of the nineteenth century, they required immensely skilled crews, men with a specialised technical competence which now, only twenty years after the last commercial voyages, has been completely lost. The last voyages were made without skilled crews and this fact comes clearly out of Anne Stanley's narrative, the story of the last woman under sail.

The world of Annie Slade had covered a longer period. The small wooden vessels in and around which she spent her life were the heirs of the older carpenter and blacksmith technology of wood and hemp seafaring. Her schooners and ketches from the mid-nineteenth century took over the deep sea and coastal trades previously operated by the smaller wooden square-rigged ships and they remained in the ocean trade to North America and to the Mediterranean until after the First World War and in the coasting trade about Britain, almost incredibly, until 1960.

Two young women in a shipwreck

Commentary

Mary Molesworth was born in India on 8 February 1811. A daughter of Major General Arthur Molesworth of the East India Company's Service, who had spent much of his time in Madras, she was a descendant of an Irish peer. She was brought up in England, but, as was the custom then and for many generations afterwards, in her late teens she was sent back to India by her family, no doubt in the well-justified belief that her chances of an early and satisfactory marriage would be as good in the sub-Continent as anywhere.

Mary Molesworth's sister Gertrude had married Francis Lascelles of the Madras Civil Service, who was later to become a High Court Judge, and on 14 October 1829 when she was eighteen years old, Mary sailed with them from Portsmouth towards Madras in the merchant sailing vessel *Lady Holland*, Captain James Snell, a full-rigged ship of 405 tons owned by C. Joad & Co, which had been built on the Medway in the year of Mary's birth. Passengers on board the *Lady Holland* included Mary Anne Keble Saunders, aged twenty-five, who was going out to India to stay with a brother.

Since 1815 the East India Company had lost the monopoly of trade with the sub-Continent and was open to competition from privately-owned shipping. In 1826 and in 1827 the *Lady Holland* made round voyages to Calcutta from Britain on private account, she was not on charter to the East India Company. Captain Snell was appointed her

master in 1827. No portrait of the *Lady Holland* exists other than the
sketch made by Mary Molesworth when the vessel was lost (Plate 3).
But it is safe to say that the photograph of ships of much the same
size lying in Swansea in the early 1840s (Plate 1) gives a fair impression
of what she looked like.

The *Lady Holland* reached Madeira early in November 1829, and
while anchored there, was forced out to sea by bad weather, leaving
many of her passengers ashore. It was some weeks before she succeeded
in making her way back to the land. When she finally sailed she was in
company with HMS *Undaunted,* Captain A.W.J. Clifford, a forty-six
gun fifth rate built at Woolwich in 1807 and notable chiefly as the
vessel which took Napoleon to exile in Elba. Captain Clifford, who
later became a Baronet and a Companion of the Order of the Bath, had
been appointed to the *Undaunted* in 1827. He was made a Gentleman
Usher of the Black Rod in 1832 and had no further naval career of
note. A coloured engraving in the National Maritime Museum shows the
Undaunted lying in Barn Pool, Plymouth (Plate 2) during the five years
of Clifford's command.

On board the *Undaunted* was a midshipman named George Smythe
whose log of her voyage is also in the National Maritime Museum.
Smythe records that she lay in Madeira to a single anchor taking on
provisions from 2-5 December 1829, when she sailed 'taking under
convoy an English merchant ship bound for India'. Mary Molesworth's
account narrates that passengers from the *Lady Holland* spent 'some
very pleasant hours' on board the *Undaunted* at St Jago in the Cape
Verde Islands where the vessel lay at anchor for some days while
Captain Clifford collected the latest available information about the
local pirates. In fact Smythe's log shows that they lay there only one
full day, putting in on 13 December and leaving on 15th and Mary
Molesworth's clearly favourable impression of Captain Clifford was
almost certainly based on contact with him at dinner on 14 December.

Mary's record of the separation of the two vessels when 'we parted
from her, or rather lost her, while she was chasing a pirate or slave
vessel' is confirmed by George Smythe, who wrote of the incident
'22nd December am at 6 saw a vessel on larboard bow 6.30 beat to
musters and rounded to on the starboard tack lowered both cutters and
boarded the *Gallina* of Havana 8 mod cloudy last sight at convoy 11.30
up boats noon mod and fine made sail'.

The dramatic loss of the *Kent* in 1825, the story of which Lascelles
was reading to Mary and her companions in their cabin just before

their own vessel struck, was illustrated in two paintings by William Daniell, exhibited at the Royal Academy in 1825 and 26. She was an East Indiaman engaged in taking the 31st Regiment to India; while in the Bay of Biscay her cargo shifted, a cask of spirit burst near a lighted lamp and set her hold ablaze. A medal to commemorate the rescue of 547 people was later struck and presented to Captain William Cook and the crew of the 200 ton brig *Cambria* which took the survivors to Falmouth.

At 10 at night on 14 February, according to Mary Molesworth, and the night before in the account written by Mary Anne Saunders, the *Lady Holland* went ashore on Dassen Island, forty miles north of Cape Town. Her loss was the result of a navigational error of a type very common until well into the twentieth century. Although the ship's latitude, north and south, had always been known accurately in favourable weather from observations of the sun or stars, her longitude east and west had not been known accurately because of errors in the chronometers. These sea-going clocks, normally extremely accurate, enable the navigator by comparing the local time on shipboard, derived by observations of the sun or stars, with the time at a known meridian to which the chronometer has been set, to tell how far east or west he is of that meridian and therefore where he is east or west on the earth's surface. By the early nineteenth century a British vessel almost always used the time at the meridian running through the centre of a telescope (transit instrument) sited in the Old Royal Observatory building now part of the National Maritime Museum at Greenwich, London, England, because this was the time used in the *Nautical Almanac*.

Captain Snell knew that his chronometers were inaccurate ever since, as Mary Molesworth records, he had unsuccessfully attempted to make a landfall at the island of South Trinidad. Well over on the western side of the South Atlantic, this island seems to modern eyes a long way off the course from the Cape Verde Islands to Cape Town, but square-rigged sailing ships did not follow the shortest geographical - great circle - routes. Unlike modern racing dinghies, they were very bad at sailing close to the wind so that it was quicker and safer to sail with favourable winds many hundreds of miles round the areas of known adverse winds rather than to spend weeks attempting to sail against them.

Mary Saunders records that an observation had been taken at noon on the day of the wreck which established that 'we were then far from land'. What she had not learned in four months at sea was that this observation can only have fixed approximately the *Lady Holland's* latitude and that her position east and west, vital to a vessel approaching a coastline running north and south, must have been based partly on estimated distance and direction sailed and drifted over several weeks, and probably partly on lunar observations which Captain Snell should have been taking whenever opportunity offered. These measurements of the distance of the moon from certain stars, followed by laborious calculations lasting sometimes for several hours, gave even an expert navigator a longitude position much less accurate than that of a chronometer (if that were accurate) and never accurate enough for approaching an unlit coast, as was disastrously proved not only by the *Lady Holland* because she stranded only a few hours later but many times in the late eighteenth and in the nineteenth centuries. But it was the only 'observed' position available when chronometers failed. Captain Snell probably made an error in a delicate observation or in a long and complex calculation or both. But his fundamental error was to hold on his course under a considerable amount of sail and strong breeze when he was approaching an unlit coast at night and not completely certain of his position.

Though the vessel was a total loss, all the passengers and crew were landed on Dassen Island, an achievement which may be taken to indicate a high degree of professional efficiency on the part of Captain Snell, the mates and crew. The wreck took place late on Saturday and with the exception of Captain Snell, the two mates and two men who remained to salve what they could, all were taken off Dassen Island the following Tuesday morning by HMS *Falcon*, Captain H.G. Colpoyse, which had come up from Cape Town after the doctor's arrival there with news of the wreck.

Captain Snell may have been rough by Mary Molesworth's standards and his arrogance not justified in her eyes by his social origins, but the handling of the wreck situation suggests that Mary Saunders' assessment of him as a man who inspired confidence is nearer the mark. For all its interest and the considerable ability of the writer, Mary Molesworth's account of the wreck is the less convincing. One feels she wished to provide her readers with the maximum excitement to talk about. She attributes the saving of the long boat to Lascelles, but Mary Saunders simply records that 'one of the sailors dashed into the water and caught the rope just in time to save it'. If Lascelles had been responsible it is scarcely likely that she would not have learned of it. Moreover, had the long boat been in so bad a state as Mary Molesworth represents it could scarcely have made repeated journeys to the wreck during the next two days.

Dassen Island was described in 1930 by the naturalist Cherry Kearton in his book *The Island of Penguins*. He found the skeletons of four whales there, took a photograph of a fin bone such as Mary Molesworth and her companions used for a tent and wrote, in a chapter called *Storms*, 'It is because of these constant south-westerly winds that the seas are rougher and the coast is rockier on the western side of the Island. It is on that side that ships have often been wrecked: a piece of metal casing from one of them lies on the part of the island now, and two penguins habitually rear their families in it!'

HMS *Falcon*, which Mary Molesworth described as 'the smallest sized King's ship, only two guns', was in fact a ten gun brig, built at Pembroke in 1820. Some claim to fame rests in her conversion as an experimental steam vessel in 1833. She was sold out of the Navy in the late 1830s.

At Cape Town, Mary Molesworth and her party remained for a month. They were fortunate to secure an onward passage to Madras in the bark *William Glen Anderson*, Captain McMillan. She was a barque of 392 tons built at Richibucto, New Brunswick, Canada, in July 1827 by R. & J. Jardine. Owned in Britain, she was bound for Bombay at the time the shipwrecked party came into Cape Town, so Mary Molesworth's statement that Lascelles 'chartered' her is scarcely acceptable as it stands. In fact he procured her diversion to Madras *en route* for Bombay and probably had to pay at a high rate for it.

In August 1830 Mary Molesworth sent her account of the voyage and loss of the *Lady Holland* home in the *Alfred*, whose Devonshire master, Captain Thirsk, took personal charge of the letter to her father who had retired and was living in Exeter. Mary Anne Saunders had already written a long account of the wreck to her brother Robert which she sent home from Cape Town in late February. Written by young women of very different personalities, these accounts reveal much of their authors' social attitudes. We have already commented on the few significant discrepancies.

The *Alfred* in the care of whose master Mary Molesworth sent her letter was a very fine full-rigged ship of over 700 tons built in India of teak in 1818 and sheathed with copper against tropical and other marine wood borers. The *Childe Harold* by which Mary Saunders sent her news, was also a full-rigged ship, built in 1825 in Ipswich and engaged in trade between Britain, Mauritius and Bombay. Her master was Captain W.W. West.

Neither of these young women passengers seems to have learned anything of the technicalities of sailing ship handling and navigation. In this they resembled the modern traveller by sea or by air but with a great deal less excuse. During their cramped four months in the *Lady Holland* the minimum of intelligent interest in their environment could have taught them a great deal about ships and the sea. Mary Molesworth was used to a narrow social circle but in the 1820s no amount of protection could save a young child from exposure to a great deal of what we should now call horrors, especially in India, and the casualness with which Mary writes of the wrecks at Funchal and of her cabin mate's death (although she composes a sentimental poem she does not even mention the young woman's burial) is an indication that she was relatively immune to what would now be considered traumatic experiences. But she clearly retreated from the inevitable squalors of the *Lady Holland* into an exaggerated regard for her brother-in-law and an unreal disdain of Captain Snell, whose responsibilities as a merchant shipmaster engaged in long range trade before the development of any means of communication faster than his own vessel were much greater than most people are asked to undertake today. Nevertheless, Mary Molesworth's letter is valuable and interesting for the human weaknesses and character it reveals. She was an able and energetic creature, very self-assured for eighteen, even at a time when the expectation of life was such that people matured early. But Mary Saunders was the more realistic of the two.

A year later Mary Molesworth married Nathaniel William Kindersley, Principal Collector of Tanjore, who was seventeen years older than herself and a widower with two sons. He was a competent administrator, a district rather than a secretariat man, and they appear to have been a happily married couple. She bore him five sons and two daughters and she has numerous descendants alive today. It is from the widow of one of them, Mrs Tom Maurice of Marlborough, that we obtained the copy of Mary's letter from which the present transcription was made. Mrs Maurice, in her late eighties at the time of writing, has strong recollections of two of Mary's children. One of them, Mary Agnes Kindersley, Mrs Maurice's mother-in-law, bore and raised thirteen children. She was a very small person as Mary herself is reported to have been. She died in 1919, ninety years after her mother's shipwreck.

Mary Anne Saunders married Auguste le Gonès in 1840. She had three children of whom one, Marie Louise Keble, born in 1842, lived into the present century. Her letter to her brother Robert passed through the Saunders family to Lady Roome, a great-great niece of Mary Anne, by whose kindness we were allowed to reproduce it here.

Letter from Mary Molesworth, August 1830

My dear Papa,

I feel assured you will read with pleasure a narrative of our voyage to India, which I have endeavoured to draw up; and knowing you and Mama, with the dear little family circle, will be interested to hear all the particulars, I have given you a detailed account of our singular career these last twelve months since we left the shores of 'dear old England'. I intended to have it sent sooner, but various circumstances occured which prevented its being despatched. I have, at last, however, found a good opportunity in Captain Thirsk, of the *Alfred,* who resides at Chudleigh, and he has been kind enough to promise me to have it forwarded from thence to Exeter. The *Alfred* sails on the 15th. I am therefore unable to send some sketches which I took from Dassen Island, and which I hoped to have finished, but I enclose you parts of two rough sketches taken on the spot.

On 14 October 1829 we sailed from Portsmouth, but did not succeed in clearing the Channel before the 31st; soon after which we ran against a large vessel in a fog; it was a complete wreck; all hands seemed to have perished.

Our voyage was as monotonous as most others until the 17th November, when we arrived at Madeira, where we were obliged to remain one month, occasioned by our ship having been blown out to sea in a storm. Most of the passengers were fortunately on shore. During this storm we witnessed two ships dashed to pieces, and only three hands saved. So completely dashed to pieces were they against the rocks that many persons who came down to render assistance could perceive no remnants of them, except what was floating in small fragments on the sea, or had been thrown on the beach below. The people on the island were standing within fifty yards of one of those ships when she struck on the rocks; it was blowing a gale, and except in the case of our own shipwreck I never witnessed such a scene. We

could distinctly see the distracted countenances of the poor sufferers as
they clung to the rigging, their faces turned to the rocks on which their
ship was dashing, every wave covered the greatest part of the ship,
striking from the deck the sailors on board, each wave leaving still
fewer, until the strength of the strongest gave way to the force of the
water, and the ship was soon after dashed to pieces. Here and there we
could perceive a poor fellow struggling with the waves to reach a
floating spar or cask, but the water breaking over him hid him from our
sight and launched him into eternity.

We were sufficiently near to throw a rope over the bowsprit, which
was the means of saving three sailors.

The island of Madeira was in a wretched state. Popery in full vigour,
and the Government most arbitrary; An attempt was made while we
were there to poison the troops by putting poison into their bread. It
was fortunately discovered before many suffered, but it tended much
to irritate the already insolent soldiery. The baker was accused and
tried by the Inquisition, but nothing was extorted from the poor
sufferer.

The climate of Madeira, however, is delightful. The myrtle, the
geranium, the rose, and the violet grow in all the prodigality of
primitive nature on the borders of the narrow horse paths (you can
hardly call them roads), being narrow paved passes through the vine-
yards and the mountains.

The town of Funchal stretches along the margin of the bay for
more than a mile. It strikes an English eye as being the centre of filth,
although it is by no means so dirty as the Portuguese like. The English
residents are so influential there, that they have been able to exercise a
tyranny of cleanliness which the natives sullenly endure at the hazard
of catching cold.

We visited every part of the island on horseback, the only mode of
conveyance made use of except a very disagreeable kind of palenkeen,
the hills being too steep to admit of wheel carriages.

When you intend to make an excursion at Madeira you send a
servant to the corner of the street to summon the muleteers, at which
down come scampering the crowd of boys, mules, horses, and ponies,
and a regular fight commences. Often when you are getting up on one
horse, the bridles of two or three others are put into your hand. At
last when you are seated, the *vara* in hand, and all ready, the muleteer
catches hold of the tail by the left hand and begins to goad the flanks
of the animal with a small pike in the right, shouting 'cava, cava,

cavache, caval,' and away they go at full speed up the pebble-paved streets.

The greatest sight on the island, perhaps one of the greatest in the world is the awful *Corral*. We visited this place, and I will endeavour to give you a description of it, although a pen of more descriptive powers than mine is needed to give you any idea of the scenery. We had to ride miles into the interior of the island. The road was a steep ascent almost the whole way; at first winding under traceries of vines and among groves of oranges and lemons. At length we came in sight of a valley which was luxuriantly carpeted with heaths and furze, intermixed with violets and geraniums. The ends of the valley closed up with mountains round which our road lay, and hard work it was for our horses to pick their steps through the masses of granite of various kinds, that were lying in all directions. We rode round one mountain and over another until we attained the top, when we were suddenly surprised by the unexpected scene so immediately before us - an enormous chasm opened of some miles in length, and about 4000 feet in depth; the bottom was a narrow plain, with a river running through it, and in the centre of this plain there was a Nunnery with its chapel. Right opposite, the rocks rose perpendicularly and shot into the sky in tottering precipices. At first the clouds lay motionless below, then rapidly careering amongst the craggy pinnacles sometimes entirely buried them, and then descending again revealed the stupendous mass piercing the heavens.

Lascelles and another gentleman scrambled a great way up one of these pinnacles, much to our tremor below, and one of the clouds I before mentioned came sweeping along and quite hid them from our sight - it had an exceeding grand effect. They seemed to have been walking or rather gliding down through the sky and appeared to be looking over the highest cloud. We wandered about for some hours. Unfortunately we had neither paper nor pencil to take a view, having forgotten them, but we were fortunate with our cold dinner, which the refreshing air of the mountains and our long ride gave us a great *gout* for, and we soon despatched Mrs Gordon's savoury pies, fowls, etc, which in no small measure relieved the porters, whom we sent away like AEsop with nothing but empty bottles and baskets to carry home.

We left Madeira on 4th December, and were convoyed by HM Ship *The Undaunted* (Capt Clifford) to the Line. On board this ship we passed some very pleasant hours while at St Jago, one of the Cape Verde Islands, where we were anchored for some days in order that Capt Clifford might make every inquiry respecting pirates with which these sea are so infested.

St Jago is a convict island where there is a poor miserable English Consul, who has not another European to open his lips to, as very few ships ever touch there except pirates.

The Island is very barren, but produces great quantities of the finest oranges and other tropical fruits. It is also famous for turkeys of a prodigious size. There are very few inhabitants, and the few that there are are a set of wretched negroes. I believe they had never seen a European lady before we landed, and when our boats arrived they all came running down to see us, staring as if they were half afraid of us, and whenever we approached near to them they ran away laughing in the wildest manner. They have so little communication with any other part of the world that the use of money is hardly known, and they have refused it for their goods. They prefer to barter their fruit, etc, for knives, empty bottles, and the oldest clothes or bits of canvas.

Lascelles accompanied Capt Clifford on a visit to the British Consul and the Governor of the Island. These two authorities amused them with numerous anecdotes regarding the pirates. I recollect one which we had from Capt Clifford at dinner on board the *Undaunted*.

It appeared that a short time before we arrived at St Jago, a celebrated Captain of a pirate vessel - I forget his name - put into port and demanded of the Governor *fifteen of the convicts to man his ship*. The Governor very properly refused to comply with so impudent a request, but the pirate was resolved on recruiting from among these sons of atrocity, and therefore landed his men, determined upon taking by force what was refused him, and the Governor knowing that the convicts were all anxious to join the Corsair, and not being able to resist, was forced quietly to witness the convicts paraded and *thirty* instead of fifteen of the most active and desperate were selected to

'Gaze where some distant sail a speck supplies
With all the thirsting eye of enterprise,
To tell the tale of many a night of toil,
And marvel where they next shall seize a spoil.'

The Undaunted had been ordered out to search for pirates. We were therefore very grateful for the protection. It also broke in some measure the monotony of board ship, for she used sometimes to sail quite close alongside of us, and occasionally the band played, which we could distinctly hear, and which had a very sweet effect upon the water. We parted from her, or rather lost her, while she was chasing a pirate or slave vessel, and not long after we fell in with a suspicious-looking vessel. Oh! What I would have given that day to have *The Undaunted* with us. All were preparing for action, there was great bustle and confusion. The ladies were to have been placed down in the hold, and the gentlemen kept at their quarters (I think many of the former were as much alarmed as they were at the shipwreck.) We now regretted much having refused Capt Clifford's kind offer of a passage back to England in *The Undaunted*, which he made us in consequence of his perceiving the very unpleasant circumstances we were placed in on board the *Lady Holland*, occasioned by our having a *very disagreeable* Commander. (You may form some idea of his character when I tell you that in consequence of some slight misunderstanding between him and a young officer at the cuddy table he threw two full bottles of wine at the gentleman's head, and nearly killed him.)

Fortunately for us a calm came on, and in less than twenty-four hours a breeze having settled in in our favour, we were soon completely out of sight of our supposed enemy.

About this time we had a great trial in the illness and sudden death of a young lady on board. I dare say you remember a Miss Nash who shared the cabin with me, and whom Lascelles had promised to take care of during the voyage. She was a very sweet girl; circumstances had made her peculiarly dear to us, her mild and amiable disposition was developed in every action, and was seen in her handsome and contented countenance. We found great pleasure in each other's society, and she used frequently to talk in great delight of meeting a favourite sister in India - but consumption, that fatal canker-worm of youth, carried her off when she had just completed her nineteenth year. She had been ill with a cough for a few weeks, which the medical men (there were. two very clever on board) apprehended from the first was consumptive, but they did not suppose it would have been so rapid or fatal as it proved. Being of a rather full habit, she burst a blood-vessel from the force of coughing, and the bursting of a second (notwithstanding every precaution) carried her off in the middle of the night - I trust to one of the Mansions of bliss which Christ has prepared for them that love Him. For some weeks before her death the Doctors had ordered me not to sleep in the same cabin with her. I was therefore not with her when she died. She could not speak after the vessel burst and only breathed a few minutes.

> 'My lost companion, my dear friend, adieu,
> Your toils, your pains, your dangers are no more.
> The tempest now may howl unheard by you,
> While surges drive our trembling ships on shore.

Oh! happier thou escaped to endless rest
Than those who still survive to err and weep,
Since grief and pain and sorrow still molest
Thy wandering shipmate on the faithless deep.

Unfelt by you, hot Afric's sun may send
His scorching powers on earth, with baneful heat,
On you the blast surcharged with showers of sand,
From 'Dassen's desert isle' shall never beat.

The rolling surf against that rock-bóund isle
Has dash'd our ship to pieces on its coast,
Unseen, unheard, by you alone of all,
For thou, my friend, art breathless, lifeless, lost!!!'

I may now place our shipwreck, and as this will interest you, I will give you a more detailed account of it.

On 14th February we were endeavouring to make the Cape of Good Hope, but the wind being contrary we were obliged to tack, hoping however to reach the Cape in two days. The 14th was a fine day, the breeze was fresh and all sails set. During the evening Lascelles had been reading to us in our cabin the narrative of the *Kent* East Indiaman, while the rest of our party were working, which was the general way we spent our monotonous evenings on board. At 10 o'clock, the hour for retiring to rest, Lascelles had just finished the narrative, and while we were standing taking leave for the night, and making observations on the dreadful state of suffering which all must have experienced on board the *Kent*, we were alarmed by the Captain calling 'Helm hard down, Breakers ahead'. We rushed towards the cuddy, but before we reached it - it was only a few yards, our cabin being the round-house, - the ship struck, running seven knots an hour. Everything was thrown from its place, and in less than ten seconds the cuddy was full of the passengers. Many of them had retired to rest, but the shock had awoke and alarmed them.

Broken bottles and glasses, chairs and books covered the floor, while about thirty persons - half of whom were ladies disturbed from their sleep - stood looking at each other with distracted countenances.

Some of the gentlemen had gone on deck in hopes of being able to render assistance, but there was, if possible, more confusion there than in the cuddy, and they soon found that no assistance of theirs could be of much use. We found ourselves surrounded by large rocks, which the sea, breaking over, occasionally hid from our sight. We only knew we were on the African coast, and believed ourselves north of St Helena's

Bay, among the savage tribes of that inhospitable region, but as our chronometers had been proved to be incorrect from our having endeavoured and not being able to make the coast of Trinidad, this was all conjecture. It was the opinion of all that the ship could not hold together many minutes, for the waves were washing over her, and she appeared to have rested on a rock, which was breaking her up. We rolled much upon this rock, and saw that if the ship worked off we would immediately founder as we had deep water on each side of her.

To cut away the masts, or lower down the long-boat, was the first disputed point on deck. The Captain had lost all authority over his men. Some were so hardened that they went below-stairs and, opening the lockers, began plundering them of spirits. Providentially, however, some were steady, and the masts were cut away. They fell on the deck with all the sails set, rendering the ship a complete wreck, having broken everything that came in their way. I can only compare the breaking of the masts and yards to a long and loud peal of thunder, which having struck the ship was tearing her to pieces.

The ladies went to the lower deck until the masts fell, for there was some apprehension that they might have gone through the upper deck in falling. While there we joined in prayer to the Lord to protect us, and those lines of Newton's came with great comfort to my mind:-

'Incarnate God, the soul that knows
Thy Name's mysterious powers,
Shall dwell in undisturbed repose,
Nor dread these trying hours.'

We again got on deck. The moon enabled us to see the deplorable state of the ship; it also showed us that land was very near, although it was impossible for any boat to reach the shore in sight.

About this time I went down to my cabin to endeavour to save any little trinkets I had about my person by putting them into my pocket. I succeeded in saving my watch, and dear Mama's hair necklace, which she gave me on leaving France, and also that little ring which was the joint present of the four darling children, and which was so valuable to me, having their hair in it.

I also took the opportunity of locking my boxes, and taking away the keys, for seeing the system of plundering that was going on, I knew that if there was a chance of saving anything afterwards, the boxes would be better locked. Gertrude put into her bag a few small trinkets, but forgot her diamond ring, which was the most valuable article she had. Lascelles prepared two guns to put in the boat, partly in case of our landing among savages, and also to kill game. This was all he saved when he left the ship, except his watch.

The two small boats were now lowered down, and one was sent to find a place to land at, the other was stationed with sailors in it at a short distance from the side of the ship to be able to render assistance if necessary.

In order to make the wreck roll less, everything that could be moved from the deck was thrown overboard and after our guns had gone through their last duty of firing signals of distress, they were also rolled over.

It is impossible for me to give you an adequate idea of the state of distraction we felt when the ship was dashing to pieces amongst the rocks. We were lying about thirty yards out of a heavy surf, and each swell lifted up the ship and let her fall with such violence as almost to throw us off our feet.

Perceiving that the ship's back was broken, and that she would soon divide and probably founder, every exertion was made by all hands to launch the lifeboat over the side of the ship. With much difficulty and labour this was accomplished at twelve o'clock, but the boat was in such a state, the falling masts having broken her sides, and from having been long exposed to the sun that it was not expected it could swim. They had filled up many of the cracks with candles and tallow, but were afraid these would soon be washed out by the sea. Two men were put into her to bale out the water with which she began to fill immediately on being let down - but when they had only begun a wave struck the ship and tore the long-boat from her side. ALL HOPES of being saved were now given up, and the Captain *bursting into tears retired to the poop*. From this time he gave up giving orders. *This indeed was a trying moment. All* were alarmed at the sad news! We had a Missionary on board of the Kirk of Scotland and he proposed all hands being assembled to prayers, which many acquiesced in, and we gathered in the cuddy and resigned ourselves to the Lord.

In the heat of the battle I believe it is possible to forget death, but the cool and protracted hours of a shipwreck (as it is beautifully expressed in the Retrospect) 'there is often nothing to engage the mind but the recollections of tried and unsuccessful labours and the sight of increasing and unavoidable harbingers of destructions; it is not easy to forget ourselves in a future state.' I have, often been surprised at the cool collectedness of many when I have been reflecting on our

peculiarly trying situation. Dear Gertrude spoke feelingly of her little
Mary, [her daughter left in England] left, as we thought she would be
soon, an orphan. Another lady, when the ship's rudder was torn off
and the water began to rush in, spoke of an only child she had left in
England. All seemed to have some strong tie they thought of as much
as of their own suffering, and you, my dear Papa and Mama, were
indeed often present in my thoughts as Gertrude and I clung to poor
Lascelles, for we were resolved not to part on any account.

While we were at prayers an idea struck Lascelles, who was outside
the cuddy, that the long-boat might yet be saved. Not a moment was to
be lost; twice the breakers had broken over her and hidden her from
their sight.

He rushed up to the poop where he remembered having seen the
log-line lying, and throwing it into the little boat on the lee side of the
ship, it was conveyed by it to the long-boat when she was within twenty
yards of a rock on which a tremendous surf was breaking, and Lascelles
having kept hold of one end of the log-line, the long-boat was soon
pulled alongside of the ship, amidst the loud and hearty cheers of some,
and whilst the silent tear was dropped by some in gratitude to Almighty
God for this singular mercy.

This was pleasing intelligence to those in the cuddy, immediately
after rising from their knees, at the time we had no hopes of being
saved. It at least mitigated our fears, although we could see that to get
into the long-boat was little better than getting out of one wreck into
another.

Nothing could exceed the exertions made by Capt Story of the
Madras Infantry, and Lascelles during this trying period; their great
presence of mind and active exertions cheered us all.

Buonaparte had the credit of saying there was only one step from
the sublime to the ridiculous, and we had rather a ludicrous illustration
of this the night of our shipwreck.

Capt Story, while the alarmed ladies were deploring their situation,
came running into the cuddy requesting of them to bring him a knife.
All ran to find one, supposing it was to cut a rope or some part of the
rigging, but upon the knife being produced, he requested the next one
to him to cut off the skirts of his coat, finding them, I suppose an
annoyance in his labours - his request was immediately put into
execution by the trembling 'fair one' with great eagerness, as if the
safety of the ship depended on it, and Captain Story escaped as if
relieved of a burden, leaving the skirts of his coat in the hands of the

1 The *Countess of Bective* and the *Mary Dugdale* in Swansea Harbour in about 1845. These vessels resemble those in which the women travelled whose passages are described in Parts 2, 3 and 4 of this book

2 *HMS Undaunted*, Captain A.W.J. Clifford, which escorted the *Lady Holland* from Madeira to beyond the Cape Verde Islands where 'we parted from her, or rather lost her, while she was chasing a pirate or slave vessel'

lady.

The ship was by this time fast going to pieces, and the little boat that was sent to discover a landing-place not having returned, it was therefore proposed to put the ladies into the long-boat and anchor it at a short distance from the ship. The swell breaking over the quarter-deck made them anxious to place the ladies out of the wreck, but how to accomplish this appeared difficult.

The deck was covered with the masts, yards, and sails of the main and mizzen masts, which having fallen against each other much lumbered the ship, and the surf increasing and breaking on the quarter-deck, it was with much difficulty and danger that even the gentlemen could scramble over the ruins. It was therefore deemed impracticable to put us into the boat from the deck. The plan of leaving the wreck before daylight was opposed by the Captain, for his opinion was that the boat could not be 'kept alive'. It was, however, at last agreed upon that the ladies should be put out of a port-hole and carried along the side of the ship until they reached the stern, when a rope was to be placed round their waists and they were to be lowered into the long-boat. The small boat was stationed by the long-boat to assist in saving any person that might fall into the water during this critical operation. Gertrude was the first to be put down, and all remained in breathless anxiety to learn when she was seated in the long-boat. This was the first time we had been separated since the ship struck, and when left alone, although it was only for a few minutes, for I soon followed, I cannot tell you how desolate I felt. We were received by Lascelles on the outside of the ship. He had nothing to walk upon for ten or twelve yards but a narrow ledging not more than three or four inches in breadth. (I am not conversant, as you may perceive, with marine language, but perhaps even if I was, it would be as unintelligible to you as it has often been to me on board ship). I believe, however, the ledging I allude to is called the 'Ship's Bends'. Assisted by a rope, my dear brother and sister reached the stern, and after having been bound round by a rope, she was safely landed in the boat. All the ladies in like manner left the ship, only some, on being lowered down, missed the boat and reached the water and had to be dragged in, in the best ways practicable under the circumstances.

One of those who fell into the sea was Capt Story's wife. I before mentioned his name. I never saw his courage fail until that trying moment when he thought he saw his wife sinking for ever beneath his eyes.

However, we were all safely handed into the boat in about an hour, during which time the long-boat had nearly been swamped several times by the wreck rolling over when it had been brought near to receive the ladies. Just as we were all in with three gentlemen (the only married men on board), the little boat, sent to discover a landing-place, returned and delighted us with their report, which was that about three miles to the westward there was a safe landing-place. That the land we saw was Dassen Island, about twelve miles from Saldanha Bay and forty miles north of the Cape of Good Hope. That there were no inhabitants on the Island, it being quite a desert, but that they had met three or four men who came there occasionally from the Cape for the purpose of catching seals and collecting the eggs of the penguins and other birds, and who, having been roused by the signal guns, had come down to the shore, and that these men would give us the use of their hut, which was the only habitation on the Island.

This news was altogether cheering to us, and we as had got the boat full of all the ladies (fourteen in all, three gentlemen, two sailors, a box of biscuits, two double-barrelled fowling-pieces, and some powder and shots), we left the wreck - towed by the boat which had just returned and stood away for the west side of the Island.

From the rapid manner in which the boat was filling with water, the distance we had to go and the very slow pace at which we moved, many of us wished ourselves again on the wreck, but this was not a time for standing idle. Excepting two hands employed at the only two oars we could make use of, all were engaged in throwing out of the long-boat the water which was coming in, in every quarter. This was done with a set of japanned dish-covers, the only articles at hand when we left the wreck, and which were thrown into the boat out of the cuddy just as we were setting off, and with these we baled away and succeeded in keeping the boat from sinking, but still we were knee-deep in water. We had wrapped round us blankets or any other warm clothing we could find on leaving the wreck, but they were soon so wet that we took them off and endeavoured to fill up some of the leaks with them - by this means we were able to prevent an increase of water. For two hours we were kept in this state before we reached the land. There was a very cold wind blowing, but the state of suspense and anxiety we were in prevented us from feeling the great annoyance we should otherwise have done from the wet and cold, and gratitude to God for having done so much for us in having answered our prayers by giving us the means of being saved, assisted in keeping those who were stayed on Him 'in that peace of mind that passeth all understanding.' We left the wreck about two o'clock and it was near four when we approached the land.

The moon was a great comfort to us, it enabled us to see some men on the Island, warning us to avoid the place we were making for, and pointing to us a spot where we could run our shattered sinking boat.

We were now soon released from our wet and perilous situation, and the fishermen conducted us to their hut and gave us as hospitable reception as their uncouth manners would permit.

I stop here for a moment to recall to my recollection this habitation and since I cannot with a pencil delineate its interior I must endeavour to do so with a pen.

It in many respects resembles the account I have so often heard dear Arthur and Selina read you of Robinson Crusoe's abode on his desert island.

It was constructed of bones of whales and shells and covered in with turf. There was a little lamp burning on one side, which threw a dim light on us as we crept in and made us appear more ghastly than our fright had already done. The walls were covered in with half-dried seal and rabbit skins, which with the bad oil in the lamp can easily be fancied not to emit a very refreshing smell.

Fishing tackle, tobacco pouches, and an old torn garment took up one corner, another was occupied by a rude image of the Virgin Mary, and it seemed to be the favourite retreat of all the vermin in the Island. It only contained ten persons in a sitting position, but so exhausted were we that some of us rested and even slept until daybreak. The boats returned to the wreck to bring off the remainder of the passengers and crew.

How true it is that 'they who go down to the sea in ships and occupy their business in great waters see the works of the Lord and His wonders in the deep', and also that as there is little to break the monotony of the surrounding scene, a state of mind is produced - from the temporary absence of all wordly scenes and employments - peculiarly adapted to receive strong and lasting impressions. So much is this the case, that I have before me the whole scene. Six hours only have elapsed since we had been employed in working and reading in our cabin, our vessel had struck on a rock and had become a total wreck, we had been out at sea in an open frail boat, had landed on a desert island, and we were now sitting in a dark miserable hovel as wet as could be, talking of the past occurrences, but I have not room in a letter to relate one half of the many little circumstances that occurred.

As soon as the day began to dawn we walked out and found the Island covered with hares and penguins, so much so that I do not think the Island could afford three square yards to each animal. The former were so tame that we could have caught any number of them. We walked to the side of the Island where the wreck was lying, and could approach within three hundred yards of it, but between us there lay large rocks on which a heavy surf was breaking, rendering all communication extremely dangerous. We saw the remaining part of the passengers and the crew standing on the poop anxiously waiting the return of the boats which were bringing a party on shore. The swell had in some degree subsided, and the day was fine; there was therefore little apprehension that the ship would go to pieces before night.

About eight o'clock we returned to our encampment and found that several of our fellow passengers had landed and had brought with them some biscuits and a ham; the biscuits at first brought off had been spoiled by the water in the boat, as was also the gunpowder. We had no means of boiling the ham, having no cooking utensils, and there was not a drop of fresh water on the Island except a small quantity which the fishermen had brought from the Cape and which they shared very sparingly amongst us. The only food we had this day was ham half broiled and seaweed and a little biscuit, both of which were bitter and bad.

Lascelles, assisted by the fishermen, made a sort of tent of the ribs of an enormous whale which had been thrown up by the sea, apparently some time before, for they lay on the shore quite bleached by the sun. They placed them in the ground at equal distances, and threw a sail, which had been drifted on shore, over them, and under this tent fifteen of us slept. It was a wretched abode. We were burnt by day and chilled by night.

The boat continued all day to bring from the wreck all they could pick up, but as it took four hours for each trip, and as there were about fifty to sixty persons to bring away, very little on this day was saved.

They succeeded in picking up a pipe of Madeira (of which wine there had been 300 on board). This was a great comfort to the gentlemen and sailors in their toils.

About midday, the second small boat being idle, some sailors volunteered to row any person to the mainland, which was about eleven or twelve miles distant, and from this the fishermen informed us they could, in twenty-four hours, ride to the Cape and send us assistance.

The doctor of the ship was the person selected for this duty, and the second officer with six active men undertook to row the boat to Saldanha Bay.

During the evening the ladies employed themselves in spreading out the clothes, books, etc, which had been brought off the wreck, or had been washed on shore by the tide. It was an amusing scene to those who had lost little (for there was little to lose), to see the waves washing up millinery, boxes of artificial flowers looking quite fresh, having been well washed with salt water; superb military hats, gold and silver lace, and a variety of finery of all sorts, but what was of greater value to us at the time, a basket of rice and onions, with many other things too numerous to mention.

Before night came on everyone had reached the shore, *not a life lost, not an individual hurt.*

Some were anxious that thanks should be returned to the Lord for our deliverance, but the disorderly state of intoxication in which some of the men were, made it desirable for the thanksgiving to be delayed till the following morning - the same reason made it necessary for the gentlemen to keep watch during the night over the small quantity of property saved, for plunder seemed the main object with many; some of the crew, however, remained steady, and were afterwards rewarded.

Keeping guard was a tedious undertaking, for the gentlemen had been exposed to the heat of the sun all day, and the cold night air had such an effect upon them that *some of* them slept during the watch. One corner of the tent we made as comfortable as we could under the circumstances there. Gertrude and myself, with her old ayah and our greyhound (Winifred), all slept better than we expected.

Monday morning - Early this morning I joined Lascellès, who had been keeping guard, in a walk into the interior of the Island, accompanied by Winifred (I daresat you recollect our beautiful blue greyhound of that name, which was such a favourite of dear little Frank's); she had saved herself by swimming, and appeared in great delight in getting again on land. She made great havoc amongst the hares; she soon caught seven, and we returned with our acceptable provisions to the tent. Lascelles acted as cook, and soon produced an excellent stew with the rice and onions which had been washed up the evening before. Many of us had eaten nothing on the previous day except biscuits. After breakfast, thanks were returned to Almighty God, by the Rev Mr Duff, for all His mercies to us. During the whole of this day, also, the boats continued to ply backwards and forwards to

the wreck, bringing off everything that was obtainable, and the ladies
continued to spread out to dry the articles brought off. About two o'
clock in the afternoon the little boat returned from Saldanha Bay. The
officer informed us that the Doctor had proceeded to the Cape, having
been assisted by a rich Dutch Boer with a horse and servant, and that
we might expect relief the next day (which was Tuesday) from the
Cape. In the afternoon we all dined together in the tent - the first time
we had all met at meals since we dined at the cuddy table on Saturday.
They had succeeded in getting a few necessaries which enabled us to
have a comfortable repast. Picture to yourself twenty-five persons
sitting on the ground close together, without knives and forks, only a
few plates and one dish to drink out of. The Island is covered with that
kind of pointed shell-fish, which they call in Ireland 'Bornaugh' but I
am not aware if you will know it by that name. They grow to a great
size, and these shells we collected and made use of for drinking vessels
and spoons. We collected a quantity of oyster-shell, very large and flat
for the purpose of plates. True is the vulgar adage: 'Necessity is the
Mother of Invention.'

I could not help reflecting on the great change that had taken
place in a short time. Our *ci-devant* Captain was now no longer the
busy bustling Master of the Ceremonies, but a quiet, unobtrusive
spectator of the whole, pitied and despised by most of us. After dinner
we explored the Island; it appeared to be about two miles in length and
about one mile in breadth. Not a tree was to be seen, not a blade of
grass; the only thing that grows on it is a small shrub, a species of fern
on which the hares feed. The greatest part of the Island is composed of
rock, and white sea sand, which the least puff of wind blows up into
clouds. This, you may suppose, with the glare of a scorching sun, was
extremely disagreeable and painful to our eyes. The water was swarming
with water-fowl of all descriptions, from the majestic white pelican to
the little diminutive sea-gull. The penguins (which are extremely
numerous) are very singular birds. They stand perfectly upright, and
are about three feet in height, constantly making a wild disagreeable
cry, something resembling that of a young ass. They build their nests in
small holes under the rocks, which they protect with great firmness.
Their eggs are pulled out from under them with a hooked stick, and
carried to the Cape in boats full, as food for the slaves. They are
amphibious and live upon fish. We also visited the fatal point where the
wreck lay. It had divided into two. The fore-part had almost
disappeared, but the stern still stuck on the rock on which she had

originally struck.

From this point, at about the distance of fifteen or twenty miles, could be seen on the horizon, like a cloud, the dark-blue mountains of Africa, the tops of which were gilded by the last rays of the setting sun, which was fast disappearing behind them. I sincerely wished our party at the foot of one of these mountains with some hospitable Dutch Colonist, for many of the sailors had become disagreeable, I may say dangerous characters. We had dreaded this from the beginning, and Lascelles had consequently used his best endeavours to form a strong body of the most active and steady of the men. These remained useful and obedient until we reached the Cape, when, by the kind assistance of the Governor (Sir Lowry Cole) and others, we were able to reward them. This night we passed in the same way as the preceding one.

Tuesday morning. - Lascelles started early with Winifred to get another supply of hares, and had caught five, when observing a sail to the eastward, standing into the Island, he made all haste to the tent with the welcome news. The stranger soon anchored in our little bay, and the Captain sent a boat on shore to inform us that he had been sent by the Governor of the Cape to give us every assistance and to convey us there. Our joy indeed was great when the First Lieutenant landed and desired us to make all haste on board, which order you may fancy we made all haste in obeying - they had breakfast prepared and everything comfortable for us. It was the smallest-sized King's ship, only two guns, *The Falcon*, commanded by Captain Colpoys. We were only one night on board, and on Wednesday evening we anchored in Table Bay. As soon as it was known at Cape Town that *The Falcon* had anchored in the bay, and that she had brought the shipwrecked passengers of the *Lady Holland*, boats were sent off to us, and the beach was covered with spectators to see us land. Lascelles engaged a boat for our party, in which we were soon seated, dressed in our board of ship clothes, which we had not taken off since Saturday morning. *Our faces and hands were without any skin on them, our eyes red and inflamed with the white sand of the Island, and our feet were so swollen and blistered that it was with much difficulty we could walk.* You may now form some idea of the figure we presented on landing at this strange quarter of the globe, but that which weighed most upon our minds was our being in want of everything, having no money, and as we thought *then* no friends. It was one of those beautiful evenings in autumn which are so seldom equalled, and never surpassed, in the colder latitudes. There was not a breath of air on the bay; the Mountain, which is the

Barometer of the Cape, appeared every moment to change its shape and lines. At one time it was covered with a large white cloud, which hung like a drapery over the Town; at another, the bold outlines of its Tableland, which makes the Mountain so remarkable, and from which it derives its name, could be distinctly seen. While reflecting on our distressing situation, and the peculiarly grand appearance of the scenery, *I was never more startled nor rejoiced,* on approaching the landing-place, than by hearing a voice call out, 'Lascelles, how are you?' and seeing a gentleman hand us out of the boat into his carriage. He was an old college friend of Lascelles, in the Bengal Civil Service. We were soon comfortably settled, and supplied with everything we could desire, by many kind friends whom Lascelles and Gertrude had known in India. I now request of you, my dear Papa, to picture to yourself a very different scene from the one which I last placed before you. Stripped of our clothes, and made comfortable in every respect, we are seated with a large party at dinner in a superb boarding-house in Cape Town, attended by numerous slaves dressed in the Indian costume, and surrounded by every European comfort and every tropical luxury which the season afforded. You cannot imagine how much we enjoyed ourselves. We visited all the sights at the Cape. We rode into the country almost every evening; it was looking beautiful, dressed in all the golden hues of autumn. At Constantia we drank the far-famed wine on the spot on which it was made, and in the morning we employed ourselves in making up another equipment, as we had lost *almost everything* in the wreck of the *Lady Holland.* I felt the sudden change so great that I cannot describe it, having no words sufficient to express my joy. I really fancied I had found what was supposed to be peculiar to the lovers of the Garden of Eden. But, perhaps, if we could be transported thither without the inconvenience and annoyance of a sea voyage, it would not charm so much. We left England in October, shivering and melancholy, under a rain of more than a month's continuance, for if you remember the autumn was particularly cold and wet in 1829 - foul winds, tossing in the Bay of Biscay, constant tacking and then shipwreck, made us long for the Cape as for a land of promise.

Captain Colpoys returned to the wreck to endeavour to save some more property, but did not succeed in getting anything; the wreck was scarcely perceptible at high water, and upon it appeared a steam boiler and Lascelles' little phaeton. We received great kindness from Sir Lowry Cole and Lady Frances. Sir Lowry offered his services in the kindest manner to Lascelles, and his protection to any ladies whom L. thought particularly required it, and two being named to him as being without friends, he took them to Government House, where they remained till we sailed. I can never forget or feel sufficiently grateful to Lady Frances Cole for all her soothing attention to Gertrude and myself. In short, we spent a very pleasant month at the Cape.

I certainly think it is one of the most enviable spots that I have ever seen, but there is no spot without its alloy, no place or situation without its annoyances, and here, alas, I felt for the first time the sting of the mosquito and the parching thirst of the land wind.

Seeing no prospect of getting a passage on to India in a regular ship before the winter, which was now fast approaching, Lascelles chartered a Bark, *The William Glen Anderson*, 400 tons burden, and having made our party, which consisted of seven ladies, thirteen men, fourteen servants, thirty-five sheep, thirteen horses, and five milch goats, fowls, pigs, ducks, geese, etc, we weighed anchor from Table Bay on the 13th of March, to contend once more with the storm and dangers of an element emblematical of the sinner's mind, never at rest.

In this ship we were comfortable in many respects. We had peace and harmony all the voyage.

The whole economy of the ship was arranged by Lascelles. The Captain and Officers sat as guests at the cuddy table. We had only one gale which, perhaps, after our shipwreck, appeared to be greater than it was. It was bad enough. You have been in a storm off the Cape of Good Hope, so it is not necessary for me to give you a detailed account of the manner in which the dark, heavy clouds, surcharged with rain rolled over the ship, apparently divided by flashes of lightening which only made the darkness more terrible, the ship rolling from side to side, and almost lying on her beam-ends, each broken swell striking her sides, and breaking boxes, etc, away from their lashings; water washing backwards and forwards, followed by tables and chairs; women screaming, sailors laughing, officers swearing, and the sea roaring. I daresay you have also witnessed a dinner at sea on such an occasion, and seen a pie and two ducks roasted to a cinder, the former attempting to reach the lee side of the ship on a thick stream, and the two latter swimming to and fro in their natural element on the deck of the cuddy, with a thousand other incidents equally absurd and inconvenient.

On the 18th May we got the first sight of Adam's Peak on the Island of Ceylon, and soon afterwards of the Mount of Madras, and never can I forget what I then felt. It filled my heart with the joy which no one can feel who has not taken a long voyage on the ocean. On the

19th, early in the morning, we anchored in the Madras Roads. There our kind friends (the Cockburns) waited to receive us, to whose house we were welcomed, and remained there six weeks.

What a contrast between the twelve months' past experience and the years of my former life. Then the life of one day was nearly that of the 365, but the narrative I have just given you must show how different a life I have led lately. It is now over, and we are enjoying rest and every possible happiness, which has been much increased while writing this letter, which has brought very forcibly before my recollection the many instances of the Lord's preserving care over us.

And now, my dear Papa, I must conclude, hoping that this may arrive safe, and trusting it may find you all enjoying every happiness is the sincere prayer of your unalterably attached Daughter,

MARY MOLESWORTH.

Letter from Mary Jane Saunders, February 1830

                                        Cape of Good Hope
                                        Tuesday, Feb 23, 1850

My dearest Robert,

I did write a few hasty lines to James by the *Childe Harold* two days ago when it was literally impossible for me to do more, but I trust at least that the contents of it will have been forwarded to Eltham, as you will, I am sure, have felt as much for me as anyone, if you have heard, as no doubt you have, of the melancholy loss of our ship.

Much as I have heard of shipwrecks, yet I am convinced that no one who has not experienced it can form any adequate idea of all the horrors of it.

We had been going on prosperously until the evening of Saturday, the 13th. We had been for some days annoyed by contrary winds which prevented our reaching the Cape. On the day in question, an observation was taken in the middle of the day and we were then far from land, but the wind and the violent current, carried us with such rapidity, added to the darkness of the night, that at 10 o'clock, there was a cry of 'breakers ahead' - immediately the helm was put down and every effort made to back the ship, but alas it was too late, and in two minutes we struck.

I had been in bed for half an hour, and with the exception of one lady, were the only ones of the party who had unfortunately taken off our clothes. A few seconds sufficed to assemble all the party on deck, where nothing can equal the scene which took place, the married ladies all clinging to their husbands. We all assembled together, not venturing to go forward to speak to anyone occupied with the ship. The masts were cut down, but the repeated and severe shocks of the ship were such as to make us all tumble about, nor was there anything secure by which we could hold. A small boat was lowered, and the second officer sent in it to see whether there was a possibility of getting on shore anywhere. We were to remain in the ship to the last moment, deeming it safer than risking our lives in the boat, surrounded as we appeared to be on all sides by breakers, but before any tidings arrived of the boat, the shocks of the ship became so frightful that we literally stood on the deck expecting every moment she would shiver to pieces.

She was filling fast with water and it was then declared that our last hope rested on getting into the longboat and keeping out at sea until the moon should give sufficient light for us to ascertain nearly where we were.

The bulwarks were cut down, and the boat launched into the water upon which there was a cheering hurrah from all the men at its being safe in the water but this was followed by a moment of awful silence and intense agony when one voice was heard to ejaculate 'our last hope is gone, the boat has gone off, and is upon the breakers'. At the same moment one of the sailors dashed into the water and caught the rope just in time to save it, it was brought round to the stern, and we were all taken out at the gangway, carried along the side of the ship, and then with a rope secured and lowered down one by one into the boat. We were fourteen females, three gentlemen accompanied us, being all it could contain with any degree of safety. By this time the small boat hailed us, they had found a landing place on a desert island, took us in tow and conveyed us to it.

There were three men in the place, who came for seals, and one miserable mud hut, in which only six or seven could cram. The elder ladies took this, and we were so numbed with cold and so dripping wet, for the boat was nearly swamped while taking us all in, that we were obliged to wander about. We bent our steps towards the point where the wreck was and before sunrise we got very near to it, and a more melancholy spectacle I never witnessed. The passengers had come away when the boats returned, but the Captain and the crew were all still on the wreck endeavouring to save what luggage they could, although they were almost in momentary expectation that the ship would go to pieces. We could not quit the spot so great was our anxiety until we saw all safe, which was not till three-o-clock in the afternoon, the Captain remaining some time after everyone else thought it very unsafe.

That same evening the Doctor was sent off in a boat to the mainland about twelve miles distant to convey the intelligence without delay to the Cape, in order to send us provisions, and the means of getting away. We lived the first day upon eggs of the penguin, a bird which abounds in Dassen Island, picking up shells to use as spoons and cups, although we had scarcely a drop of water, for there is none in the island. We got each one about a thimbleful in the day, and then contrived with a sail we got on shore, and the aid of the bones of some whales to make a sort of tent, under which we all passed the night, shivering with cold, for the dews are very heavy, and our canvas not very thick, besides which owing to its supporters being short it was so low that we could only get into it by crawling on our hands and feet. The next day we got some biscuits and wine from the ship, so that we were better off although obliged to be sparing, not knowing how long we might be there, and having upwards of sixty mouths to feed.

On Tuesday morning we received the pleasing intelligence that a man of war, the *Falcon*, was in sight. She came to an anchor, and Captain Colpoys with two others in boats came off to the shore having been sent by Sir Lowry Cole immediately he heard of our misfortune to bring us all away. We lost no time in going on board, where we were regaled with a most delightful breakfast, and soon set sail for the Cape, leaving only the Captain, his first and second officer, and two men on the island to save all they could from the wreck.

We were all, as you may believe, most dreadfully tired and many of us with our faces blistered with the heat. Mine has not yet recovered, nor should I probably be recognized very easily by anyone at home. My face is as red as possible and my hands brown. We were two days on board the *Falcon*, which returned immediately we were landed to render Captain Snell all the assistance possible, and to bring him back here. They are to leave Dassen Island tomorrow, and we shall probably see them on Wednesday. Most heartily rejoiced shall I be to have Captain Snell with us, for he is, of course, very much depressed by what has occurred, and really ought not to be left much alone to brood over his misfortune, and he is also such a kind and steady friend to me that I scarcely like to do anything without his advice and assistance.

All the passengers are very anxious if it were possible that he should charter another ship and take them on to India, for I believe there is scarcely one who would not prefer going in a ship commanded by him to any other.

My paper and my time both remind me to close, and with my best love to Isabella and the children to assure you my dearest Robert that I am ever your most affectionately attached sister,

MARY JANE SAUNDERS

PART 3

A Victorian Family moves to New Zealand

Commentary

Jessie Campbell sailed from Greenock on August 25 1840, in the barque *Blenheim*, Captain Gray, 375 tons, built at Jarrow in 1834 and registered as of the Port of London, bound towards Wellington, New Zealand, which harbour was reached on December 27, eighteen weeks less two days later. She sailed with her family, her husband to whom she refers in her journal as Captain Campbell or Capt C, and her five children, John, Colin, Louisa and the infant twins Susan and Isabella. The last named, almost always affectionately called Tibbie, was to die on the passage, judging from the detailed descriptions of the symptoms of infective enteritis probably culminating in peritonitis. The primitive methods used by the ship's doctors to attempt the child's cure is a horrific reminder of the state of medicine less than 150 years ago. She had the assistance of two women servants, a maid Mary Cameron and a nurse referred to as 'the Skye woman'. Both began the voyage badly but improved in their mistress' eyes later. Travelling with the Campbells were another couple, a woman whom Jessie Campbell invariably calls J.B.S. and her husband Drimintoran, who had their own family and a servant. There were a number of other cabin passengers whose names occur from time to time.

Jessie Campbell's account of the voyage gives a complete picture of the life of a cabin passenger in a wooden square-rigged sailing ship. The full journal is detailed and inevitably repetitious. We have selected extracts amounting to one third of the original which cover the essentials, the living conditions, the food, the shortage of water, the problems of travelling with children, the heat of the tropics, sanitation, the work of Campbell and Sutherland the two ship's doctors, some of the problems of ship management with which Captain Gray had to cope and the emigrants who occupied the greater part of the accommodation.

Jessie Campbell was a strong-minded woman who took the death of her child with apparent equanimity but its real effect comes clearly through her writing. She is much less confident afterwards. She minds the weather more and is inclined to worry. On the whole, despite her attitude to her servants at the beginning, she is less snobbish about the other occupants of the cabin accommodation and about the emigrant passengers than was William Johnstone, whose journal of a similar passage forms Part 4 of this book. Her statements about them tend to be factual rather than contemptuous, those of a woman familiar with and sympathetic towards all degrees of a rural community. Her position was special - she was a Scot and this seems to have been an almost entirely Scots migration.

Captain Gray emerges as a competent shipmaster beset by considerable troubles from time to time. His navigation is careful and accurate. The difficulties of sailing in remote parts of the world, still comparatively unfamiliar to Europeans, are emphasised by the problems met with in finding Wellington harbour. Because of their particular interest we have reproduced these entries in full.

The *Blenheim* spoke a number of vessels on the passage. She stayed in company for some days with the barque *Tam O' Shanter*, Captain Ellis, 270 tons, built at Workington in 1836, and with the schooner *Naiad*. That this latter, a vessel markedly smaller than the *Blenheim*, kept company with her on and off for some time is an advertisement of her sailing qualities and especially of her superior ability in sailing to windward. She was an early example of the use of this type of vessel by British owners in long-distance trades.

The most interesting of the vessels spoken was the *Vernon* (Plate 6), a full-rigged ship with paddles and an auxiliary steam engine. She was built at London in 1839 by the famous company of Richard Green, whose history is shown in a special display at the National Maritime Museum, Greenwich, on the opposite side of the river to Blackwall where the *Vernon* was built. The merchant shipping historian, Basil Lubbock, in his book on the London-Calcutta trade, *The Blackwall Frigates*, says that the *Vernon's* side paddles and steam engines were removed before she sailed on her maiden voyage but Jessie Campbell's observation suggests to the contrary that she was still equipped with them when the *Blenheim* spoke her in late 1840.

The Campbells settled at Wanganui. It is by kind permission of one of their descendants, Mr E.A. Campbell of Wanganui, that we are able to publish these extracts from the journal which has remained in the family. Mr A.G. Bagnall, the Librarian of the Alexander Turnbull Library in Wellington, first drew our attention to the journal and we are most grateful to him for his help. A complete transcription is now in the National Maritime Museum

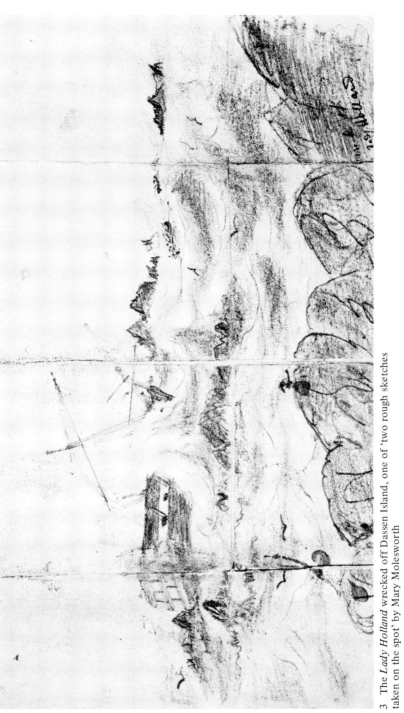

3 The *Lady Holland* wrecked off Dassen Island, one of 'two rough sketches taken on the spot' by Mary Molesworth

4   Mrs Nathaniel William Kindersley, formerly Mary Molesworth

Journal kept on board the ship Blenheim *by Jessie Campbell, August – December, 1840*

August 25th: Embarked this day on board the *Blenheim* at Greenock, had a bad commencement to our voyage by getting drenched with rain while waiting for a steam-boat to take us alongside the ship. I was agreeably surprised at our good accommodation.... Put the five children to sleep in the berth in the cabin and had a bed made for Captain Campbell and myself on the floor. Cabin in great confusion, put up with it very good humoured with the hope of being more comfortable the following night. The children very good altho they had nothing to eat but part of a loaf we brought on board with us.... A steam-boat came at 11 o'clock at night to tow us out twenty miles, a beautiful calm night. Children slept pretty well. Capt C and I slept wonderfully well considering the uncomfortable bed we had. Sailors astonished the children in the evening by the noise they made heaving up the anchor.

August 26th: Awoke this morning about six, got up about seven and assisted Mary to dress the children. Capt C got up and dressed before this. The twins very cross from hunger, steward told Captain C nothing for the children's breakfast but coffee without milk and biscuit and a little bread, he did not know how to make the stirabout and had no oatmeal, reflected on Capt C for not taking a small quantity of meal and molasses for the children. While feeding the two little ones with sops made of our own bread Capt C announced breakfast, could not go to it and feed the bairns at the same time, took a cup of coffee when the children were at their breakfast, wee bodies complaining of the hardness and toughness of the biscuit.... Very little motion in the vessel all day, wind against us. Saw Capt Gray at distance for the first time, very dull, suppose from parting from his wife, thought I should like to know him, sat next him at dinner, Dr Campbell on the opposite side. J.B.S. next to me, Capt C next to her; got very squeamish in the evening and very low spirited. Lay on the bed, Colin and Tibbie with me and very sick, Susan on deck and quite well. John sick for half an hour, Louisa fell asleep on the floor but quite well. J.B.S. and most of her children very sick in bed. Mary Cameron fortunately continued pretty well and very active. Their maid got sick in my cabin and vomited on the floor, very angry at her and sent her to the water-closet till she was able to go to the steerage, passed another miserable night, all serene in the cabin, would not take off my clothes....

August 28th: Awoke at the usual hour after passing a most comfortable night. Twins never woke the whole night, Tibbie peeping out in the morning and laughing to Papa. Capt C always rises first to make room in the cabin. Twins breakfasted heartily upon sago and in very good humour all the morning; fine day, with a light wind in our favour... Capt Gray told us at dinner he had only been a month in Britain (including the time he was coming down from London to Greenock and while at anchor there) since returning from his last voyage, he said he was not so ill off as his mate who had only been six weeks with his wife for five years. Drimintoran asked if the mate had any children which caused a great laugh. J.B.S. was much shocked at her husband's question; dined at the usual hour between 3 and 4 and drank tea at 7, went to my cabin after the children had tea to assist Mary in putting them to bed. Skye woman of no use, always sick, Swinging of the cots sets the twins asleep immediately after they are put into it. Capt C lighted a taper in the lamp to burn all night in case of either of the wee bodies wakening and working their way out of the cot....

Wednesday, 2nd September: Blowing very hard, at first not favourable still crossing the Bay of Biscay, ship rolling and tossing a good deal. J.B.S. very sick for a short time; often thought of Ewen's account of the Bay of Biscay, in tacking some of the rigging gave way, not frightened in the least. Gray astonished at our not being sick. Tibbie not very well yet, Susan quite well. Had the best sherry at dinner I ever tasted. While sitting at dinner part of a wave broke in upon the deck which made me nervous for a little while, I saw the Capt and all looking so unconcerned; great lamentations among the bachelors about their beds getting wet from the sea getting in at the port-holes. Dr Sutherland says he is better than any of them. Mary Cameron so frightened at the rolling of the vessel burst into our cabin at four in the morning; during the afternoon the wind was favourable going along at a great rate. Have asked so often when we will be free of the Bay of Biscay, ashamed to ask it again. After the children were in bed wrote awhile to bring my journal intend to carry it on regularly after this. Had my drink of porter as usual and went to bed.

Thursday, 3rd September: Passed a very uncomfortable night, vessel rolling and pitching so much could not sleep, sometimes thought when she went to the side she would not rise again. Laughed at by Capt C. Fine day, light breeze but favourable. First thing we heard in the morning that Mrs Fraser the smith's wife from Ardgour had been brought to bed of a fine stout boy, both doing well as possible. Capt Gray said she must have had a rolling time of it. Child gets no other name than Blenheim. Like Capt Gray more every day, find him so obliging, he saw that the children's cot was not properly made, set his sailmaker to alter it all day yesterday and gave surveys himself.... One of the sailors was complained of for the 4th time to the Capt for being lousy and eating the lice, Capt put him in irons on the poop, the rascal struck the capt on the face he still wears the mark, one of the emigrants impertinently interfered and wished to rescue the sailor. Capt Gray was going to punish the emigrant likewise until he begged his pardon and acknowledged his error. J.B.S. quite nervous at the idea of the crew being mutinous.... Beautiful evening a great change in the warmth of the climate. One of our sheep broke his leg on Wednesday last, had to be killed, had part of it for dinner today, capital mutton, everything for dinner so well dressed, our cook understands his business remarkably well. Pipers began to play in the evening, Capt Gray set all the people to dance, he got hold of my Skye woman and forced her up, could not get her to continue dancing, he obliged an old wife to get up to our great amusement, instead of accepting the partner he gave her she got hold of Capt Gray and forced him to dance the reel with her which he did very good humouredly. Children and all so happy, could not help saying how much I would give that my beloved mother and sister could get a peep at us. John a great favourite with Captain Gray, says it does him good to shake hands with him, he has such a *paw*, teaching Jack, as he calls him, to climb up the ropes; John so delighted with the ship, says he would rather be here than on shore. Louisa the wonder of everybody being so well and her appetite so good. Got clear of Bay of Biscay half past six tonight.

Friday, 4th September: A beautiful morning with a light favourable . breeze. The barque we saw yesterday afternoon close to us, Capt made signals found she was the *Tam O Shanter* from Liverpool for Port Jackson with a general cargo, a smaller vessel than ours; saw a lady on board we guessed to be the Captain's wife; kept us company the whole day, beat her at sailing. Stayed a long time on deck, children so well and happy...

Saturday, 5th September: Saw several vessels in sight, two of them Russians. Capt Gray never saw so many vessels as at this time. Weather very warm, a delightful breeze sprung up in our favour, delighted at it, dislike the heavy rolling of the ship when calm very much. Quite astonished that I never feel afraid and sleep so sound. *Tam O Shanter* not in sight today. J.B.S. very nervous at night, frightened when she hears sailors run which they always do when doing anything about the ship, she tried to conquer this but cannot, complains of her want of faith, her husband complains she does not allow him to sleep. Children all made an excellent dinner on preserved soup and lobster, twins recovered their appetite and looking well. Capt Gray nursed Tibbie in his arms for a good while, astonished at the luxuriance of her hair. He takes great trouble in making the emigrants come on deck and cleaning out their places below, complains of the indolence and filthy habits of the Highlanders, the few Paisley emigrants keep themselves cleaner and are more easily managed, he says Dr Campbell is a great deal too easy with them... Just as we were sitting to dinner felt a bad smell from J.B.S.'s cabin, strange they will not use our convenient closet...

Sunday, 6th September: A beautiful morning with a fine breeze in our favour, rather late on rising, angry at Mary for being so long of coming with the water, dressed in one of gingham gowns, Capt in his best suit very much admired, boys in drill surtouts and trousers, slippers, the 3 girls in light frocks, all the gentlemen dress better on Sunday. Capt Gray in white trousers, puts on a long coat to dinner Capt C does the same... Heard today that we had nearly got on sand banks off the Irish coast from the stupidity of the man steering, he mistook the light from Wexford lighthouse for a light of a steamboat, fortunately they sent down to ask of Capt Gray if there should be any lighthouse in sight, he sprung out of bed and found ten minutes more would have put us on a sand bank. Capt Gray said our lives might have been spared but the vessel would have been lost, glad I did not know till we were so far from land... We had for dinner today roast ducks, boiled fowls and curried fowl and pea soup and pickled pork, this is the first day we have been without beautiful cabbage for dinner since leaving Greenock, the potatoes are still very good, our having such a good cook adds much to our comfort; all the steerage passengers got flour, suet and raisins served out to them yesterday to make puddings for their dinners today, most of them did not know how to use the ingredients, they eat the raisins their children going about with them in handfuls, made scones of the flour. I do not know what they did with the suet, they likewise got pickled cabbage, a good many cannot be prevailed on to eat it and were caught throwing it overboard....

Monday, 7th September: Catherine had Susan at the window and allowed her to throw the lid of the tin pan overboard in which we keep the fresh water, very vexed about it, blamed Mary's sister for not hanging up the pan where she got it. Mary defended her sister very impertinently, told her to hold her tongue I did not want to hear her opinion about it. Mary continued to answer very impertinently, said a letter would reach Dr Macleod yet to tell how she was used, told her instantly to walk out of my cabin that Dr Macleod forgot his duty when he did not teach her the respect due to a Mistress, that I would oblige her to make out the time she was engaged with me after that she might go about her own business. Had preserved soup, roast ducks and fowls for dinner....

Tuesday, 8th September: ....Was horror-struck to hear that a man was ill on board with what the doctor thought was small-pox, he has been 3 weeks on board the ship, all astonished that the infection would remain so long about him before showing itself, only complained of being ill Saturday last, the rash came out today, he has been put into hospital and quite separated from all the others. It is a fearful prospect a disease of this kind breaking out in such a crowded ship and when just coming into the hot latitude. May the Almighty protect us all. Capt Gray in great dismay about this, neither he or a young boy his brother have had small pox, would rather lose his own child than anything happen to his brother, it would kill his mother, came to sea at this time against her wish. I trust in God it may yet turn out not to be small-pox. ...I am sitting at the scritoire writing this with my clothes off down to my waist and the 3 cabin windows open; passed Madeira today, did not see land, ship going very fast and not so much motion as you would expect; have just drunk off my tumbler of porter and am going to bed. Lat. at noon 33-41 N. Long 18-4 W. Made sops of rusks for the children's dinner today and meal, the twins were delighted with it, intend to keep a cup of tea for them from my own breakfast and tea water is so bad and scarce....

Wednesday, 9th September: ...1st and 2nd Mates had a dreadful quarrel tonight. Capt Gray was called out to pacify them. Lat. at noon 30-53 N. Long 19 W.

Thursday, 10th September: Not much wind today but very hot, an awning put up on the poop which makes the deck delightful, sat a long time under it, children playing about. Saw a large shoal of flying fish.... Capt Gray very busy today from his mates being under arrest, he blames the 1st Mate most, he struck the 2nd Mate and followed him from side to side of the deck striking him altho he knew the other dare not return the blows if he had he would have been put in irons, it seems to require all Capt Gray's firmness to keep his crew in order, what a blessing to us he is so determined, he did not go to bed last night. Mary Cameron has been very submissive since we had the quarrel. Nothing like keeping her in good order... I am so frightened for small-pox that I got Dr Campbell to vaccinate my arm today, he was not half the time that Chrichton used to be. We have had such merry-making on the deck this evening, the Capt set a part to dance to the sound of the bagpipes, on the other side a party played at leap-frog. My husband, Drimintoran and Mr Macfarlane were the only males that did not join in either past-time. Capt Gray was most active at leap-frog, I enjoyed looking at the fun from the poop exceedingly. It is a glorious evening, bright moon-light, a soft balmy breeze, it requires a more eloquent pen than mine to describe such an evening, the ship looks so majestic with all her sails set. Capt Gray complains woefully of the indolence of the emigrants, he has such a work every day hunting them out of their beds and keeping them on deck, particularly towards evening that their berths may cool before they go down to sleep.

Friday, 11th September: A fine morning with rather less wind than we could wish. Capt C as usual got up first and went for our washing water, he got better measure than Mary gets if English pints is our allowance, viz a pint for each, we are obliged to be very careful of it as this is all we get during the day except a little to drink when we ask it from the steward; any water we require for sago etc I must take from our washing allowance... the spots on the small-pox man beginning to dry up Dr says there is no fear of him now.... Little Blenheim and his mother were on deck today...

Saturday, 12th September: ...Capt Gray baths every morning at least has pails of salt water thrown over him on deck. Today he put John up threw 2 pails of water over him, John stood it manfully forsooth he would not go without trousers. One of the flying fish fell on board, had no idea it was so small. Capt Gray and the doctor complaining woefully of the filth of the Highland emigrants, they say they could not have believed it possible for human beings to be do dirty in their habits, only fancy their using the dishes they have for their food for certain other purposes at night, the Dr seems much afraid of fever breaking out among them, this would really be a judgment on us, poor as I am no consideration on earth would tempt me to trust my little family in a ship with Highland emigrants if I still had the voyage before me...

Monday, 14th September: ...felt so oppressed with heat this forenoon that I sat a long time without my stays on. Had dancing to the pipes as usual tonight. I enjoy the deck very much after the sun sets it becomes so cool...

Tuesday, 15th September: All felt the heat very much during the night, this morning got a large tub filled with salt water and bathed the children. John as usual had buckets of salt water poured over him. Capt C has commenced having a bath in the same way. When Capt Gray observed Tibbie in the tub he went himself to bathe her. Capt Campbell dressed today in his french shirt, it is very much admired as a suitable dress. Capt G says he will provide himself with a good many next voyage. Louisa is today in a blue frock with only chemise on under, not even her stays, twins in blue striped frocks and their chemises. Last night it became so calm we were terrified the trades were going to fail us, already to our great joy today a breeze has sprung up, it defies me to do any work, the heat makes me so languid. I have got the *Water Witch* from John Galgarry, even with the reading I get slowly on, I would be very grateful if I could go without my stays or shoes. Two vessels in sight today, one of them our friend the Austrian polacca [which was named *Prince Rubarez*; Plate 5 shows a similar vessel] the other we are making signals to Capt Gray never saw so many vessels as at this time...

Sunday, 20th September: Very little wind, vessel scarcely moving, very great heat. Had prayers as usual. John read, said his questions and hymn, read a story to him afterwards. Mutton so much tainted at dinner could not eat it, made up for it on pudding. A great deal of sheet lightening, very beautiful, this evening. Two ships in sight all day, one of them came close, would not answer our signals. Such a violent squall came on about 11 o'clock, one of the largest sails was rent from top to bottom; altho the night was very dark it was replaced in half an hour. The Smith's infant who was very ill considered out of danger, no apprehension of small-pox spreading, the man who has been ill with it quite well but still confined to the hospital.

Monday, 21st September: Fine morning, all well. Dispute between our servants and the steward about the quantity of water for the children, said he had orders from the Capt to give them the reduced quantity, told him the jug he had for measuring the water was not the proper size, on getting the proper pint measure from the hold found that even on the reduced quantity we got as much water as formerly. This has caused an unpleasant feeling between Capt C and Capt Gray, the latter in very bad humour but continues very polite to Mrs Macdonald and company. He is short tempered forgets it soon but does not like to acknowledge that he is wrong.

...

Wednesday, 23rd September: It has been rather a stormy night but all well. Wind still unfavourable but the ship always making some way. 12 o'clock a schooner near us going the same course. 2 o'clock she is up to us and spoke to us, she proves to be the *Naiad* from London bound to South Australia, out 30 days, appeared to be only about 120 tons. 8 o'clock, retiring in good spirits a good deal of Gaelic singing and dancing among the emigrants.

...

Saturday, 26th September: All well, a good deal of wind and favourable all night. 12 o'clock incessant rain since 8 o'clock, all the emigrants below except some that are collecting rain water for washing. The Dr and Capt insist on the emigrants keeping below, getting wet with the tropical rain being very bad for them. Awoke this morning quite free of toothache. Saved a large tubful of rain water intend to have a washing on Monday, washed all the children's heads. The *Tam O Shanter* abreast of us at 8 o'clock, ship on her course and a good breeze.

...

Wednesday, 30th September: All well, head wind. A niece of my Skye maid very ill, threatened with water in the head, she was sickly when she came on board, she is about 30 years old. Forgot to say got a good many things washed on Monday, today one of my domestics is ironing them. A long time on deck with the children.

...

Friday, 2nd October: Beautiful morning, wind ahead. My little darling Tibbie is very unwell today, she has a bowel complaint, is very feverish scarcely raised her head all day, her gums are inflamed, her eye teeth must be the cause of her illness. The Dr had ordered a warm bath for her and a dose of Calomel in the morning with Senna leaves to work it off.

...

Tuesday, 6th October: The Macquarrie child has just expired, her complaint general debility and latterly water in the head. Tibbie still continuing better, I trust she may continue. The body of the Macquarrie child committed to the deep. Capt Gray read the prayers over it. Crossed the line at 2 o'clock. Passed the schooner *Naiad* which we had not seen for several days. Ship going at a good rate. Discovered a Baker from Paisley stealing soap in the hold, he is confined to the poop.

Wednesday, 7th October: She made great progress last night. My little darling not quite so well today. I begin to feel very anxious her father is very desponding. God grant his fears may not be realized, she has no pain but continues very weak and reduced, her appetite gone again. Dr Campbell unremitting in his attention to her, a great comfort she has everything she could have on shore except milk which she would not be allowed to take in her present state.

Thursday, 8th October: Fine morning, ship making great progress, Tibbie much the same. John and Louisa not well, took no breakfast, suspect John has put his stomach wrong by going down to the hold with Capt Gray's brother (who has charge of everything out the provisions) and eating a quantity of raisins and sugar. Louisa was found in the steerage yesterday and confessed she had been eating raisins and flour scones there; a doze of medicine will put both to rights. Lat 4-55 S. Long 27-4 W.

...

Monday, 12th October: Dear little Isabella much worse. I can see the Dr has little hope of her. I never despaired of her until today. I trust I may be strengthened to bear this severe trial which I fear awaits me. Capt Gray came into my cabin to see her; ill and weak as my little darling was she stretched out her hands to him, he nursed her for a long time, she has a little of the bowel complaint, what she passes is very green and bilious. Fine morning, strong breeze. Spoke a Brig from Rio Janeiro to Trieste. Capt Gray boarded her and we all wrote letters he refused to take them as he would be obliged to ride quarantine 14 days if he carried them. No observation.

Tuesday, 13th October: Isabella still the same, continues free from pain, sleeps a great deal, the pupil of her eye contracts so naturally Dr does not think her head affected, her evacuations not frequent but very green and bilious, think her digestive organs so weakened they do not digest her food, her appetite quite gone but drinks a great deal, takes arrowroot for a drink as thick as she can ... (Beautiful morning) drinks it with a very little white wine in it, pulse about 90, skin quite cool. A son of Frazer the smiths ill of the jaundice. Lat 16-39 S. Long 32-9 W.

Wednesday, 14th October: ...The man that had the small-pox allowed to come on deck for the first time, his bedding thrown overboard and his clothes towed after the ship for several days. Lat 18-44 S. Long 32-5 W.

Thursday, 15th October: Isabella rather better, her pulse a little stronger, still very little hope of her recovery, still drinking a good deal, gets thin chicken soup occasionally; for a change she did not sleep well last night but did not seem to have any pain. Dear little lamb she likes so much to have me beside her in bed, even during the day she gives me her little hand to hold or sometimes puts it across my neck; she does not vomit, altho she does not eat she takes a good deal of nourishment in drinks, nothing seems to put her bowels right, she still passes very green stuff but has not a stool oftener than twice in 24 hours. Beautiful morning, ship going at a great rate at 12 o'clock. Lat 20-8 no observation for Long. A cry of land turns out to be Trinidada, an uninhabited island in Lat 20-20 S. Long 29 W seen at the very time Capt Gray expected which is very gratifying as it shews how very correct he is in his calculations. It seems to be a complete mass of broken rocks, puts me in mind of a large fortification.

...

Saturday, 17th October: ...½ past 2 o'clock spoke to *Naiad.* Capt Gray wanted a particular chart from him which the Capt had not; if she calls at the Cape is to report us....

...

Sunday, 18th October: ...We are now out of the tropics, *Naiad* in company. Lat 23-26. Long 25-1.

Monday, 19th October: Poor Isabella much weaker ...I think if I had her on shore I would not be half so distressed, altho she has every comfort here she could have anywhere...

Friday, 23rd October: My dear little lamb lingered in the same state all night, she expired this morning at 8 o'clock; she resigned her breath as quietly as if she were going to sleep without the slightest struggle. What would I give to be on shore with her dear little body, the idea of committing it to the deep distresses me very much, she has made a happy change from the cares and miseries of this world, it is hard to say what misfortune may await us from which she has escaped. The Doctors did not seem to understand what her complaint was, both agreed it was brought on by teething and that she would have had the same on shore. She will make a sad blank to me for a long time. 12 o' clock - My little darling's body has just been committed to the deep. Capt C tells me Capt Gray was so much affected he could hardly read the funeral service; he made such a work about her, she was very fond of him, would hold his face between her little hands and kiss him. John seems to feel her death a good deal, the others did not mind it. Her father feels this sad bereavement very much.

...

Sunday, 25th October: Lat 31-25 S. Long 19-14 W. Fine morning, wind the same as yesterday, went into the cuddy for the first time for a fortnight to attend divine worship and went on deck afterwards; find myself much the better of fresh air; day so cold, put on my tartan cloak; have got a blanket put on each of the beds, put on my flannel petticoat this morning. Boys have got their tartan surtouts on, girls have got their flannel petticoats. Susan missing her dear little sister very much, searched the bed for her, it was like to break my heart hearing her calling 'where's poor Tibbie?' Wind more favourable, ship going 7 knots an hour. Attended the meals in the cuddy for the first time.

...

Wednesday, 18th October: ...A Paisley woman delivered of a daughter, the women do not seem to suffer as much as at home.

Thursday, 29th October: ...Row between the mate and one of the sailors, the sailor put in irons....

...

Sunday, 1st November: Stormy but all well. Alarmed last night by a call for Capt Gray who with his usual dexterity was immediately on deck; it seems a heavy squall came on which laid the ship over till they took in most of the sails; it relieved one very much to hear Capt Gray return to his cabin whistling. A dreadful smash at breakfast all the cups and saucers and plates on one side of the table took a rapid journey to the other and several were broken and Capt Gray nearly scalded by the quantity of hot coffee that came upon him; three of the gents followed their cups till the side of the cabin brought them up together; it was a very laughable scare particularly for me who sit so snug. Gale did not abate till evening, no public worship today, children and I passed most of the day sitting in bed telling stories on part of the Bible to the 3 big ones. Capt C took a good sleep in the boy's cabin. We got very little rest last night. Lat 25-12. Long -.43 W.

Monday 2nd November: Passed a comfortable night, a fine morning, wind not favourable. Mr Macdonald had a long conversation with the culprit in irons, advised him to ask the Capt's forgiveness, said he was told it would be in vain to do so, said he could read but had no Bible, would be very glad to read one if he had it. Mr Macdonald gave him one and a prayer book; poor wretch he is to be pitied, he is brought off the poop to the cuddy every night, it is melancholy to hear his irons clanking every movement he gives. I am busy mending Capt C's stockings in the heel; have a washing of the children's things today. The mate saved rain water for us on Saturday on condition of washing a few shirts for himself. Lat 35-10. Long 28 East.

Tuesday, 3rd November: ...The prisoner has been released I am glad to say. Colin is making progress at school as the lessons are given in my cabin I always hear how they are coming on. Catherine has a very good method with young children. Louisa has commenced hemming her papa's coloured neck-clothes, she is nearly as far on with her lessons as Colin. Lat 34 - 40.

Wednesday, 4th November: ...Forgot to mention the first pig was killed Saturday last, children had a roast of it on Sunday with which they were delighted, no one more than Susan, it was as delicate as lamb, so different from the pork on shore. The children were tiring of preserved meat which they were getting for some time. We are to have a sheep and pig killed every week, the pigs are very small; we have good soup every day and the children the same and fresh meat every day, preserved beef; our potatoes are done, except a few we get when there is any fish on the table; we have a curious dish for breakfast once a week, a fish pudding, the day we have that we get no rolls. Lat 36-6. Long 2-29.

...

Friday, 6th November: ...Capt C has brought from Capt Gray a wooden water pail with a lid to it of good size. We manage to save a little of our allowance of water every day and by keeping it in the pail we have as much at the end of the week as washes a few things, so that tho I did not get my washing at Rio Janeiro we can keep *ourselves quite clean,* till the end of the voyage.

...

Saturday, 7th November: Beautiful morning, light breeze for us. Mrs Macdonald and I went down to the steerage and women and girls berths for the first time. Quite delighted with the cleanliness of them. Capt Gray takes a great deal of trouble in obliging the emigrants to keep their places in order, he drives them on deck in good weather with a small cane in his hand calling '_ _ _' the only Gaelic word he can say. The ship in company for two days is the *Isabella Stewart* from London to Sydney, out 35 days. The wind is now fair all sails set, we have such a great many large whales today some of them quite close by the ship; saw also the little Blenheim today in the steerage, firm, stout, thriving, babies...

Monday, 9th November: Beautiful morning, all well, a calm. Capt C as usual desponding at the long voyage we are likely to have. Have got Cook's *Travels* from Dr Sutherland, very much interested in his account of New Zealand as I can depend on his having written the truth.

Tuesday, 10th November: ...John is quite a sailor, knows the name of every rope and stick on board; the other day his father went on deck and was horror-struck to see him near the top of the main mast he was afraid to scold him till he got on deck.

...

Thursday, 12th November: Fine morning, ship going at a tremendous rate, 9 miles an hour all night rather too high a wind to my taste. Capt Gray calls it a glorious breeze. 12 o'clock off the Cape Horn farther south than 300 miles. The gentlemen form two card parties every night in the cuddy, as I have more light to read or write in my own cabin I always go there at 8 o'clock. Mrs Macdonald comes to me with a bit of biscuit and cheese and a glass of porter or ale; if I do not pick up it will not be for want of good things, I am now as strong as ever again. Mr Macdonald never tastes spirits and instead of the brandy and water the others take at meals he divides a bottle of malt between himself, his wife and I; the water for drinking is all filtered and most excellent, I never would desire to take better, the Thames water always improves after a while, during the hot weather it was rather warm, now it is quite cold. I do not feel so comfortable tonight as it has the appearance of being rather stormy. Lat 39-45. Long 18-33.

Friday, 13th November: Rather a stormy morning but much more moderate than it was during the night. The mate put under arrest last night for insolence to the Capt when found fault with for not taking in the mainsail during a heavy squall that nearly tore it to pieces...

Monday, 16th November: Fine morning... 11 o'clock a very large ship in sight. 2 o'clock spoke her, she is the *Vernon* (Plate 6) from London to Calcutta, left 17th Sept. she has a steam engine and seemed about 1000 tons, she is a splendid looking ship, saw 8 or 9 ladies on board so gaily dressed; when they left London the Egyptian Question had created a sensation likely to end in a rupture with France; The Capt promised to report us from Calcutta overland. All day on deck, much warmer. Lat. 40-25. Long. 33-12.

Tuesday, 17th November. Stormy morning, sea running very high, ship going at a great rate can carry very few sails; Capt Gray still calls it a glorious breeze. Another added to our number by the birth of a daughter to a man from Risley. Mother and child doing well, this is the 5th birth on board all doing well. 8 o'clock the gale increasing shockingly, the Capt anticipates a stormy night, does not intend going to bed for some time. I expect a very sleepless, uneasy night. John, on my asking him about the wind was forsooth amused at my being frightened and told me the sailors thought nothing of this breeze. Lat. 40-23. Long. 37-29.

Wednesday, 18th November: ...The night was very stormy I could not sleep I was so frightened; I often thought when the vessel went to the one side she never would rise again; a great deal of vivid lightning; the children slept quite soundly, even if I were not alarmed it would be impossible to sleep the sailors made such a noise shortening sail etc. add to that the tremendous noise of rushing of the water at the stern and the noise of the wind. The ship has been going at the rate of 8 or 9 miles an hr.... We nearly lost one mate last night the vessel gave such a tremendous lurch to one side he was thrown with so much force that he went completely out of her into the boat at the side, if he had fallen a little further up or lower down he must have gone overboard...

Thursday, 19th November: Fine morning with a light breeze in our favour. Had such a comfortable night's rest last night, went on deck and had a good walk, air very chill. Children all running about so healthy, we have from 50 to 60 children on board under fourteen; there is a great change for the better in the appearance of most of them. Read a good while Wilson's *Tales of the Border,* they are very stupid. Still mending stockings in the heel, work gets on slowly on board ship. At noon our lat. was 40-35. Long 44-34 East. Breeze freshening, ship going about 8 knots an hour, this is what I call a comfortable breeze. I forgot to mention that when a sheep is killed my Skye maid is employed to make the haggis, and very good she makes it.

Friday, 20th November: ...Had a black pudding for breakfast today and some small ones of pig's blood garnished with fried pork, a strange dish you will say, however it seemed to be very much relished; one of our pigs met with a strange death yesterday, it was choked in a small cask of yeast the cook had prepared for baking bread.... Capt Gray has hopes of being in New Zealand by Christmas Day. 6 o'clock blowing a strong gale, Capt Gray just making the ship what he calls snug for the night...

Saturday, 21st November: ...A strong breeze in our favour last night, was very stormy tho not much afraid; I could not sleep neither could Capt C from the noise. The children fortunately are never disturbed. We have had a good run since yesterday, upwards of 200 miles, if I had my wish I would prefer *quieter sailing* tho not quite so fast... 6 o'clock wind increasing, in daylight I am quite ashamed of the nervous fears I have at night. I sometimes fancy that the man at the helm is falling asleep and not steering, then that we have too much sail up and a squall will lay her on her beam ends, next I begin to smell fire. Every vessel I ever heard of lost at sea comes to my recollection. I was not in this state when I came first away, my mind I know is weakened, but thank God my bodily health is now quite good. 8 o'clock busy looking out clean things for the children and giving them a Saturday washing. Wind has fallen considerably. Capt Gray very angry at Skye woman for refusing to make haggis on Sunday. I did not interfere. A great quantity of sea-weed passed the ship, Capt says it has come from Desolation Island.

5 *Tuesday, 15th September, 1840* – 'Two vessels in sight today, one of them
our friend the Austrian polacca'. This illustration shows a Mediterranean polacca,
L'Heureuse Marie, painted by Nicolas Cammillieri in 1810

6 *Monday, 16th November, 1840* – '...the *Vernon* from London to Calcutta,
left 17th Sept, she has a steam engine and seemed about 1000 tons, she is a
splendid looking ship, saw 8 or 9 ladies on board so gaily dressed'

9 William and Matilda Johnstone and their family painted during a visit to Scotland in 1855

7 *Saturday 6th November, 1841* – 'We were leaving home, country, and all the beloved companions of our youth, to seek our fortune in a strange and distant land –'

8 *Christmas Day, 1841* – 'in the evening the Emigrants got up a little dancing amongst themselves to the tune of an old cracked fiddle which happened to be on board'

Sunday, 22nd November: Desolation Island. Passed a very comfortable night. Wind still fair and blowing a stiff breeze, threatening rain and altogether a very cold, comfortless day; passed most of the day in my own cabin; John learnt his questions etc very well. Had public worship as usual. A very large whale seen quite close to the ship. Catherine has come to the cuddy for the first time for several days. 2 o'clock so cloudy could not take an observation; just been superintending the children at dinner and a capital one they had; pea soup capital roast pork and rice and baked plum pudding, I fear they will miss the good fare they have when they get on shore. Colin is the only one of mine that takes the preserved milk with his porridge he likes it very much. Immense numbers of birds about the ship.

...

Friday, 27th November: Blowing rather hard in our favour with a heavy swell, a very strong wind during the night, ship going at a great rate. About 3 o'clock this morning the wind changed so suddenly from one side of the vessel to the other that she was in danger of being taken aback, the man at the helm was thrown completely over the wheel. Capt Gray was on deck immediately and to save his masts (it was blowing strong and a good deal of sail up) he put the ship as quickly as possible round to the wind, until they shifted the sails. I was very much frightened at the extraordinary rolling of the vessel and the noise on deck.... I was reading during the forenoon Colbourne's Magazine extracts in it from Mrs Trollope's amusing novel the *Widow Married*...

Sunday, 29th November: ...All beginning to talk now a great deal about our arrival, our destination and discussing our future plans. Capt C bought from Capt Gray two large stone butter jars for 4/- each, we have had the best salt butter I ever tasted on board. At noon we were in Lat 41-19 S. Long 83-29 E.

Monday, 30th November: A gloomy morning, strong favourable breeze; ship rolled such a lot during night Capt C got no sleep; she still continues to roll very much. In my own cabin all day running children's stockings in the heel. Astonishing how quickly the time passes, there is so much sameness. So cloudy no observation could be taken today. Capt Gray expects a hard gale tonight, the glass has fallen very low. 6 o'clock wind has increased very much, every prospect of a stormy

night, sea running very high; Capt Gray making or rather getting things
snug for the night....

Tuesday, 1st December: Such a night as we passed, the wind was high
till 12 o'clock, when it shifted a little and blew very hard indeed. I
could call it a storm *if I was allowed.* About daylight it modified a little.
Capt C never closed an eye from the rolling of the vessel and the noise
of the sea and wind. Fright made me pass a sleepless night; a cask of
empty bottles on the deck was thrown down and rolled on the deck, it
made a tremendous crash. One old religious man of the emigrants said
he was sure we would all go to the bottom as a judgment on the Capt
for ordering a pig to be killed on Sunday. Children slept quite soundly
through it all. John does not mind blow high or low. Colin does not
like a hard breeze for the fear the ship 'cosses', Lucy does not suffer
any inconvenience except when she finds difficulty in keeping her feet.
Susan keeps her feet better than any of them when it defies her to
stand she sets herself sitting on the floor...

...

Thursday, 3rd December: A strong favourable breeze, it is 3 weeks
today since we passed the Cape, in that time we have run 3,800 miles.
Capt Gray never had such a run except coming round Cape Horn once
in winter. I must confess I would prefer quieter sailing, even if it was a
little slower; the reason given for our having such constant high wind
is our being so far south. So much motion cannot venture on deck;
children contrive to run about the low deck. 6 o'clock glad to hear the
glass is tending upwards, wind moderating. 8 o'clock prospect of a sound
sleep tonight. This morning Colin looking out of window announced a
shoal of bottle nosed whales. Lat 42-32 Long 100-60.

Friday, 4th December: ...J.B.S. keeps entirely to her own cabin from
having only one servant she is obliged to nurse a good deal...

Saturday, 5th December: Blowing hard still with a high sea, we had a
harder gale last night than we have ever had yet. Capt Gray is my
authority for this, fortunately it was favourable; the emigrants were
much alarmed, the vessel shipped a good many seas, some of the water
found its way down the hatchway which made the people think she was
sinking. They are like me easily alarmed; we are most uncomfortable

today from the rolling of the vessel. I am obliged to sit in bed as the steadiest place to write this. Lat 43-36. Long 108-35. The last week has accustomed me so much to high wind and I was not frightened last night and even slept a good deal. Capt C never can sleep when the vessel rolls. What an awful place this must be in winter, if you ever cross the seas you must leave Britain in August or September so as to be in the high southern latitude with summer weather; we never have had good weather for more than 2 or 3 days at a time; in winter there are often weeks of it...

...

Wednesday, 9th December: A strong favourable breeze. You would have laughed if you had seen me dressing this morning; I had a basin of water on the locker washing myself, another large basin of water beside me Capt C was going to use, he was leaning against the scritoire strapping his razor, the vessel gave a tremendous roll, in attempting to save both basins I lost both and my footing, to the bargain, basins, water and I were thrown against the side of the cabin with such force that Capt Gray thought some of us were going to pay him a visit. Before I could recover my feet the next roll drove my accompaniments and I with equal force against the other side. I think I hear you say where was Capt C all this time, just looking on laughing heartily, his excuse for not assisting he could not risk spoiling his good razor by throwing it down. In the hurry fortunately I escaped all but the water. I often think of Mary's weakness in her limbs, if she was here she would be obliged to find strength in them. Our Lat 43-48 S. Long 122-54. 12 o'clock bright sunshine, had thought of going on deck till I heard it was very cold. Capt Gray killed a large porpoise before dinner and the liver of it was very nicely dressed and put down on the table. I tasted a small bit from curiosity and would not know if from sheep's liver. The sailors consider a porpoise a great treat they say it eats like beef steak but dryer and coarser....

Thursday, 10th December: ...The carpenter when pumping the ship this morning brought up some sand from the bottom of the vessel, one of the emigrants who saw it said it was easily seen we were drawing near land when the sand was coming into the ship with the water, we could not see that two weeks ago. Capt Gray says it is time *to look about us* if the ocean has become *so shallow*....

Friday, 11th December: Beautiful bright day blowing a hard but favourable gale. About 8 o'clock this morning, squall with a heavy shower of rain which obliged them to furl some of the sails. We have had a fine run since yesterday. At 12 noon to 12 today 204 miles, we are in lat 43-51 S. Long 131-56 E. Some of the emigrants are much afraid we have passed New Zealand, we are so long of arriving, their remarks are very amusing, one old 79 year old pensioner from... who was 20 years in the regiment is quite an oracle among them, he certainly shows he had *doubled the Cape more than once.* I am busy giving the last mending to John's surtout that it will bear. Colin quite whole altho he has worn it as much as his brother; it is too cold for their french shirts. Louisa has fairly worn out her dark silk, she is wearing her crimson velvet, it looks well with a clean pinafore; she has still two of her prints clean; my saxony is my constant wear it is the most useful and my black cap equally so. J.B.S. begins to be rather ill off for caps, she envies me my black one, she wears an old black merino and a shawl handkerchief, on Sundays she puts on an old black silk. A collar keeps a long time clean here, I wear mine a fortnight without being at all dirty....A tremendous row tonight again between the 1st mate and Mr Macdonald's culprit (I mean the sailor to whom he gave the Bible) the rascal got hold of the mate because he had found fault with him when both were up the rigging and threatened to throw him overboard. The Capt gave him a sound drubbing with a stick and hung him for an hour by a rope round his waist over the ship's side to clean the chain plates near the water edge. Then he was pardoned.

Saturday, 12th December: I forgot to mention that we have a Venetian and Russian on board as sailors, the former is the cleanest and best behaved sailor on the ship, and the latter is the dirtiest, both speaking a little English. Busy in the evening giving the children their Saturday washing and looking out clean clothes for tomorrow. Curious how reconciled the children are to the ship, they never ask when they are to see land except Colin. I am certain John will regret leaving the *Blenheim...*

Sunday, 13th December: ...Catherine does nothing but read except while giving lessons to the children and occasionally some slow worsted work, she fiddles at it. It is alleged by the other young men that Dr Sutherland is looking sweet at her... His fortune is between £400 and £500 and 100 acres of land. Dr Campbell may be a good doctor but you would never think so from his manner, he speaks with such a Highland accent and expresses himself so ill you would think he had not spoken English till he was at least twenty. I must say he is most attentive to his duties and most obliging; we have always found him particularly so at all events we have not a very polished party, we have what is better a very merry and social one....

Monday 14th December: A fine fair morning but cold, a favourable breeze carrying us about 7 miles an hour, everyone on the *qui vive* expecting to see land, a constant lookout from the mast head. Capt Gray on making up his reckoning at noon found he was further south than we expected, consequently we will only see land from a great distance. About ½ past 12 there was a cry from the mast head of land in sight, shortly afterwards those with *sharp eyes* could see it from the deck, you cannot fancy what a sensation this caused among people who for 16 weeks have seen nothing but sky and water except the desert island of Trinidada. As we were about 30 miles distant I only saw the land like a dark cloud, it was the south part of Van Dieman's Land. Capt Gray says we would be in Hobart Town last night if that had been our destination. While off the land in the evening we had heavy showers of rain and the smoothest sea we have had since we left the tropics. We were delighted to find Capt Gray was quite correct in his reckoning. 6 o'clock the land more distinctly seen, some of the gents saying it was like the point of Ardnamurchan. We have only been 32 days from the Cape to Van Dieman's Land an unprecedented quick passage; we have now been 34 days without an adverse wind, this is looked on as quite extraordinary.

Tuesday, 15th December: A beautiful morning, much warmer, the favourable breeze still continuing tho not so strong as we have been accustomed to, still we are progressing 5 or 6 miles an hour. A woman delivered of a son last night, this makes the sixth child born on board and all very fine, thriving children, this woman with all her former confinements had long and difficult labours, yesterday evening she did not feel herself very well, the Dr desired her to go into the hospital, she thought she would have plenty of time to remove after she was taken ill, however matters came so quick upon her that the child was born before she could be removed; Dr C was very angry at her and no wonder, think how unpleasant for him going about her before so many women and married men who sleep in the same place; to crown all not one stitch had she prepared for the child, it was rolled in an old petticoat of the mother's. She is a carpenter's wife from Skye. All the other women had their baby things so neat and tidy, particularly the low country women; they come up on Sundays so clean and dressed some of them with white frocks and nice little hoods.... After tea the Capt killed with a hook and line 6 large albatrosses, one or two of them measured 10 ft 8 inches between the tips of the wings, some of them, almost pure white were beautiful birds they are valuable on account of the quantity of down on them....

....

Friday, 18th December: Beautiful bright day, sea as smooth as the Clyde a light breeze favourable, for some days the crew have been employed scraping the masts before giving them a new coat of paint, discovered this morning the fore mast was very much decayed and sprung under the top, the carpenter is putting a piece of wood in where the decayed part was dug out, it will help to strengthen it; this will oblige Capt Gray to remain a month in New Zealand to get a new mast put up, most extraordinary it did not give way with the strong winds we had and the press of sail we sometimes carried. Capt Gray is sure we will have our Christmas dinner on board, he says if we are only making the land on that day he will be so anxious and constantly on the poop he will not enjoy himself. I have been occupied a great part of the day making out a list of every article we have on board, it is a tolerable long list. Lat 43-3. Long 157-12. This morning about 2 o' clock I was startled out of a doze by a mouse that was scrambling about the bed, falling on my shoulder, it then got under my night-gown; I nearly went distracted when I felt it creeping on my body, I jumped out of the berth and it required some persuasion to get me into it again; I give myself great credit for not screaming. You would be amused to see my Skye woman and Capt C hunting the mouse in the cabin this evening, they got hold of it after a hard chase.

Saturday, 19th December: ... Our cannons, which amount to 4 were taken out of the hold today (except one which is always on deck) to get them in readiness to fire a salute on casting anchor at Wellington. Capt Gray applying to J.B.S. and I for old flannel petticoats to make cartridges; I told him mine were too good to use for such a purpose; it is so warm we are sitting with all our cabin windows open. Lat 42-35

Long. 161-12. J.B.S. very busy packing all day. I proposed beginning on Monday, on saying something about it Capt Gray said none was allowed to pack till just about to cast anchor, that packing early was sure to bring on foul wind. J.B.S. proposing to take her things down again for fear of reflections. Great preparation in steerage of bonnets, caps, gowns etc for landing. Our party will not give the New Zealanders a high opinion of Highland beauty; I never saw so many very plain looking.

...

Monday, 21st December: ...Both my domestics busy today cleaning out my cabin, washing down the paint on the sides and roof, determined to deliver it up in good order. I got, by Capt Gray's orders, 3 gallons of water for this purpose; intend to have the boys' cabin scrubbed to-morrow....

Tuesday, 22nd December: A beautiful day, Capt Gray complaining of the want of wind, afraid the change of Moon on Wednesday may bring a gale, we expect by that time to be in Cook Straits where it will be anything but pleasant to encounter bad weather. This forenoon a great many whales in sight, some of them came so close to the vessel I could have tossed a biscuit on their backs, even I, blind as I am, saw their mouths and the air holes through which they blow the water quite distinctly; they were sperm whales, Capt Gray said some of them must have been at least 80 ft long; the children were astonished beyond measure at their size and the noise they made spouting up the water; even Susan called out there was 'Jimmy Ducks' this is a Bogie they tell her lives in the sea. At dinner, quizzing Mr Macdonald at the figure he would cut driving his sheep and four hens he has bought from the Capt into Wellington.... Louisa in deep distress at having lost a purse given her by the carpenter for a kiss; it was made of the skin of the foot of an albatross; by Colin's advice she tied a line to it and towed it out at the cabin window and of course lost it....

Wednesday, 23rd December: ...Capt Gray turned all hands up in the steerage at 4 o'clock this morning to commence the scrubbing, such a chattering and noise as the women made.... *A cry of land about ½ past 10 o'clock,* everyone in such a state of excitement so anxious to get the first peep of the land of our adoption. It was Cape Farewell on the north of the South Island; it appeared to be very high land. We soon lost sight of it. Cooks Straits are 80 miles broad at the entrance. We have fairly entered them. The sea is quite green in colour. Capt Gray hopes to anchor in Port Nicholson tomorrow afternoon if the breeze continues as it is at present. The land we saw today was so far off that we could only see the outline. Lat 40-18. Long 172-24. Capt C. Had his straw hat blown overboard tonight.

Thursday, 24th December: During the night we had a strong favourable breeze. 11 o'clock the ship lay too still, 3 o'clock in the morning when the day begins to dawn, Capt Gray took this precaution because he had never been here before and the Straits are so narrow in some parts that the navigation is rather intricate. Just when the moon changed last night a very sudden squall came on, it was violent while it lasted. Fortunately it didn't continue long from the ship laying too, we felt it more I confess I felt very anxious and often wished myself out in the blue water again. Capt Gray sat up all night, he seemed very anxious, this place is so subject to sudden gales of wind. This morning almost calm, great fears spring that we will not cast anchor today. About 11 o'clock a smart breeze sprung up to our great disappointment right ahead of us; we have been taking all day and making no progress. Capt Gray says with this wind it will take us 4 days to make out Port Nicholson, a fair wind would bring us there in 6 hours; this is very tantalizing, we are about 60 miles from our destination, we have had land in sight in both sides all day; about 7 this evening we came within about 8 miles of the North Island; it is very high land and very precipitous. Near the coast we could see large trees on the tops of the hills altho there were none on the side next to the sea. A large butterfly (of course a New Zealand one) was seen on board the ship; we smelt the land quite distinctly this evening and saw fire on shore. I have been busy packing all day. Capt Gray quite disconcerted that he will not be able to enjoy his Christmas dinner from not being at anchor. 8 o'clock the breeze has died away completely, it is a complete calm.

Friday, 25th December: A beautiful bright sunny day, so warm cannot bring myself to think this is Christmas Day. A very light breeze sprung up about 11 o'clock against us. Capt C saying we may be a week of anchoring. All very merry at dinner, a favourable breeze came on about 6 o'clock which, with a good allowance of wine, put the gents in famous spirits. A lovely evening, went up on deck to look at the emigrants dancing, they got some grog to keep their Christmas. Capt Gray expects to anchor tomorrow at breakfast time. Sat up till 11 o' clock at which time the vessel had just got through the narrows and lay to for the night.

Saturday, 26th December: When we went to bed last night it was blowing a light breeze, a beautiful starry night; judge of our astonishment on awaking this morning to find it blowing a very hard gale right against us. Capt Gray mistook another bay for Port Nicholson; instead of anchoring as we expected at 9 in the morning we were obliged to pass Port Nicholson and were drived out 30 miles from the land; it was quite one of the storms Pollock describes as so frequent in the straits; altho blowing hard not a cloud was to be seen in the sky and the sun shining so bright. I was dreadfully alarmed, if we had been in an open sea I would not have minded it. I dreaded one of the sudden shifts of wind that Pollock describes, likewise which might drive us on shore; my fears got so much the better of me I believe I afforded great amusement to the gentlemen. The gale commenced at 2 o'clock this morning. Capt Gray thinks it will moderate about that time.

Sunday, 27th December: A beautiful mild morning, just as Capt Gray expected. The wind went down and changed in our favour about 2 this morning. The Capt is in rather a dilemma about finding out the harbour; there is not proper chart of it published; he is not sure which of the bays it may be. Very stupid of the Company not to have some signal put up to shew the proper entrance. Went up on deck after breakfast, we were off the bay thought most likely to be the proper entrance. To make sure the Capt lowered a boat with six hands, they were to make a signal if they found we were in the right place; besides this we had five cannon fired with the hope of bringing a pilot to our assistance. Before the boat had gone any distance from the ship Somes Island and Wards Island were discovered from the mast head which made the Capt so sure he had at least found the proper place that he made sail into the bay. You may fancy the state of excitement we were all in, the children calling out everything they saw or imagined they saw; Louisa even the length of saying she heard the New Zealanders speaking. At length a ship was seen at anchor which was the first symptom we had of being near Wellington. The town consists of a number of small houses some wooden and some thatched, both on the sea beach and a few on an elevated plain behind. We were much disappointed at the wild appearance the country presented. The Bay is so very extensive it would contain the British Navy and more, and surrounded on every side by hills wooded to the top. The climate would be delightful but for the high winds that prevail. I am told a very short way inland the weather is so much milder that you will scarcely feel a breath of air when blowing a hard gale in the harbour. We counted 12 ships of all sizes at anchor before the Town. The moment our anchor was out a number of boats came off the shore to us. Some of the gentlemen were very superior in appearance and manner to what I expected to see. We were much disappointed to find that the Surveying Department had been so slow in its operations there was no chance of getting our sections for some time, even those who came in the *Royal Merchant* have not been provided with theirs. Our land will be 80 (130?) miles from Wellington, at Wanganui. To make up for this we are told by all who have seen that part of the country that the land is more level and much easier cleared. Indeed the fine harbour at Port Nicholson is all it has to recommend it. Up the river Hutt about 8 miles from Wellington there is very fine land but heavily timbered and of course a great expense, the clearing of it from being so near the chief town where this is always a demand for everything it will pay the expense well. Some of the natives came on board dressed in European clothes. As I have brought the ship to an anchor I will now close my journal. Our proceedings from the 27th I will give you in a letter which I will dispatch by the first ship which sails and that I hope you will receive long before this comes to hand, as I intend sending my journal home by Capt Gray and he returns by Manilla and China. I hope this will afford you some amusement, I have been very particular in putting down everything, as I know nothing would be too trifling to interest you. I have enclosed for your amusement an invitation card I got to a Ball. Now that the voyage is over I must say I thought very little of it, and were it not for the severe trial we met with I think I would have even enjoyed it; to be sure we were most fortunate in weather, ship and Commander; to give you an idea how attentive Capt Gray is, from the Tuesday we entered Cooks Straits till we anchored in Port Nicholson on Sunday he never went to bed; he is rather blunt in his manner, I always liked him and found him most attentive and kind, were it nothing more than the love he had for the little lamb who is no more I would always feel a deep interest in his welfare....

And now my dear Mother and Sister I will bid you goodbye and may God bless you.   Your most affectionate JESSIE CAMPBELL

PART 4

The Husband's Story

Commentary

William Johnstone was born in 1819. His wife, Martha Matilda Birnie, was born in 1822 of a family apparently professionally connected with the sea. The couple were married when William was twenty-two, Matilda only nineteen. Shortly afterwards William sold up his possessions and sailed with his young wife for Tasmania in the barque *Arab*, Captain W. Westmorland. The *Arab* had been built at Southampton in 1827, fourteen years earlier. She was just under 300 tons and owned in London by Godwin and Company at the time of the Johnstone's passage in her.

The diary which follows was written by the young couple on their way to Australia. Like the other journals and letters in this book, it mirrors the social climate of its time. William Johnstone was a merchant and he was bound for Australia with sufficient capital to establish a small retail business. The *Arab's* decks must have been so confined that all the passengers, however they travelled, were forced into close proximity, but the social gulf between the Johnstones and the Somerset labourers who formed the bulk of the *Arab's* passengers was a wide one. These emigrants were the very people whom William Johnstone, the emigrant with·capital, would be seeking to employ in his business in Launceston.

The Johnstones appear to have been well-satisfied with the ship although their accommodation must have been very cramped. At the

end of the journal there is a list of the supplies on which the cabin
passengers lived during their four month's passage and this does not
suggest that their diet lacked either in quantity or variety.

The *Arab's* departure was delayed (in the manner of the departure of
most merchant ships until very recent times) and while they were lying
in the Thames at anchor off Gravesend waiting to sail, the young
couple were visited by William's mother, his sister Emily with her
husband George Stephens and two other relatives. The *Arab* towed the
boat containing these visitors some way down the river before 'we cast
them off and were finally left to our now somewhat melancholy
reflections'. But the Johnstones were to see Emily and George again
soon for they shortly afterwards sailed for Tasmania themselves.

The gale the *Arab* met with in the Channel moved William Johnstone
to write in vivid terms of the conditions on board a small wooden
sailing ship in bad weather. Like other writers of his period, he refers to
the general noisiness of the experience, the now forgotten but obvious
'creaking of every part of the vessel'. Another traveller of the forties
wrote of these noises at greater length. 'Imagine', he said, 'a huge
wicker basket of the driest materials, filled with heavy weights,
suspended by each end, and put into rapid motion by being violently
jerked backwards, forwards and sideways, its creaking and screaming
will very nearly resemble the grating of the new mahogany panelling in
the cabin, which succeeds so loudly and so incessantly to drown all
conversation'.

The hard-pressed little *Arab* put into Falmouth, as many a vessel has
done before and since. Six weeks later, just south of the equator, the
Arab met the *Cambridge,* also of about 300 tons, then a nearly new
vessel and under the command of Captain S. Graham. She had been
built in Nova Scotia in 1840 and was bound from Buenos Ayres to
Glasgow. The meeting of two such vessels at sea after many days without sight of another ship was always an important event to be talked
about long afterwards and William's description of this particular
meeting conveys the drama very well. The *Lady Emma,* seen by the
Johnstones from the *Arab* in the harbour below Launceston was a
barque of 231 tons, built at Portsmouth in 1824 and owned in London
by R. Betts.

The passage was uneventful. Hundreds of similar voyages to Australia
were made throughout the nineteenth century. This was the longest
passage in the normal run of ocean commerce and it was to be the last
great sailing ship route, as the journal of Anne Stanley, reproduced in

the last section of this book, shows. It was also the last sailing emigrant route, for though the emigrant trade from Britain across the North Atlantic passed out of sail to steam as early as the beginning of the 1860s, passengers continued to sail to Australia until the early years of the present century. There were good reasons for this. For all its dangers and difficulties a sailing vessel passage to Australia was, in relation to its length, a far easier proposition than one westwards across the North Atlantic. The average westward North Atlantic passage in the nineteenth century under sail was about six weeks. Although the distance is much more than two and a half times the breadth of the North Atlantic, Australia was only sixteen weeks away from Britain and many passages were made in three months or even less.

The Johnstones prospered in Tasmania. Their original home in Launceston is presently occupied as a private house. William founded a retail general merchant's business in the town in partnership with Stuart Eardley Wilmot. This developed into the firm of Johnstone and Wilmot Pty Ltd which still employs direct descendants of.William Johnstone. William and Matilda had six children, three boys and three girls, and at least twenty-one grandchildren. Miss Eleanor Johnstone, of Mildura, a great-great-granddaughter, kindly allowed us to use this journal and the photograph of the painting of William and Matilda with their family which was made when they returned to Britain on a visit in the 1850s (Plate 9).

*Journal written by William Johnstone on his 'Wedding
Journey' to Launceston, Van Dieman's Land, November
1841 – March 1842*

After the extreme kindness I received from my family and friends
during the last two months of my residence in England, the least return
I can make is to write a short sketch of our proceedings on board the
Barque *Arab*, Capt W. Westmorland, bound from London to Launceston...

    We left Gower Street on Monday morning, 1st November 1841 - I
proceeded by the 11.o'clock Steamer to Gravesend - circumstances
detained the *Arab* there during the week, which time we spent very
happily in lodgings in St George's Terrace, in the society of those kind
relatives who had accompanied us from London. 'All that's bright must
fade however', and accordingly at about 10 o'clock on Saturday night
we were once more compelled to take a sad adieu from our friends, and
escorted by I.I.M.J. Hills and Gets and G. Biewe entered a small boat at
Gravesend Pier, which quickly put us on board the Arab (350) tons
Capt Westmorland, bound for Launceston, Van Diemen's Land. Our
feelings at this moment, may, as the newspapers would say, be more
easily imagined than described. We were leaving home, country, and all
the beloved companions of our youth, to seek our fortune in a strange
and distant land...(Plate 7). After arranging our cabin, the rest of the
party left us to the sad reflection of 'Our Friends are gone'.

    We employed ourselves for some time in perusing the scraps inscri-
bed on the walls of our cabin, and soon afterwards turned in. About
5 o'clock on Sunday morning, we were aroused by the sailors heaving
up the Anchor - jumped up, and were soon most agreeably surprised by
the sound of voices immediately under our windows., They proved to
be John and George Stephens, who had come off in a boat to pay
their last respects. Finding that we were up they returned to the Hotel
and brought off my Mother, Sarah and Emily. This was indeed a cheering sight. After having towed their boat some distance down the river,
we cast them off and were finally left to our now somewhat melancholy

reflections. This day was chiefly spent in arranging the furniture of our cabin, discovering the contents of the several packages, and making everything fast ready for sea. The emigrants, about 200 in number, including men, women and children chiefly on deck, and mostly engaged reading their Bibles and Tracts - some of them had mounted on the Poop, from whence they were most unceremoniously expelled by the Captain, who commanded them never to have the impudence to shew their faces there again. We dined at 3, and a more woefully gloomy table it was never my lot to sit at. All seemed occupied with their own thoughts, and the Captain our Chairman, never opening his mouth unless spoken to, or except for the purpose of *roaring* out to the people outside the cuddy to take that *noisy squalling* brat out of the way, silence continued the language preferred by all. At 6 pm we brought up in the Leigh Roads, about 7 miles from the Nore Light. On Monday 8th Nov a thick fog prevented our sailing till 10. At 8 in the evening we anchored opposite the North Foreland Light House - spent the evening in preparing letters to send on shore by the Pilot. Matilda found the motion of the boat somewhat unpleasant. On Tuesday morning we again got under weigh, and anchored early in the afternoon just off Deal. Here the Pilot left us taking our letters with him.

The wind continuing adverse we were detained in the Downs till Sunday Morning 14th Nov...

The weather during these few days being moderate, the motion did not in-accommodate us, and we became a little better acquainted with our passengers - but I shall reserve my descriptions of them for the present. The Deal boatmen came off to us every day bringing fresh supplies of bread, beef, vegetables, and herrings, which found a ready market amongst the emigrants, as a relish with their salt provisions. They also brought us the newspapers with the intelligence of the birth of an heir to the British Throne - Long Life to His Highness. But better than all, on Sunday morning they were the bearers of two most acceptable packets of letters for us from London...

Whilst reading our despatches a heavy gale suddenly sprang up, and having with great difficulty recovered our anchor we dashed on under double reefed topsails, and fortunately succeeded in avoiding all the numerous vessels actively engaged in weighing anchor, shaving one of them so closely that a sailor might have jumped from our bowsprit on to her quarter. We ran close in to Dover, and landed our Pilot who came on board at Deal - paying the boatmen who were on the look-out for him, £4 for landing him, though we were close upon shore. We still kept up our 9 knots beating a large steamer that was ahead of us at starting. The gale continued to increase in fury, and after passing Beachy Head and Isle of Wight, we could not make a fair wind of it, but under close reefed topsails were running backwards and forwards across the Channel, keeping always out of sight of land, the vessel pitching and tossing most cruelly and waves swathing over the bulwarks. The between decks where the Emigrants were all stowed away (sometimes a man and his wife and two children in one bed) were in a most horrible condition. The seas had washed down the hatchways and the floor a complete pond, many of the beds drenched through ; ˙d through. In addition to these delights, with some four or five exceptions, they were all violently seasick - some of the women fainting, and two going into convulsions - all calling out for Brandy, which they had been told by the Emigration Agent had been put on board for their use - but which they now found was 'nonest inventus'. The squall had come on so suddenly that their boxes were all adrift, flying about from one side to the other, with nearly 50 whining sick squalling children to complete their misery.

One day we were sitting at dinner, or attempting to do so, when a heavy sea broke over the Poop, smashing in our skylight, the vessel laying over almost on her beam ends - a lamp which was hanging up in the cuddy was thrown down broken to pieces, and though we had by this time acquired some dexterity in the art of balancing our plates in our hands, yet to-day one or two of us had the pleasure of a lapfull instead of a spoonful. It was a curious scene outside the cuddy. Our cook, who always looked more like a Mulatto than an Englishman, which he maintained himself to be, was hanging over his caboose, his face perfectly black from the smoke of the funnel; dealing out pea-soup to those of the Emigrants who were well enough to fetch. The heavy seas which broke over the side, occasionally extinguishing the fire, or pouring into the coppers by way of seasoning the soup. Their salt beef is boiled in seawater or they would have suffered much more from this cause. In endeavouring to walk from the galley to the hatchway with their bowls in hands, three out of five were thrown down, by which they not only gained a complete ducking, but lost their dinner as well, for away sailed the carrots, beef coulli and etc, much to the delight doubtless of the porpoises surrounding our vessel - and provisions once served out could not be replaced.

The Emigrants, chiefly Somersetshire Labourers, all lamented their foolishness in leaving home - 'Catch I at sea again' groaned a newly

10 Appledore in the early 1920s. The schooner with sails set is the *Haldon,* then owned by the Slade family

11 Appledore quay as Annie Slade knew it when she first went to sea. The vessels are the cargo smack *Happy Return,* built at Fowey in 1846 and the schooner *Countess Caithness* of Wick, built at Garmouth ten years later.

12 & 13 Wedding photographs of Tamzin and Edward Williams. On July 24, 1850, they set out in the barque *Joseph Cunard* on their honeymoon passage towards Quebec

married lassie - 'No, not for all the men on the face of the earth.' 'Just give I the chance of getting ashore, and don't you wish you may get me here again' replied her loving husband. Such affectionate remarks abounded. By degrees we had got down the Channel, weather dreadfully cold, and on Saturday 20th November, were a few miles west of Lands End. Nearly the whole of this week Matilda remained in bed, occasionally getting up to tea. On 18th, being in want of a candle, I cautiously opened the doors of the book-case in which they were stowed away, when in an instant the whole contents, books, parcels, candles etc, were saluting my head in a most unpleasant manner. Everything was turned out - and all the exertions of myself and steward being insufficient to replace them, so much were we lying over - and we were compelled to leave them lying about on the floor. The only light in our cabin was admitted through a small bullseye in the deck both our stern windows having deadlights up. Sleep at night was out of the question. The awful creaking of every part of the vessel, hollering of the sailors and roaring of the sea, with noises of every description, completely preventing it. The Captain (who said he had never had such a thrashing in the Channel before,) did not take off his clothes for several days together, remaining on deck nearly all night.

The gale not abating on Sunday, he determined to shape his course for Falmouth, and accordingly on Monday morning we were delighted by finding ourselves just entering the Carrick Roads. At 8 we passed Pendennis Castle, and half an hour afterwards dropped our anchor in smooth water in the Bay between St Mawes and Flushing in full view of the town of Falmouth. Close alongside was moored the *Indian,* a vessel which left the Downs at the same time with us, also bound to Launceston with 40 Emigrants and a few passengers. She had been here ever since the Friday afternoon preceeding - Oh, how we envied her. The yell of recognition set up by the *Arabians* was answered by the *Indians.* The 74 gun ship *Illustrious* with Sir Charles Bagot the Governor of Canada on board had also put in for shelter. - Many others were there - one with bulwarks washed away, another with a mast gone - and several more or less damaged. This morning Mrs Wm breakfasted in the cuddy for the first time since coming on board.

Our first employment was to write home, with a request for despatches by return of post. Our next to order a boat to take us on shore. This not arriving till late in the afternoon we postponed our visit till the next day, which unfortunately proved a regular Cornwall day - Lloyd's Agent, however, coming on board to enquire for orders, the

Skipper and I jumped into their gig and went ashore. The mortality amongst our stock having been so great that he wanted a fresh supply, and accordingly purchased 18 more fowls, 3 pigs and some fresh beef etc. After rambling about the town and securing a few London newspapers, we dined at Pearce's Royal Hotel and returned to the *Arab* about 5, when we found the Doctor and fellow passengers had gone off to St Mawes. They soon returned, and we passed a tolerably merry evening after our excursion.

On 24th, the westerly wind still prevailing, Matilda, I and our three companions, somewhat to the Captain's annoyance all went on shore together. He would not allow the Doctor to accompany us as he said 'he could sail without us, but could not dispense with the services of the Surgeon', We thoroughly enjoyed our little excursion, again dining at Pearce's - laying in a store of fine St Michael's 'and a few other little creature comforts'. Vexatiously enough for us who were expecting the arrival of another budget of 'Pennyworth's' in the evening, we found on awaking the following morning that the wind was sufficiently favourable to enable to slant off. The majority of vessels in the harbour were bending their sails, and weighing anchor, so that the Captain (who was also anxious to hear from London) had no excuse for delaying our departure. We had just time to write a hasty epistle or two when the Pilot left us, and bidding a final adieu (at any rate for many years) to the shores of Merry Ould England, we once more stood out to sea, disconsolate enough at losing our letters when so nearly in our grasp. This being 25th, we did not forget to drink Mrs B's good health.

The breeze which tempted us out of harbour, died away in the evening, leaving us to enjoy as best we might the uncomfortable rolling of a heavy sea. The following day we spoke to a vessel from Quebec - terribly leaky, the crew working lustily at the Pumps to keep her above water. During the next ten days the wind continued so adverse that we did not make 100 knots on our course during the whole time, leaving us exposed to the force of the gale and an ugly sea. On 6th December however, the wind once more veered round to a favourable quarter, and the swell moderated so much that we were enabled on 7th to have our stern deadlights taken down, which was a great comfort. The same evening one of the Emigrants' children died, having been ill ever since it came on board, and was buried at 8 o'clock the next morning, the Surgeon acting as Chaplain. The weather was already getting much finer and warmer and we were brushing over the Bay of Biscay very briskly, dimly sighting the coast of Portugal. As in duty bound, we did not omit to congratulate you George B. on the return of 8th. The 10th proving a most lovely day, Matilda got up to breakfast, and we became very busy all the morning in rearranging our traps after the late confusion. Spent the afternoon very pleasantly on deck. On Sunday 12th December we both rose in particularly elevated spirits - the weather like a fine June day in England - everybody arranged in *Sunday* attire - the Emigrants donning their blue coats and bright buttons in lieu of their weekday smock frocks. Divine Service was performed on deck for the first time, and was attended by nearly all on board.

In looking over my portmanteau I found a packet from G.A.S. with a very kind note, enclosing a set of tablets which will be always valued. In packing our boxes, our kind friends had distributed a considerable number of notes and other little remembrances, which were indeed refreshing and gratifying to discover. We used them sparingly, and so contrived to have nearly two every week up to this time (2nd March 1842, when we have one left, and expecting to see land, either the Australian Continent or Kings Island in 8 or 10 days). The morning after 14th was very fine and warm - R.M.E. we duly remembered you - and Matilda commenced working a chain for you. In the afternoon we arrived off Porto Santo, the first of the Madeira Islands, and could just discern the Husky Cliffs. On the following morning we found ourselves off Madeira, but too far off to see more than the hills. In the afternoon we passed about 20 miles to the east of the two Deserters, which appeared like very high rocky mountains rising out of the sea. This was a most delightful day - the sun shining brilliantly - thermometer on our cabin standing at $70°$, sea very calm, with a light breeze taking us along at the rate of 7 knots an hour. On 16th we again discovered land in the Island of Palma, one of the Canaries. Bidding adieu to this, we crowded all possible sail and on 21st made St Antonio, the westermost of the Cape de Verds, bearing about 10 miles east of us - the very lofty hills being quite distinct and having a very picturesque appearance. Therm standing at $76°$ but getting up daily.

On the following day, all the children were mustered, and with the help of a few alphabets, tracts and testaments, school was commenced for two hours every morning. Some of them made little progress - but the great benefit we derived was in the temporary relief it afforded from the dreadful noise and riot they created from morning till night. 23rd was marked by having little more rolling than usual - Therm $80°$. Saturday 25th December at noon placed us in N. Latitude 7" 38′ W Longtitude 22½° - the heat *rather* oppressive (Ther $85°$ in the shade and 125° in the sun) though we were still progressing at between 7 and 8 knots an hour. This was perhaps the dullest Christmas Day we had ever spent. Almost the only notice taken on the ship was performing Divine Service in the morning, and in the evening the Emigrants got up a little dancing amongst themselves to the tune of an old cracked fiddle which happened to be on board (Plate 8). I employed myself in the morning in writing a letter in readiness for any homeward bound ship we might fall in with, which unfortunately we had no opportunity of putting on board.

As may be supposed, we spent this usually convivial day in thinking and conversing about those friends by whom we felt convinced we should be more than usually spoken of and affectionately remembered at their hospitable boards. The sailors also took a holiday and feasted on Plum Dough and an additional glass of grog. Our Turkey at dinner was rather the worse for the high temperature - half of it having fallen away before coming to the table. Sunday 26th, a lovely day, but heat excessive. Remained on deck during Service under the awning. On Monday 27th we lost the North East Trade Winds and became completely becalmed. The discord caused by two flutes and a triangle, besides the fiddle, contrived to amuse the Emigrants in the evening, and incite a little more 'stepping out' as our tars say. About midnight, we were awakened by some of the most awful claps of thunder we had ever heard, accompanied by most vivid flashes of lightening. The storm lasted for about half an hour. In these latitudes they are a very common occurence - but grand and spectacular. The lightening reflected on the water truly is, making the vessel appear to be surrounded on every side by one vast furnace, the thunder rolling close over the ship with a noise equal to the discharge of a whole broadside of artillery, are indeed appalling. They make you stand trembling, breathless and awestricken - it is impossible not to feel affected. Even our swearing second mate, who never brings out three words without an oath, was effectually silenced during its duration.

For four days we were completely becalmed, then contrived to crawl on till the morning of 6th January, when a breeze gradually sprung up which eventually settled into the South East Trades. During the whole of this week the heat proved excessive, quite knocking up Matilda, who was not able to leave her cabin from Monday till Friday. One of our fellow Passengers in celebrating the birth of another year, contrived to stow away sufficient grog to cause him to reel about the decks for an hour or two, when two sailors kindly carried him down to bed. On 1st January 1842, we commenced the day by wishing each other a happy new year, the same to all our friends and many happy returns of the day to our chere ami Wade E.C.B. Just before dinner we caught a shark 8 ft 3 ins long - having four rows of teeth perfect, consequently four years old, as it is said they gain a fresh set every year. The jaws were preserved, cleaned and hung up in the rigging to dry ready for presenting to Mrs Wm. Provokingly enough the upper jaw was stolen during the night, but we secured the teeth from the under one and will send them to you when an opportunity offers.

Whilst becalmed, we had three or four 'heavy wet' days, enabling us to fill up all the empty water casks - giving the ducks and geese a delightful swim in the lee scuppers and affording a rich treat to the sailors and emigrants, who ducked each other to their heart's content. On Sunday 2nd we saw two more sharks and the spouting of a whale, which did not however, shew itself on the surface. With the exception of a most lovely magnificent sunset on 3rd, nothing of note occured till 4th, when our eyes were once more regaled with the sight of a sail in sight about 12 miles off, going the in same direction. *Wednesday, 5th.* Yesterday's sail still in sight - spent the evening in teaching Doctor chess. About half past 2 on 6th January we crossed the equator. No notice of it was taken by the sailors, as our Captain never allowed 'Father Neptune' to come on board. On 7th, we saw another vessel ahead, and on 8th, whilst sitting in the cuddy about 1 in the afternoon preparing a letter, we were again aroused by the cry of 'Sailho'. On running up to the Poop, by the aid of the glass, we could discern a vessel rapidly bearing down upon us with all studding sails set. This was a truly exciting scene; the long speaking trumpet was brought up - the signal flags got ready in case we were only near enough for a 'bunting talk', and all set busily to work to finish despatching in the hopes of being able to put them on board her. In the course of three quarters of an hour she came up with us and proved to be the *Cambridge* of Glasgow from Buenos Ayres bound to Falmouth. It was truly tantalising to find that though she was skilfully steered within 20 yards of us, we were yet unable to ship any of the numerous despatches ready, on board of her, for both vessels being able to make a fair wind and scud along at the rate of 8 knots per hour, neither Captain would do more than furl the mainsail for a few seconds whilst we exchanged the usual queries of 'Whence Come? Where bound for? How long Out? What's your Longitude?' to which our old Skipper added a request to be reported at Lloyd's as *'All Well'.* A wave of the hand and they were gone. We watched the vessel as it gradually lessened the distance and finally faded from the sight, with mingled feelings, somewhat tinged with sadness. You may *possibly* be inclined to laugh at my romance, but I cannot help quoting Tatsy's favourite lines-

'The Bridal is over - the guests are all gone
The Bride's only sister sits weeping alone -
The wreath of white roses is torn from her brow -
And the heart of the Bridesmaid is desolate now.'

to describe our own sensations at that moment. The excitement and happy feeling at the commencement, and desolation at the close of the 'Ceremony' being so precisely similar. Meeting with a homeward bound ship is no slight event in a long voyage - its very name has a charm - and the thought that in a few weeks your new acquaintance will probably arrive at that happy land from which you have so lately departed, is alone sufficient to make you feel an interest in her.

Sunday, 9th January, was marked by intense heat and by all becoming more talkative than usual. Matilda amused the Captain by donning a white muslin dress for the first time, quite coming out in bridal attire as he termed it. On 10th our 'lookout' again refreshed us with the cry of 'Sailho', and on straining my eyes I could just discern a white speck in the distant horizon, which gradually gained upon us till 6 in the evening, when she came up with us, and declared herself the *Gertrude* from Liverpool to Valparaiso, out 38 days, whilst we had been 46 from Falmouth. Poor Tillia was so unwell all day that she could not leave her cabin. Spent the evening in giving her a first lesson in chess. Two other sails in sight a long distance off. 11th - Ma Chere still so-so. A fine breeze taking along merrily at 180 miles per diem. 12th - Till better - weather cooler. Ther 81 - played chess with Dr. Skipper proposed a game of whist in the evening, which was negatived - all disliking cards. On 13th at 7 in the morning another child which had been long dreadfully ill - 'the Spotted child' - died and was buried at Sunset. It is astonishing how soon such an occurence is forgotten on board. Much more stir was created by the discovery of some stolen flour on one of the Emigrants, for which he was put in irons and confined. Chess with Mrs Wm in evening.

On 14th the above mentioned thief was unkennelled and duly admonished. The single men diverted themselves in fighting most awfully - in which one man received such a severe black eye as to require immediate lancing. Dyce (one of the apprentices) fell down on deck in a fit which the doctor fancied was produced by a 'coup de soleil' - Tillia on deck till ½ past 8 talking with Skipper about Van Dieman's Land, Society, Etc, etc. A long lost treasure was discovered today in the shape of a cask of chloride of lime - which had been sadly wanted daily ever since our departure. Had not our stock of vinegar been good, the consequences of not having found it till now might have proved disastrous. On 15th, the sun was vertical and atmosphere very hot indeed. Till again confined to her cabin the whole day. Bridgewater offensive - poor Mr Playter sadly put out by the Captain - declared he would rather beg his bread than sail another voyage in the *Arab*. Saw the far famed Southern Cross for the first time this evening and were greatly disappointed. The stars are none of first rate magnitude and greatly surpassed in brilliancy by many northern constellations. 10 weeks tonight since our embarkation at Gravesend. On Sunday 6th January, we were about 40 miles east of Rio de Janeiro tho in the same latitude. Matilda much better - Ther 82°. We enjoyed the afternoon and evening together on deck chatting over past scenes. 17th delightful weather - sunset ¼ before 7 moŝt splendidly. 18th sighted two vessels in the distance 19th Ma Chere sadly ill - Ther 79°. 20th better. Invited the doctor into our sanctum - played chess. 21st - A marked change in the weather - strong breeze, heavy sea and squally - showery and much cooler. In the same latitude as the Cape.

At four bells in the dog watch in nautical slang - or in sober English, 6 o'clock in the evening, the Captain was astounded by the sails suddenly bounding and flapping about as if we had been caught by a white squall, for five minutes previously our good ship was cutting right merrily through the water with a fine breeze and all press of sail. On the gaining the Poop to enquire the cause, he discovered it to be merely a manoeuvre of the helmsman to be relieved from his 'trick of the wheel', the mate having omitted to call the watch. On 22nd we were once more becalmed - only making one knot per hour. Were favoured with the company of an Albatross for the first time - Shark round the vessel unshipping fine weather and putting up storm sails. Third mate refused his duty. 23rd Sunday - wished Mr Wm Brownley many happy returns of the day. Very cool and pleasant. Ther 66° - first albatross shot. Wet afternoon, but wind again sprung up. 24th - progressing famously - our fellow passengers amusing themselves in shooting at Albatrosses - 25th - Squall at 4 in the morning - shortened sail. Numerous seabirds flying about. Wind again left us in the evening - Skipper rather personal to the 'Porkies' about smoking. 26th - Again becalmed - glorious sunset - sublime moonlight. 27th - For several days we had been talking of Commodore Glass the Governor of a small Island named 'Tristan D'Acunta' (having a population of about 40 individuals) and were anxiously hoping to sail near enough for him to come on board - his invariable practice when any vessel approached his dominions. The wind was unkind, however, and all that could be discerned of Tristan was a sort of mist or cloud rising from the horizon at 7 o'clock in the evening. Captain appeared quite disappointed.

Strong breezes prevailed on 28th, followed on 29th by heavy showers throughout the day. The Emigrants caught a swallow, which the Doctor stuffed. About 7 this evening we were on the meridian of Greenwich, and we felt it quite a delightful treat to know that our time was again the same as smoky London's. The thought seemed to diminish the distance between us by thousands of miles. Till not very well - Sunday 30th, very wet morning, but fine afternoon. Till not on deck from yesterday, till Thursday afternoon 3rd February. On 4th another calm accompanied by a most uncomfortable heavy swell from the southward - On 5th a fine 8-knot breeze again sprung up - a lovely day, the deep blue ocean again became green, though still out of soundings. The Doctor spent the evening in our little boudoir playing chess. Rolling dreadfully all night, but morning of 6th fine with cheerful sunshine.

At last we were able to congratulate ourselves on our arrival at the Cape of Good Hope although we could not persuade Capt Westmorland to touch there as he had intended when at Gravesend - for our provisions and water were still ample, and a fair breeze for proceeding on our voyage. In five weeks more, thought we, we shall be at Launceston. On 7th another child of about two years old, died after an illness of two months. A very heavy sea - pitching and tossing awfully, the Skipper thought even worse than in the Channel - poor Emigrants all sadly ill, and a repetition of many of the early scenes. Ma Chere ill in bed for several days. By way of lessening her headache, the Capt ordered the carpenter to commence caulking the decks just over Matilda's head - the noise was unbearable, and it was not till after the repeated remonstrances of myself and Doctor that he would allow him to desist. So much for sea brutes.

For several days the squall had gradually been increasing, and on 11th it blew a complete gale - seas dashing over the Poop - thunder and lightening - close reefed topsails - and altogether 'nasty weather' - On 12th the wind abated, but swell continued unpleasant. On 14th caulking was again commenced, Tillia being rather better, dining in the cuddy for the first time for these 10 days. Very busy on 15th shooting Albatrosses. 17th, Cold unpleasant day - another little ocean daughter born. 19th, rolling continues - Sunday 20th fine. Tillia had pleasant walk on deck, chatting about home and the changes which would probably occur in our family 'ere we meet again'. Strong winds on 21st causing her to lay over most uncomfortably - abreast of St Paul's but out of sight. 23rd - Showery and very cold - seas over the deck, heavy lurches - bright moon. 24th - Heavy sea - dreadful rolling. At dinner leg of Pork pitched into Matilda's lap - pleasant, very - wind fresh - close-reefed topsails. 25th - Breeze fell - cold - but pleasant enough for Ma Chere to 'feel her feet again'.

Ma Chere commenced a few small preparations for landing. On 27th, Long. 100°, complete calm, much warmer. On deck chatting upon our favourite topic 'returning to dear happy old· England'. 28th - Calm continues - weather not so fine, and cooler. In eve played at cribbage with Captain. On 1st March a slight breeze springing up we again sped along at 7 knots, the Captain in good spirits hoping to reach his destination in 12 days at latest - but alas! the following morning ushered in another calm, scarcely making a knot an hour all day. Sailors and Officers all very busy scraping and repainting buckets, hencoups etc. 3rd March, wind not yet arrived - day cold, damp and smaller rains. Evening Till very sprightly, telling our fellow passengers' fortunes etc. All greatly amused by a mistake made in the dusk of the evening by the sailor at the helm - an amusing Portuguese, who mistook the Captain who was sitting on the Monkey Poop close behind him for one of the passengers, and confidently whispered in his ears 'I say, Our old Woman' (the Skipper's nickname in the forecastle) 'ess dronk' - You might imagine his look and start on discovering his error, by the Captain's angrily exclaiming 'What do you mean, sir?'

On 4th and 5th we contrived to drop a little further into the South in search of a wind, and on 6th drifted down as low as 42½°, rather too much to be pleasant, as we had to encounter such a heavy sea, causing a most uncomfortable pitching and rolling the whole night - breeze very strong. Felt pleased by the idea that once more we were within a few hundred miles from land, being at length abreast of New S Wales - weather very cold, and much too rough to allow of service being performed. 'Perkies' amused themselves in catching Albatrosses, smoking and novel reading. 7th - Sea continues heavy - squally throughout the day. Scudding under double reefed topsails. 8th - Night most uncomfortable rolling - another of the Emigrants was blessed with a small encumbrance - hundreds of Albatrosses and other sea birds about the ship - passed the carcase of a dead whale. Ma Chere had another present at dinner, in the shape of a lapful of gravy - the dish containing a leg of Pork was capsized, and the leg fell on to the seat, whilst Mrs Wm was treated with the other contents. 'Nothing when you're used to it'. At 4 o'clock am another arrival (the fourth). Painting Poop, and the whole vessel being made shipshape. About 1 a sudden squall came, and the tars being at dinner would not turn out to reef topsails so readily as they ought, which caused a regular 'row'; Chief Mate quite furious. Skipper again rejoicing at the fair wind - which is completely aft, blowing in unpleasantly enough at our cabin windows.

10th - Still going famously. Ma Chere very so-so. 11th - Sea continuing heavy. I commenced the accompanying chart, being pitched about unmercifully from side to side of our small cabin as the vessel lurched. Birds abounding. 12th - Very busy packing up. All rather down at change in the wind, which towards evening was much against us. 13th - Doctor feeling quite certain that before the expiration of another week we should have reached our haven, preached a farewell sermon this day, which attracted a full attendance. All put on 'going ashore' dress. In the afternoon fell in with a whole school of grampuses, which accompanied us for half an hour. Tillia better, but wind too high to permit her going on deck. From 13th to 18th we were all sadly disappointed by a directly contrary wind coming from the very quarter we wished to reach - numerous and constant were the repinings and murmurings during this weary time - for to make bad worse, the weather continued cold, the sea running 'mountains high' - the ship leaning over and tossing about most cruelly - every watch wearing ship even during the night.

This was perhaps the most wretched part of the voyage - all had been so looking forward to landing long ere this that they were getting quite worn out with expectation - hope deferred sickening their hearts in proportion etc, etc. When some weeks' sail from port a day's delay seems to be of no consequence, but with the wave worn traveller approaching so nearly his future home, the case is far different - an hour's illness appears an age. 18th was a much finer day - sun shining, and from the appearance of the heavens, the mariners all portend a change of wind - 'Old Betty' more cheerful in consequence. 19th - Wind changing still more in our favour, almost making our course; but sea dreadfully heavy. Great stir among the Emigrants - two accused of thieving.

Sunday 20th - Both up early and remarkably happy, thinking of this day next week when we fully hope to swell the congregation in Launceston Parish Church - fair wind going on well - quite warm and pleasant - rolling continues. On the afternoon one of the apprentices was jerked off the foretry sail-boom and fell on to the deck. He set up a most dismal yelling, but escaped without any serious injury. The morning of 21st was most lovely - bright sun, gentle breeze just warm enough to be pleasant. At breakfast the Captain informed us that at about 10 (if his Chronometers were correct) we should first catch a glimpse of *terra firma*. As may be supposed all were on the *qui vive* - telescope was mounted and brought up and a lookout sent aloft. A few minutes before 11 we heard the Mate's joyful cry 'Land ahead on the Larboard Bow', and true enough a dim mist could just be discerned rising out of the water in the distance - the old boy was quite cranky with delight. Another hour and the coast was quite distinct. The Capt frisked about the deck and rubbed his hands with all the glee of a schoolboy returning home for the holidays - 'Ah sir', he said to me, 'what a wonderful science is navigation. To think of having come 20,000 miles over the trackless ocean and yet to be enabled to name an hour and almost to the minute when we should again discover land, is indeed most astounding'. A few minutes later a fine baracouter (how d'ye spell it?) was caught and in half an hour was smoking on the cabin table - a fine white fish, something like cod in taste.

On mounting the Poop after dinner, Cape Bridgewater was full in sight - a truly refreshing sight to our eyes. Bore away for the night. In the morning 22nd weather still delightful light winds but not fair - in sight of land all day. The Lawrances and Lady Julia Percy's Islands all visible. Had a good view of Portland Bay, and were driven close in shore at Port Fairy - a spot thickly inhabited by the Aborigines. Our Skipper became quite fidgetty - not a breath of wind to carry us away from the land - to *our eyes* the scenery though really rugged, flat and sterile appeared extremely picturesque - the trees looked so truly refreshing. Hoping to make Kings Island or Cape Otway tomorrow - but tantalising enough the wind continued contrary, and on Wednesday night we found ourselves in just about the same position as on Monday, when we first caught sight of land.

On 24th, we made but little progress though we sighted Kings Island. Up early on 25th thinking and talking much of all in England. Baffling winds still prevailing, though we contrived to creep on a little in spite of them. Signalised a vessel going to Portland Bay - the first we had seen for two months. 26th - A lovely day, warm like summer - made a good slant during the night - making for Circular Head, *may* yet land tomorrow. The three Hummocks in sight at 12. By some mistake in examining his chart, the Capt had an alarm when off Kings Island. A fresh breeze was blowing and we were scudding along merrily with bentroyals, when on a sudden the lookout cried out lustily 'Breakers Ahead'. The Skipper was instantly on the alert 'Down helm, about Ship' and in a few seconds we had turned our back upon the dangerous rocks, which another quarter of an hour would have carried us upon had they not been perceived. On 27th, the wind very variable but by constant tacking were brought near enough to Van Dieman's Land to make out Circular Head - a curious looking projection, looking from the sea like an Island of the shape of a goodly Twelfth Cake, whence it derived its name. 27th was spent in fruitless attempts to reach the entrance to the Harbour. Capt Westmorland this and the following day exceedingly anxious, not being able to determine the exact position of 'Hebe's Reef', a perilous rock situated close to the entrance on which the *Hebe* was wrecked many years ago.

At night we were cheered with the sight of blaze of several large fires upon the shore, and a long discussion took place concerning the Lighthouse, several of the 'Landlubbers' declaring they could clearly distinguish the light, whilst the Officers could not perceive it. A lovely moonlight night. At daylight on Tuesday morning, 29th March 1842, we found ourselves still in sight of Van Dieman's Land - a delightful morning, the sun shining brightly and but little wind. We beat close in shore all the way from Circular Head, and by dint of constant tacking and a freshening breeze, approached the Heads towards afternoon. The appearance of the Coast is wild and rugged, but altogether different to any place I have seen in Britain. The hills are very lofty, covered thickly with trees and brushwood, and running in tiers. About 3 o'clock, signalised the Light House, and at ½ past 4 were boarded by Williams (one of the Pilots). We watched his boat as it came nearer and nearer, with some emotion, rather different in character to that with which we caught the last glimpse of a dearly freighted boat at Gravesend - and narrowly scrutinised him on stepping on board as the first specimen of a Van Dieman's Lander. The three Convicts who manned his boat also attracted much attention from their costume and expression.

For a considerable time our eager questions concerning the *Indian* and several acquaintances were left unanswered - the Pilot walking the Poop and giving his orders to the Sailors with the most amusing coolness and nonchalance, and an observer might have fancied he had been our fellow voyager over the deep - so indifferent did he seem. By 25 minutes before 6, aided by constant tacking, he cleverly brought us inside the Heads and as far in as Lagoon Bar. 'A sullen splash, a harsh ringing sound, proclaimed our Anchor gone, and our weary barque securely rode in the bright blue waters of the Convicts Land', to quote Burns's expression in his history of V.D.L.

The first thing was to send on shore for milk and bread, whilst the Emigrants and sailors set about enjoying themselves with singing and dancing. Up at 5 the next morning, and were delighted with the *Corsar* Steamer which had just come down from Launceston on her way to Port Phillip. At 9 again weighed anchor and proceeded slowly up the river - perhaps a short epistle to go by the *Lady Emma* to London hourly expected down. Shortly after passing Georgetown, we narrowly escaped a serious accident, the vessel being carried within a yard of a most dangerous rock in the middle of the stream, on which several vessels have already been wrecked. Our anchor happily held fast at the critical moment, or the consequences might have been lamentable. The river varies considerably in width, the entrance being very narrow, whilst at parts it is nearly as broad as the Thames at Gravesend. The country on either side is but partially cleared, a large portion of it being thickly wooded to the water's edge. The farm and cultivated land in some parts you may imagine was not slight refreshment to us. We were boarded by three or four gentlemen going up, who brought presents of Peaches, Apples, Grapes, Cabbages etc. At 8 pm we dropped our anchor once more at Coulson's Bend, about half way up the river, and soon after were visited by Dr Pugh and McGleadow - the chief doctor and solicitor of the place, brothers-in-law to our Capt, who politely introduced us. They left us at half past 9 taking Mr Lawrence with them.

At daybreak next morning, 31st March 1842, we finally weighed anchor and reached our moorings in full view of Launceston, at ¼ past 8. The scenery improves as you approach the town, though the latter is not seen to advantage on board. We were soon boarded by Dr Pugh, and at 9 again sat down to our last meal on board. The Capt and Doctor went ashore together at 10, and at 11, having comfortably arranged our traps, Matilda was hoisted up in a chair made out of a cask, cut and decorated with flags, and gently lowered into a boat alongside, amidst the cheers of the Emigrants. Vance and I instantly joined her, and another half hour sufficed to put us safely on *terra firma* - and thus ended our voyage on *Arab*.

Our Mess was composed of eight persons, viz -

Capt Westmorland
Mr Playter, Chief Officer
Mr Corbould, Surgeon Supert
Mr Lawrence
Mr Vance
Mr Stanford
Mr and Mrs Wm Johnstone.

The Captain, take him for all in all and compared with other Commanders in this trade, is altogether a desirable Skipper and one with whom I should be always willing to go to sea again at any further opportunity.

Playter, a sociable and easily pleased fellow, but making himself and everyone uncomfortable by quarrelling with the Captain, and detailing his grievances to anyone who would listen to him, instead of complaining at headquarters.

Mr Corbould, son of Mr Henry Corbould, Artist of Burton Crescent, was a most gentlemanly, kind and clever young man, and proved the only one of the passengers with whom I cared to have any intercourse.

Mr Lawrence, a young man of 18 - son of the wealthiest man in this part of the world, but who had just heard of his father's death, and was now returning from England where he had been sent for education, to take charge of his father's affairs. He had lately taken a trip up the Rhine, and could discourse a little about the scenery and so forth - but beyond this his conversational powers were by no means of the highest order. 'No' and 'yes' were all that could be extracted from him at the table - a truly pleasant companion for five months at sea - 'and one sickly sheep, etc.'

Vance, a boy just turned 16, and sufficiently proud in having emerged from school and mounted a long tail coat - teasing the poor Skipper to death with his everlasting questions - having a vast opinion of his own importance - but withal an Irishman with a slight touch of the brogue.

Stanford was quite as disagreeable as the other, but far worse in many regards - and about the same age - the former all openness and fair play - the latter, a complete sneak. It was laughable to observe their gradual advance in boldness and emancipation from control increase in strength. The first night they would touch nothing before retiring to rest - a few evenings later, and they would take a little weak wine and water, a few weeks later and Stanford became such a desperate fellow at the brandy bottle, that for ten days together he could not be called sober - The very last caution he had received from his father before sailing, was never to touch spirits. 'Out of sight, out of mind' saith the Proverb.

Mr Wm Johnstone it is not for me to describe, and as for his lady, she is so well known to my readers that it would be superfluous to say more than that time and distance have affected no alteration in her character.

We thoroughly enjoyed our little cabin, often spending 18 hours out of the 24 therein, so little did we relish the society in the cuddy - tho' we occasionally invited Mr Corbould to spend the evening with us - and altogether we have much reason to be thankful for having come out in the *Arab*. Our table was excellent, indeed our only want on board was *milk* - having no cow on board, and the goat perishing in the severe weather.

Our greatest annoyance was in the Emigrants - a most awful set, about 20 respectable out of the whole number. Scenes are daily occuring, which tho' unnecessary to describe, are yet most revolting - and can scarcely be prevented. Fighting and swearing from morning till night - I would advise no-one to come out in an Emigrant Ship when another is in the berth. They were chiefly agricultural labourers from Somersetshire, who had been earning upon an average, 7s 6d a week, on which they supported their wives and families.

The appearance of the town on first landing, is dull and disappointing enough, but it daily grows upon you, and by this time we have become quite reconciled. For further particulars of V.D. Land I refer to Burns' History in the *Colonial Magazine,* which is by far the best I have read.

'Adieu, till we meet again.'

Launceston,
13th August, 1842.

NOTE OF PROVISIONS

13 Sheep   13 Pigs   10 Dozen Fowls   1 Dozen Geese   1 dozen Turkeys
2 Dozen Ducks   and   1 Goat, besides   13 little Pigs born on board -
pretty well for 8 people to feast on. Besides a side of Beef at
Gravesend - 1 at Deal, 1 at Falmouth

_____

Roast Beef	Fowl and Ham Pie	Potatoes
Boiled Do	Liver and Bacon	Greens
Roast Mutton	Sheeps Head and Trotters	Carrots
Boiled Do	Brawn	Pickles
Hashed Do	Pea Soup	Almonds & Raisins
Harricot Do	Mock Turtle	Walnuts
Mutton Chops	Mutton Broth	Grapes
Beef Steaks	Gravy Soup	Butter
Stewed Steak	Ship Soup	Bread
Roast Fowls	Fresh Salmon	Cheese
Boiled Fowls	Pickled Salmon	Biscuits
Curried Fowls	Fresh Herrings	Bottled Ale
Roast Turkey	Guard Fish	Bottled Porter
Curried Do	Baracouter	Sherry
Roast Goose	'Shark'	Port
Roast Ducks	Plum Pudding	Claret
Roast Pork	Suet Pudding	Brandy
Pork Chops	Damson Pie	Rum
Sucking Pig	Apple Pudding and Pie	Geneva
Bacon	Gooseberry do	Gin
Ham	Greengage do	Hollands
Tongue	Pan Cakes	Lime Juice
Looseonse	Currant Fritters	Tea & Coffee
Pillau	Rasp Preserve Tarts	Sago
Irish Stew	Blackcurrant do	Arrowroot
Fried Tripe	Quince do	Barley
Boiled Tripe	Pease Pudding	Eggs
Meat Pie		

PART 5

Two Sailors' Wives of Appledore

Commentary

Appledore has a remarkable history of merchant seafaring. For centuries there has been a settlement of mariners, fishermen, boat-builders and shipowners at this point of confluence of the Taw and the Torridge in North Devon where the sheltering hill protects the strand against the Atlantic gales, We have described part of Appledore's nineteenth century history in *Westcountrymen in Prince Edward's Isle*. In 1818 Thomas Burnard of Bideford sent the *Peter and Sarah* to Prince Edward Island, Canada, to put a party of local shipwrights ashore and establish a shipbuilding industry there. His nephew, Thomas Burnard Chanter established a large timber-importing and emigration business from the Torridge. The whole business was gradually acquired and greatly expanded by James Yeo, once a labourer in the parish of Kilkhampton, Cornwall, who had gone to the Island to manage Thomas Burnard's lumbering gangs in 1819. James Yeo had a great dry dock built at Appledore where vessels built in the Island and sailed over the Atlantic were fitted out for selling in the British market. Appledore prospered and became an important shipbuilding centre - shipyards were established all the way up the Torridge as far as the head of tidewater at Weare Giffard.

At this time the warren of small back streets, the 'drangs', which gives Appledore its distinctive character today, was developed. Some of them are no more than narrow paths between the high blind side

walls of houses leading to courts on to which the doors of many
cottages open. A hundred years ago and less these places were not
always so quiet and law-abiding or so friendly to the stranger as they
are now. Indeed throughout the nineteenth century Appledore was
notorious for the vigorous independence of its inhabitants and lawless-
ness which was the subject of comment in the Devon press. Assaults
were frequent and the women of the town had a bad reputation for the
violence with which they conducted disputes amongst themselves.
There were sixteen taverns each brewing its own beer. Nevertheless,
Appledore was a place of great character and charm with the small
sailing vessels lying alongside the quay, which was built in 1844, in
their dozens, the seamen and boatmen in their long knitted blue
jerseys called 'frocks', each representing hours of work by women's
hands.

In the third quarter of the nineteenth century Appledore's seafaring
prosperity was at its greatest. The vessels which lay alongside were of
two main kinds. There were ocean-going sailing ships, many of them
large vessels by contemporary standards, which traded all over the
world. These were often locally-owned, or owned in Prince Edward
Island or were frequent visitors from other ports. The last came into
Appledore for maintenance at the local shipyards and were manned at
least partly by Appledore men. And there were smaller vessels, coasters
owned by local families and sailed usually by men who had shares in
them. Small cargo smacks carried goods to all the harbours of the
Bristol Channel. The sea was the natural means of transport when
roads were few and still abominable. As industry and population
developed there were more small cargoes to carry and by the 1850s
and 60s the smacks were becoming bigger and schooners and later
ketches were being acquired by local shipowners. The steady employment and the high level of local economic activity provided by the
shipbuilding and the North American trade generated capital and
increased the size of the seafaring population. So great did the coasting
trade become that in 1864 an observer was able to watch fifty vessels go
in and out on one tide. He wrote that it was 'a pretty sight on a fine
clear morning - so many vessels crossing and re-crossing each other on
the Bar in working out, their white sails glistening in the sun, whilst
with a fine breeze they were bravely speeding through the water with
foaming billows at their bows'. In the course of the following year
nearly 2500 vessels were recorded as entering this creek of the Port
of Bideford, as Appledore had then become, the great majority of them

with cargo. But there was another side of this story. Many of the vessels were old and unsafe and kept afloat only by constant grinding hard work by their crews.

The two accounts reproduced here reflect these two aspects of Appledore's maritime interests in the second half of the nineteenth century, deep water seafaring in the ships of big capitalists and sailing on the coast in small family-owned vessels. Thomazene Williams, known in her family as Tamzin, was born in Appledore on January 10, 1823. She was the daughter of John Beara (1797-1865) and Elizabeth Bowen (1798-1864). John Beara was a prosperous local merchant and ship-owner, Elizabeth Bowen the daughter of a leading local seafaring family. In the summer of 1850, twenty-seven year old Tamzin married Edward Williams (Plates 13 & 12), born in Appledore in 1818, second son of John Williams. The Williams could trace their ancestry back for nearly two centuries and for much of the time many of their menfolk had been master mariners.

Edward Williams since 1846 had been in command of the barque *Joseph Cundar,* built at Chatham on the Miranmichi river, New Brunswick, in 1839. She was named after her builder, a brother of Samuel Cunard, founder of the Cunard Line. Joseph Cunard, (1793-1865) was a picturesque character who dominated the great wood shipbuilding industry of the Miramichi until his failure in 1848. The *Joseph Cunard* was first owned in Liverpool, trading to New Orleans and Australia. In 1850 she was owned in Newport, Monmouthshire, and employed in the trade with lumber and emigrants between the Bristol Channel and Canada. On July 24, 1850, Edward and Tamzin Williams set out together in the *Joseph Cunard* on their honeymoon passage towards Quebec. Tamzin recorded the passage day by day in a letter to a brother and intended 'not to be shown to anyone out of the family has it will not bear scrutiny'. Her brother's descendants, John and William Beara, who are still engaged in the shipping business of Apple-dore, were, despite this caution, happy to allow the enjoyment of this account by a wider audience and the text is reproduced as Tamzin wrote it without amendment to her own special style.

Tamzin's approach to seafaring was very different from that of Mary Molesworth or Mary Jane Saunders. She was the lively intelligent daughter of a family intimately involved with shipping. Although her family's position made her of the upper middle-class of Appledore, a great deal of her environment had rubbed off on to her. She had a healthy curiosity about what was going on around her and despite constant sea-sickness her interest in her husband's navigation never flags. It is probable that he did most of his paper work in his cabin, including chart work and navigation; one gets the impression that she peered over his shoulder while he was working out his observations and by the end of the passage she shows a great deal more knowledge than when she started.

Since they play such a large part in her letter, some brief explanation of these navigational methods is necessary. There were fifteen days in the six weeks of the passage when celestial observations were obtained. Latitude north and south was got in the usual way by observation of the altitude of the sun at midday. Longitude east and west was derived in two ways, by the chronometer and by lunar observations. Tamzin gives positions derived by both methods. Captain Edward Williams' lunar observations were of a simple type (Plate 14), using only the angular distance between the sun and the moon, a method only possible when both could be observed together. But he was an efficient and successful shipmaster and used his lunars mainly to check his chronometers. In 1850 many masters were still using lunars as their principal means of finding longitude - or worse still using only calculations of distance sailed.

To become for a moment more technical, the reference to the index which appears from time to time in Tamzin's account is a reference to the error in the reading of the scale of the sextant equal to the difference between the zero of the scale and the zero of the index and it had to be allowed for in her husband's calculations. The 'studing sails', she refers to in the entry for August 17th, were the stuns'ls, small square-sails set on portable extensions to the yards and intended to increase the power derived from the wind when it was on or abaft the beam.

'Combe' referred to on July 25th is the Bristol Channel seafarers' term for Ilfracombe in North Devon, a place where pilots waited between inward and outward bound vessels. 'Lunday' is, of course, Lundy, the island off Appledore, now the property of the National Trust and a natural point of departure for foreign-going ships and of shelter for coasters. The packet ship *Andrew Foster* mentioned on August 1st was an American vessel in regular service between Liverpool and New York with passengers and freight. She belonged to the St George Line of New York and was built in 1848. The barque *Countess Durham*, reported on August 7th, was built at Pictou, Nova Scotia, in 1839 and owned in 1850 in Newcastle-upon-Tyne.

She was bound towards Quebec from Bristol under Captain Hogg. The fishermen on the Grand Bank seen on August 20th were anchored while their men fished from the decks for cod to be salted down for the markets of North America and Europe. They were probably French. By this date there was little British activity in the fishery and the large American industry and the smaller Canadian and Newfoundland ones principally employed schooners.

Despite her idiomatic spelling, the various features mentioned by Tamzin in the Gulf of St Lawrence and the estuary can easily be found on any large scale map. The only other vessel she mentions by name, met late in the passage, was the *Montreal*, a full-rigged ship built at Dumbarton in 1848, registered at Glasgow and on her way from the Clyde to Montreal under Captain MacMaster.

Tamzin lived to a ripe old age, dying in Appledore in 1912. The owner of her sea log, then a boy of seven, records his 'mingled awe and sadness' because she died on her birthday. In her later years she lived in a house at the bottom of Bude Street with her husband, who died in 1903. In 1969, the Rev Alfred Green of Northam recalled boyhood memories of the couple in the 1890s. Tamzin was 'a neat little Victorian dame' and her husband 'a bouncy man', very much the sailing master, furious with any Appledore boy who rattled his stick along the railings outside the house in Bude Street but always good for threepence for the London Missionary Society.

If Tamzin was better informed on the realities of seafaring than any of the women whose accounts of passages have preceded hers in this book, and more ready and able to learn from experience, Annie Slade (Plate 15) was better informed again. She came from Appledore's nineteenth century working class, from a very poor family of the type in which the children were given dried apples and water to stem the pangs of hunger and which had, in the vivid local terminology, 'to work for their breakfast before they could eat it'. She went to sea to work as crew in the run-down, dangerous old cargo smack *Dahlia*, built in 1838 at Newport, of which her father, although suffering from chronic bronchitis, was master because nobody else would go in a vessel with such low earning power and the family had to be kept alive somehow. Her husband William Kingdon Slade (Plate 16), mate of the *Hawk*, (built incidentally not in Prince Edward Island as Captain Slade says in his account of his mother's life, but at Pugwash, Nova Scotia) was scarcely literate, yet determined, as with his wife's help he did, to become an independent shipowner.

Annie was a splendid example of the kind of working wife who lay behind many similar success stories in small seaport towns in the fifty years before the first world war. The story began with the ketch *Francis Beddoe* (Plate 17), built in Milford Haven in 1877 and Annie went back to sea with a baby in arms to look after as well as her sailor's work to do, and the ship's business on her hands. And the sailing of these ketches, products as they were of a carpenter and blacksmith technology and appearing to the modern yachtsman utterly primitive in their simple fittings and gear, of necessity to earn a living out in all weathers all the year round in some of the most difficult coastal waters in Europe, was an arduous and highly professional affair. The families' prosperity depended on the skill with which it was done and above all on keeping the vessel continually employed.

The *Minnie Flossie,* built at Pembroke in 1879 was the next step in the Slade fortune but it was part-ownership of the fine Cornish-built sister ships *Alpha* (Plate 18) and *Ulelia* that really began the family on the road to middle-class fortune and status. It took a long time, but Annie lived to see her great grand-children born into a life completely different from her own eighteenth-century style youth and saw her husband's family gain, largely as a result of her efforts, the historical distinction of being the owners of the last fleet of merchant sailing vessels ever to operate from a port in Britain.

*Sea Log written on a passage from Newport to Quebec in
1850 by Thomazene Williams*

Wednesday July 24 at 6 am left Newport in tow of the Steamtug
the weather being very fine we towed to the Ness Point and came to
Anchor to wait for tide, at 6 pm got underweigh and proceeded down
Channel
Thursday 25th light Easterly winds 2 am landed Alex and the pilot
at Combe at 8 o'clock passed Lunday. Noon the wind came to the NW
fine clear weather myself very seasick.
Friday 26th off Scilly Isles fine clear weather wind from the West 6
pm strong breezes reefed sailes the wind hauled to the North Stricken
ship to the Westward
Saturday 27th a very strong wind all day with a head sea very seasick
and obliged to keep to my bed the whole of the day
Sunday 28th more moderate made all sail wind from the NNW I was
able to sit on deck for a short time several sail in company
Monday 29, at 10 am hoisted signals to a Barque bound to the Westward and desired to be reported wind NNW fine pleasant weather, I feel
very much better, and able to sit on deck for hours.
Tuesday 30th most delightful weather almost a Calm wind still NNW
several sail in sight. I feel almost perfectly well, and quite enjoy
the delightfull scene on the broad Atlantic, I was also pleasure at seeing
a very great number of Porpoises, and sun fish, the harpoon was prepared to catch them, but they kept to far off to strike them the Mate
caught one small fish which gave us a delicious treat I have quite
recovered my Appetite, am able to eat a couple of eggs for my tea,
and also for the first time sat on deck sewing.
Wednesday 31, light airs from the NNW seven ships in company, all
bound the same way has ourselves, weather very fine, I feel stronger
and better every day 6 pm light wind nine ships in sight making little
progress towards our intended port
Thursday August 1st Lat 46, 39, Long 18, 30, in company with the

WS Packet ship *Andrew Foster,* wind West, moderate and clear 6 pm
I am just going to leave the deck, has a thick fog is falling employen
myself during the day, reading and sewing, I have not felt seasickness
for four days past -

Friday 2 not very well this morning, kept my bed untill tea time,
weather still very fine, wind NW, at 10 am observed distance between
the Sun and Moon, was 74° 30' 30", Index was 40 which gives the
Longitude, 19° 41' 45" -

Saturday 3rd a very strong breeze from the West, with a heavy role
of a head sea, not out of bed for the day, rather a little seasick,

Sunday 4th, blowing very hard from the Westward, rough weather,
got out of bed in the morning, spent a little time on deck,

Monday 5th still blowing very strong from the West, kept the Cabin
best part of the day, my head very gidy, but not seasick came on deck
for a few moments, to breath the fresh sea air -

Tuesday 6th very stormy weather, blowing a perfect gale from the
West the ship rolling about awfully, obliged to keep my bed all the day,
and to hold on with all my might to keep myself in This is the worse
days weather we have experienced since we left

Wednesday 7th rather more moderate, but still a heavy head sea
which makes the ship roll most dreadfully, I was able to get up this
morning, and came on deck to see some Porpoises, in company with the
Countess Durham, spent the day on the sopha reading

Thursday 8th a fine clear morning, the wind still from the same old
spot NNW the change of weather makes me feel very much better got
on deck before dinner, 4 pm heavy rain, the wind rather more favourable, but the heavy role of the head sea retards our progress, 2 ships in
sight -

Friday 9 very stormy weather, the ship rolling from side to side,
awfully, obliged to keep my bed the whole day, at 6 am It came to
heavy rain, and with it came the heaviest gust of wind for a few
moments I have heard It was indeed truly awfull, but fortunately the
sails were previously reefed therefore providently the ship sustained no
damage, the rain came down in torrents -

Saturday 10th more moderate wind West I have been able to sit on
deck great part of the day, but still suffering a little from seasickness
The ship making little progress the wind blowing strong direct against
us, with the exception of a few hours the wind has been ahead ever
since we left. I trust we shall have a change soon 2.30 pm Lat 47° 46',
Long by Chronometer 30° 15' 30" -

Sunday 11th Wind WSW a fine breeze and clear weather, the ship making eight miles an hour, Noon lat by observation 47° 30', 3 pm Long by Chronometer 32° 10' 30", 8 pm a strong breeze, with a thick fog wind west I feel rather better, eat a hearty dinner of Joint and plumb Pudding

Monday 12th strong wind with a thick fog, nothing interesting occur has the dense thickness of the atmosphere obscures all distant objects from view. I kept my bed the whole of the day -

Tuesday 13 morning blowing strong from the SW with heavy rain, Lat at noon by obs, 48° 53, at 3-37-30 time the Observed distance between the Sun & moon was 78 - 12 - 00 index was 45 which gives the long 37° 7' 30" - 6 pm more moderate I have been able to sit on deck for a little time, quite enjoying the treat of an hour's fine weather, no fair wind yet

Wednesday 14th 3 weeks this morning since we left Newport dock, we have only had 12 hours fair wind, a head wind and heavy sea his day after day what we have to contend with, how desirable would a fair wind be but we must wait with patience, This morning a calm 2 ships in sight Lat 48° 54', 4 pm Long 37° 40' 45", wind west an uneasy breeze I feel myself much better, and able to sit on deck and sew, It is quite delightful at sea, to be able to enjoy a fine day in good health 6 pm the observed distance between the Sun & Moon was 91° 00' 39" Index was 45 making the Longtitude 37° 40' 30"

Thursday 15 Light Westerly breeze, Noon Cloudy Sun obscured the Ship going along very steady, which allows me to sit up the whole of the day I feel myself much stronger, and have a good appetite seasickness passing off, no fair wind

Friday 16th a strong gale from the Westward, with a thick fog and rain, a most dreary dismal day, and the ship rolling very much which makes me feel rather poorly in my head, laying about on the sofa the whole day not fit for any thing -

Saturday 17th am moderate weather, wind from the North - Noon clear and fine, set the studing sails, lat by obs 49° 56' 6 pm Long by Chro 45° 52' this is the first appearance of a fair wind since we left Lunday, it is now almost a calm, but the little is from the NE I feel quite well today -

Sunday 18th a strong breeze of the SSW a very thick fog, with heavy rain Sun obscured, I spent the day in bed reading,

Monday 19th wind SSW, with a dense fog sun obscured, pm 4° 41' 53", mean time long by Chro 48° 16', - at 8 pm sounded in 85 fathoms on the North East end of the grand bank, at 8.20 pm the Obs Alt of the N Pole Star was 46° 55', which makes the Lat, 47° 10'

Tuesday 20 morning a thick fog, a light breeze from the South on the grand bank of Newfoundland, 4 pm the fog clears and we could see several fishermen one large Barque, It is a most exposed place to anchor rolling almost under, at 6 pm the fog came on again so thick has not to see the ships bows, The fog horn blowing night and day, sun still obs, 10 pm Lat by the N Pole star 45° 32' -

Wednesday 21 am very fogy most disagreeable weather, seeing nothing Noon clear lat by obs 45° 22', 3 pm Long by Chronometer 53° 18' - wind from the SSE a smart breeze, the ship going eight nots a hour, a light Barque in sight going the same way has ourselves I feel quite well and in high spirits at having a fair wind sea sickness gone and left an excellent appetite -

Thursday 22, a most delightful morning, which we all feel quite a treat after so much wet and uncomfortable weather, wind SSW the Ship going along steady eight knots, we on St Peter's bank noon Lat 45° 15° 3 pm long by Chro 57° 30',I feel quite well, every sensation of seasickness quite gone, I have sat on deck the whole day shirt making -

Friday 23, a most beautiful morning, a perfect calm, the wind WNW direct against us again, In sight Cape Britton the first American land my eyes ever beheld, I came on the house to see it, and while there we saw a large Shark quite close - Noon lat by obs. 46° 56', a little breeze with light showers - 4 pm St Pauls Island bearing north west distant 6 miles, wind WNW with very heavy rain -

Saturday 24, very fogy, wind NW by N direct ahead a moderate breeze Noon clear lat by obs. 47° 32', 8 pm, a thick fog again, nearly calm, distans from the Birds Islands, 17 miles, 2 ships passed us home-ward bound, I have indeed felt better today, than I have since we have been out, able to work about, and an appetite to eat anything comes along

Sunday 25, a light breeze from the East, a delightful morning numbers of birds come flying about the ship, they quite interested me, has they were the first visitors we have seen since our leaving Noon lat 48° 12' Brian Island bearing SW distance about 25 miles 6 pm, a smart breeze from the South East, fine and clear I have spent a most pleasant, and delightful day far more so than I can have anticipation of spending at sea, I have sat on the deck the best part of the day reading, and for two hours walked the deck this evening I have not felt anything like seasickness for some time, which is a pleasure I never thought to feel

Monday 26 morning very hazy, Noon took a pilot on board about fifteen miles to the Westward of Cape Gaspie, about 4 hundred miles below Quebec. It was the first Canadian I ever saw, he is of a dark yellow complexion, rather short, speaks English but very imperfectly, I was glad to hear he was come has I now hope we shall soon reach our destined port pm torrents of rain and the wind changed to the west and blew a smart breeze

Thursday 27 wind from the West, and although we have been in the Gulf for three days, I have not yet seen the land, the fog and rain obscuring it from sight, at present where we are it is sixty miles across Noon clear and fine, the land quite close 4 ships in company going up with us, 8 pm the ship has made very little progress today the wind direct ahead, but it is a most delightful change in the weather to what it was last night, and I trust the morning will bring a fair wind to hasten our progress -

Wednesday 28, morning quite becalmed, not a breath of wind, a most splendid morning, I was very much delighted, at seeing a great number of Whales, the first I had seen, they are most monstrous creatures, and they throw the water a great way up, many come close enough to see them nicely, a great number of vessels all around us fishing, a fresh breeze sprung up direct down 4 pm we passed a Brig that sailed from Newport a week before we left

Thursday 29th a light breeze from the West, with heavy showers of rain Noon calm and clear 4 pm off English Point about 6 miles distance Making little or no progress towards Quebec -

Friday 30th, at 7 - 36 - 53 Apparent time, the obs dist between the Sun & Moon was 90° 50' 39" Alt Sun's lower limbe 22-24, Altitude Moon uper limbe 49-44 height of the eye 20 feet, Index error 1' 00" to substract, making the Long 67° 33' 15', Point de Monts bearing E by N ½ N distance 6 miles, calm and clear, off Good Boat Inn about 2 miles, almost quite close to the land, a few houses in sight, the first houses I have seen, Ships are supliyn from these houses with water and provisions, seven Ships in sight, all like ourselves, laying like logs in the water, 4 pm a very light breeze sprung up from the East, out all sails, to embrace this favourable wind

Saturday 31 a calm delightfull morning, just in the same place has we were last night when our little fair wind left us, a great many ships in company some going up the Gulf others coming down 2 pm it comes on to torrents of rain, and with it down came the wind, a smart breeze. The ship being tacked from side to side, 7 pm still raining very heavy, but the wind a little lulled I have not been on deck for the day, which makes the time appear long, In the morning I was prevented by the poor dog having a severe fit and I gladly shut myself out of his way from fear 8 pm wind SW Birquette light bearing SW distance 22 miles

Sunday Sept 1st a dull gloomy morning, the wind blowing down the Gulf the ship tacking from side to side in company with the Ship *Montreall* off the Island of Bic the Pilot here takes charge of the Ship a dead calm throughout the day, 4 pm the fog and rain cleared up, and I was able to go on deck which I quite enjoyed after being confined to the Cabin for a couple of days a great many ships in sight, I found the sea air quite refreshing,

Monday 2nd, a light favourable breeze from the NE which intelligence delighted me, I got up to breakfast for the first time since we left England, noon quite a fresh breeze passed Green Island, a most delightful day I have been able to sit for hours on the top of the house with my sewing, the view on the shore is now very pretty, has every mile we advance, the distance across diminishes and on each side are towns and villages and a great part of the land cultivated, which gives it something the appearance of home the house are all one storey hight white washed 3 pm we passed the town of Kamourasca a very nice looking town indeed and at every little place is a chapple with a cross on it at 8 pm we passed through the Traversers the wind still favouring our progress, and at 12 pm raining heavy, a dark and dirty night Therefore until morning has at this place it is very dangerous, the ship was brought up under the Island of Orleans

Tuesday 3rd at 5 am the ship again underweigh, still raining pouring, fogy and a dead calm, I had indeed hoped this fair wind would have lasted up to Quebec, but alas how doomed we are to disappointments, for hours we are just in the same place, Noon the wind came down the Gulf there it has been tacked from one side to the other all the way up - The rain cleared up and I have been able to sit on deck, which I have quite enjoyed it is a most splendid river, and delightful scenery, 4 pm we are after a long passage off the town of Quebec, 4 gentlemen came on board with the inspecting Physician, to give you a pass without which you cannot proceed, They are the first of Quebec I have seen and are a most excellent sampal.

This ends my sea log in the enjoyment of excellent health, good spirits and a thankful heart, for our safe arrival at our destined port.

My dear Brother has I am well aware you would be anxious to know every particular of the passage, I have attempted in my imperfect way to keep an account of every days occurance, for your amusement, but I must instruct it is not shown to anyone out of the family has it will not bear scrutiny, ever then with love, from your affectionate sister

THOMAZENE WILLIAMS -

My Mother — the story of Annie Slade, 1865 — 1964, told by
W.J. Slade

I have written at length in *Out of Appledore* of my connection with
the sea and how father's family, the Slades of Appledore, fought their
way through life among the seafaring community of this hard-working
little town from poverty to small shipowning and comparative comfort.

Now I sit and think of my mother and her share in my father's
successful drive to place us all beyond the possibility of want. Her
ancestors were not born of seafaring stock, her grandfather came from
miles inland, he was born at Tawstock in Devon. He earned his living
from the soil. How her father, Richard Harding, came to Appledore
and became one of the seafaring fraternity I cannot remember. Mother's
uncles were all soldiers, all but one were regimental sergeant majors and
saw service all over the world during the reign of Queen Victoria. In
these circumstances it seems marvellous to me that mother took to the
sea like a duck takes to water.

There is no doubt that she played a major part in the family
fortunes. Her father had three sons beside my mother. Two became
sailors and eventually sailed with their father who had become in the
course of a few years master of the trading smack *Dahlia*. But like other
young men they wandered away to square-riggers and grandfather
Harding, who suffered grievously from bronchitis, was left with his
young son, a boy only fit to do small jobs and help generally, and so
mother having left school, knowing her father's difficulties determined
to go to sea with him to help keep the home fires burning. She was a
very intelligent girl and soon became a sailor in her own right. She was
taught the compass and how to steer by it, how to trim the sails by the
wind or going off the wind, but better still she knew the land and sets
of tides according to the time it ebbed or flowed. She also became a
good judge of weather conditions. In fact she soon knew enough to be
left in charge of the watch while her father slept.

In those days most of the old ships were veritable death traps. When at sea they were generally kept floating by continual pumping. The first stop after leaving Lydney was Penarth mud. There the crew would rest from the pump because the mud would get in the leaks to stop the water flowing in. Often I have heard mother talk of the hours she stood at the pumps in her high laced-up boots with hardly any time to rest or make a cup of tea till she eventually arrived at the port of discharge. Then all her spare time was taken up in cooking and feeding the crew including herself.

Notwithstanding all these difficulties she found time for enjoyment. Having a *very* good voice she was always ready to sing, often to a bigger audience than her own associates. She had a very musical ear. As a child I bought a small mouth organ with which I nearly drove the family mad, but not so mother. She promptly took it over and to my delight played it beautifully. She encouraged me to try again until I too could play it properly.

The conditions I have tried to describe eventually came to an end through the ill health of her father and now being a healthy young woman she constituted herself as the main bread winner. She got a position in a collar factory on piece work, earning approximately £1 a week, every penny of which she was delighted to take home to her mother. These two or three years were very happy ones. She belonged to the choir of the Congregational Church and in due course was appointed the leader. But time passes quickly on and quite naturally she went the way of most young women by marrying my father W.K. Slade, who was then mate of a schooner called the *Hawk,* built in Prince Edward Island.

This was really the beginning of a new life. Father had never been to school but was a very hard worker with plenty of ambition. His being illiterate didn't suit mother, she determined she would teach him to write and read letters. In a very short time he was writing letters to her and she would write to him, sending his own letter back corrected. In order to get him to read she gave him a Bible, to read in his spare time. For many years after this he read in his own way a chapter every night, but he always spelt phonetically. His letters were easily readable but he knew he was not fit to write a business letter. So mother, always ready to help, attended to anything that needed an answer.

Now father had a wonderful knowledge of the coast, but it was all stored up in his head. He had never handled a chart, but his time was coming. Mr P.K. Harris had heard of his ability and offered him the job of master of the ketch *Francis Beddoe.* He naturally talked it over with mother and it was agreed that he could do the job and of course the business part fell to her. As soon as she was able she was sailing in the *Francis Beddoe,* charts, parallel rulers, dividers, etc, all fitted out and soon the way to use them came easily enough, but mother still kept her job as chief scribe. He sent her all the money he could lay hands on and she saved all she could. It was the proudest day of her life when she went to the bank with a baby on her arm to deposit her savings and look at her first bank book.

When her first son arrived her mind was still on the sea, so at the age of three months, all tucked up in short clothes, her eldest son became acquainted with the sea in his mother's arms. On one occasion they were on the way down the north coast of Cornwall in a strong south-east wind. The mate, who was a brother-in-law, asked her to speak to father to get him to go back to Padstow because the sky looked bad. She went up on deck and was looking at the sky when father said to her, 'What do you think of the weather?' She replied, 'I can't see anything wrong with it.' The brother-in-law said, 'Fancy listening to a woman', so father said, 'She knows what she's talking about, so we'll see who is right, you or the woman.' They arrived at their destination, Falmouth, the next day.

Another of these voyages when mother was acting as third hand, she had her baby with her. They got to the upper part of Mount's Bay when the wind suddenly backed to south-south-east catching them on a lee shore. On this occasion, the mate was Phillip Quance who was a great friend of mother's. They reefed down and put the ship's head off on the port tack. Phillip said to her, 'Annie, you go below and look after the baby. I'll tell you when to come up. They passed up through the race off the Stags and mother realised that Phillip knew what to expect off the Lizard because the sea was coming on board from all directions. He didn't want her exposed to it, but shortly after passing through the race Philip opened up the companion way and shouted to her, 'Come up and have a look at the Lizard, you'll see your brother in a couple of hour's time'. Her brother was master of a yacht, whose owner, Dr Cook, lived at Flushing. Mother of course was delighted when they got in and her eldest brother came on board to greet her. All this time I was wearing nappies so that the reader will understand I had not even dipped my pen in the ink to write.

My father with whom I sailed for seven years never tired of telling me of mother and what she did for him during his early years as master. When we were all together we children thought only of father's

14 Taking a Lunar Distance, engraving from *The Midnight Sky* E. Dunkin, London, 1869

15 Annie Slade as a young woman. She took to the sea like a duck takes to water and went to work as crew in the dangerous old cargo smack *Dahlia*

16 William Kingdon Slade, a photograph taken at about the time of his marriage. He was scarcely literate, yet determined with his wife's help to become an independent shipowner

17 The ketch *Francis Beddoe*, William Kingdon Slade's first command, alongside Appledore quay in the 1920s with the schooner *Mary Rosanna*

18 The painting by Uncle George Quance of the ketch *Alpha*, the third vessel to be purchased by the Slade family. She was built as a schooner near Truro, Cornwall, in 1871 for trading to Newfoundland

struggles. Mother, of course, always loyal did not make anything of her own part in the fight for survival, everything that happened was due to father's ability but as time passed by, we all got to understand how much mother did for him. Perhaps as eldest son who sailed with him I had a better understanding than anyone else and a better reason to appreciate what part of his success was due to his wife and her ability.

Father told me how she appeared unexpectedly alongside at Lydney to make a voyage home after the crew left him. He had sent a telegram to her to send him a mate. She did her best but no one would accept the job offered. The next morning she was off by train after making arrangements for the welfare of her children. When she arrived alongside he could hardly believe his eyes and his first greeting was 'What are you doing here'. She replied, 'I'm taking the mate's job'. He was cleaning up the decks and battening down hatches after loading coal for Bideford. She didn't know where he was chartered for, but of course was pleased it was for Bideford. She was soon on board helping with the work.

The next morning they sailed and in the evening anchored off Penarth to wait for the next ebb tide. Father went to bed leaving mother to keep anchor watch. At high water she felt the bower cable dragging on the ground. She aroused father who was fast asleep, and told him what was happening. He assured her that everything was all right. They got underweigh and after the anchor was catted and the decks cleared up she gave him a meal, after which she received her orders to go below to get some rest. Being very tired she was soon asleep. When she woke up she went on deck and saw Ilfracombe close by and father at the wheel quite happy in the prospect of being home that evening. Eventually they berthed alongside Bideford Quay and went home together well pleased in the knowledge that the voyage was ended and no wages to pay.

Nothing of importance happened for several years after this. Father had changed ships. He was now in the *Minnie Flossie,* a little bigger, but mother was always at hand for any clerical work required and I do not recollect having heard of anything untoward happening until the *Alpha* was purchased. This was a step forward. I was old enough to sit up and take notice of what was happening. Mother had saved some money. She passed over every penny for the purchase of a quarter share in the new vessel for father. He was now virtually his own master and I made my first visit to a ship without mother. The ship loaded bricks for Rams-gate. She sailed leaving mother behind in tears. I wondered to see two women, mother and Aunt Mary Ann crying bitterly. They had begged him to wait for finer weather.

It was now blowing very hard south-west, a dead ahead wind. I was to find out why before long. It appears that my parents were short of money so father couldn't stop, he had to get some to feed his growing family as quickly as possible and he set out to do it. He had a hard voyage, but arrived to Ramsgate in quick time so mother was re-imbursed and paid her debts. It must have been a terrible worry to her to have to face the ordeal of finding food for three children and herself, not knowing where to look for the next shilling, but she faced this without a qualm.

This state of affairs did not last long. Mother never complained because she knew in her heart there were better times ahead. No woman ever made money go further than she did. She made her own and her children's clothes for a long time, watching every halfpenny so that when father came home again she had a bank balance which they both appreciated. She had deliberately risked everything and it paid high dividends. She was never again lacking in the necessary funds to pay her way.

The *Alpha* was a schooner and the short voyages in the Bristol Channel and Cornish ports had to be abandoned for longer and more remunerative voyages. The scope had extended to the Irish and Liverpool trades, also a voyage or two to London so that more than ever mother came into the picture, because business had to be sought. If he wasn't able to deal with extra correspondence, she took it all in her stride. He could dictate a letter and knew what he wanted. It was a splendid combination which worked perfectly. She sailed in the *Alpha* quite a lot and often we children sailed with her. She did the cooking which was pleasing to the crew, and always scrubbed the cabin out. At sea she took a spell at the wheel whenever required. If father was ever shorthanded, she filled the vacancy most efficiently. If the topsail or a jib had to be taken in she took the wheel.

I remember vividly one voyage bound to Waterford from a Bristol Channel port. There was only the mate for crew beside mother and her two little children, but that didn't worry father. We were off the Smalls and he was carrying a heavy press of sail, the ship's lee main rail in the water, everything feather white with foam flying all over her. We two children were sitting quietly together on the weather, or starboard quarter, with the Smalls lighthouse on the starboard side fairly close. Father was evidently enjoying the leading wind. Mother had been asleep and the elements had disturbed her. She sat down with us for a few minutes casting her experienced eye over the sails with her brow frowning. At last she said, 'You are driving the ship too heavy, if you don't take the topsail in, you'll lose the lot.' Father just laughed at her in a patronising way and said, 'She'll carry it or drag it and I'll be in Waterford tonight'.

Well, mother was right. She put us boys down in father's bunk and up she went on deck again. She had only just got up when topmast, topsail, yard and flying jib, all came tumbling down in a tangle. I heard mother shouting, saying 'I told you so. Now you can go up and clear that lot away, I'll take the wheel.' 'All right', he said, 'I'll soon secure that. Keep her on her course, we won't be long'. It took longer than they expected and I had more than one peep up through the companion way. What I've wondered at many times since is that mother stood there so unperturbed doing a man's job that seemed to come so naturally to her, seeing her antecedents were not born close to the sea.

The ship arrived to Waterford that same night and a new topmast was fitted. Finally the vessel sailed for Cardiff loaded with timber. In the mouth of the Bristol Channel the topmast again carried away. Mother, I suppose, did her part again but in this case I didn't know anything about it till she came down to get us dressed in warm clothes. There was a strong wind and fog. She therefore thought our place was on deck with so much outward bound traffic about.

When we reached Cardiff mother's youngest brother met us and they talked about family affairs for quite a long time. Father was rapidly improving on the business side and it was decided that mother should spend more time with her family at home. She still kept a keen interest in the financial side. A house was purchased and fitted out comfortably so the future looked prosperous for everyone. In time the schooner *Ulelia* was purchased on a fifty-fifty basis with Uncle George Quance. Father was appointed managing owner and Uncle Quance master of her. Mother now kept the books for the ships in her spare time in addition to household and family duties.

All the ship's share of money earned was kept strictly separate from that earned by the master. Mother had to be responsible for this. At no time were the dividends, earned by the ship, used for household expenses. They were banked every voyage and after all the ship's expenses for upkeep were paid, the balance was set aside for buying new tonnage. In this way, the family were always in a position to pay their way, the earnings of ships owned bought others. The *Ulelia* was bought in 1899. On Uncle George retiring in 1903, father became her master and owner. Mother now kept more in the background with only an occasional voyage at sea, but no matter what the circumstances she still kept a strict account of income and expenses. I have seen her sit and write a dozen letters and postcards looking for cargoes. Replies would be passed over to her husband for acceptance or rejection.

This state of affairs continued until 1904 when I left school at the age of twelve. I then took over all the business part of writing, reading, etc, under father's direction as I was now one of the crew. Mother often had a trip at sea. I was the one who benefitted by this as she took over a lot of my responsibilities. It was always a sad parting for me when she left to go home and my work doubled. On one occasion we sailed from Gloucester for Dublin. Mother was to be landed at Ilfracombe. It was inconvenient to do this so we carried on to Appledore. We missed the tide in over the bar, father ordered the boat out and I was told to pull from the bay over the bar against an ebb tide to land mother at Appledore and be back to the ship as quickly as possible.

It was a tall order for a boy of less than fourteen but I dare not demur, so after instructions to keep tight to the shore the lighthouse side till we reached Crow point, and then to sheer across to the Royal George slip at West Appledore, we left the ship with a heavy heart and pulled for the shore like sailors should. It seemed like hours of hard work but we got there and now I had to return at once before the tide was too far gone. Mother told me to wait, she ran to a shop and bought biscuits, sweets and lemonade. The tide was going out strongly in my favour so I got the oar over the stern and sculled off where the best of the tide was running and sat down to a well-earned rest eating biscuits and drinking pop to my heart's content. The sweets went into my pocket, the empty pop bottle went overboard to cover up my misdeeds. I was in no hurry. It was more than half-ebb when I got back on board and got a reprimand for being too slow.

Well, after this mother's sea-going experiences became less and less. She just became a passenger. She spent a fortnight with father going to Pentewan and during her stay there met and became friends with another skipper's wife. All four were ashore together having a good time, but for some private reasons the other couple were holding aloof from each other. Mother, full of fun and mischief as she always was, did her best to heal the breach, but having more or less failed she started to sing old love songs. As I've said, she really had a good voice. It wasn't long before the ice was broken. I remember the first verse.

It went like this:

> 'Why are you sorrowing here, love,
> When I am close at thy side,
> Swiftly the day's drawing near love,
> When I shall make you my bride.'

Of course there was a lot more than this and it worked the trick, they were soon back in harmony again. She had a lot of plaintive old songs in her repertoire and she could put a vast amount of feeling into her singing. These people remained her friends till the end.

One more little example of mother's wicked humour I'd like to mention. We were off Start Point and as usual in fine weather we were fishing for mackerel. As usual, also, we were shorthanded and mother was on the early morning watch with me. I had to obey orders to put out the lines at daylight so as we already had a lot of salt mackerel I grumbled to mother about it. I hated salt mackerel. It was after 7.30 am when mother said, 'Go down and get me a salt one,' which I did. She pulled the line in and I hooked on the salt mackerel which was put overboard. Father came up, went right over to the line, pulling it in and grumbling at my laziness for not doing it already, saying 'The fish has been on the line for hours.' Mother took the wheel and told me quietly to sheer off. When father dropped the fish on the deck she started pulling his leg. 'My word, Billie, you've caught a dead one' and a lot beside that. He made a jump for me, but I was close to the rigging and much quicker than father. All the time he was chasing me, she kept up the leg pull, until having failed to catch me he shamefacedly retired.

When Uncle George retired Aunt Mary Ann decided he must dress more like a retired shipowner, so amid a lot of protests he submitted to her demands that he wear kid gloves to church. Now mother, observing all this, bought him a silver-mounted walking stick, sending it anonymously through the post. Aunt Mary Ann took him a cup of tea in bed in the morning, innocently saying, 'George, it's your birthday. Somebody has sent you an umbrella.' When he unwrapped it and found a walking stick all hell was let loose. In the middle of it, in walked mother who had seen it delivered. She said with a perfectly straight face, 'What's all the fuss about, George?' At last he had to tell her and she agreed with him that it was an awful thing to do. He accused all the women living in the district and nearly came to killing all the women in Appledore. They cooled him off gradually and it was almost forgotten when Aunt Polly said with a laugh, 'Of course, I know who it was and what shop it was bought in', and so the two women had a laugh together, but *he never knew.*

Grandma Slade walked into mother's house one day. She said, 'Annie, your passage mats are not fit to look at. Why don't you get Billie to make half a dozen new ones?' Mother said, 'All right, I will'. She watched her chance and when it came she went to her mother-in-law's house and took away all the good and nearly new mats she could find. She collected the old ones from her own passage way and distributed them in her mother-in-law's house. Both houses being now nice and tidy, one with good mats and one with old ones, she locked her front door and went to Bideford. There was an awful hullabaloo when Grandma Slade went home and found all her lovely mats had disappeared and the worn out ones in their place.

Now I could go on telling yarns about mother but I'll finish with one of her last escapades which I feel both proud and amused about. She was well into her nineties when she took it into her head to have another sea trip and so she appeared one morning all dressed up carrying her case. She said to her nephew, 'I want to go to Ilfracombe in your car, right away.' On the way he kept asking her what it was all about, but she answered, 'Do as you are told.' When they arrived, he had to put her on board the boat for Cardiff. They guessed her destination and sent off a telegram to my cousin who met her on arrival. He, of course, was delighted to have his aunt of whom he was very fond. He kept her as long as she wanted to stay.

After a few weeks she decided to return home. She packed her case and her nephew's wife, Alice, saw her on board the boat for Ilfracombe. She dared them to send any message home to warn the Appledorians she was on her way back. A couple of ladies promised to look after her while on passage, so Alice went home feeling more relieved. It was blowing hard westerly so when they opened out Nash Point the passenger boat was making bad weather of it and mother's protectoresses became really ill with mother in attendance on them both. She gave them tea and in order to comfort them she said, 'The foreland is in sight, when we get there we'll go right down along shore in smooth water all the way to Ilfracombe. It won't be long.' It turned out exactly as she said. When the two ladies recovered and had some more tea, they asked her how she knew all this. She replied, 'I've sailed with my father and my husband. Those men on the bridge can't tell me anything about it.' She walked ashore with her case, caught the bus to Bideford, went to a restaurant, had a good meal, arriving to Appledore about 4 pm, quite unexpectedly but happy in the knowledge she had proved to her daughter she was capable of looking after herself.

There were many fine women who were ideal sailor's wives in Appledore, but when I look back and think of the life of my mother, Rosina Annie Abigail Slade, I feel she was outstanding as a wife, as a helpmate and a mother of whom we can justifiably be proud. Born on January 22, 1865, she died in November 1964, almost reaching a hundred and keeping all her faculties to the end. She refused to take the drugs her doctor ordered. He always had a bit of fun with her when he paid his visit every day. She said, 'I know I'm on the verge and I want to see what it's like to go out.' Not the least bit perturbed, she died fully conscious, sensible and unafraid.

PART 6

A Woman of Character under Sail and Steam

Commentary

There follow six letters from Rachel Henning. These are concerned
with passages in vessels driven by both steam and sail which operated
under both means of propulsion at once, occasionally under sail only,
rarely under steam alone.

Rachel Henning was born in England in 1826, the eldest of the seven
children of the Reverend Charles Henning, once Chaplain to the Duke
of Cambridge. Her father died when she was fourteen, her mother five
years later and Rachel then took charge of the family. Two of the
children had died of scarlet fever and the eldest boy, Edmund Biddulph
Henning, was so affected by the illness that he was advised to go to
Australia to seek better health. In 1853, at the age of nineteen, when
Rachel had looked after him for nine years, he sailed to Australia in the
Great Britain with his sister Annie. They settled at Appin in New South
Wales and a year later Rachel sailed with her young cousin, Tregenna
Biddulph, and her sister Amy to join them. The passage was made in the
steamship *Calcutta* of which a sailing bill is reproduced at Plate 19, and
the first letter, like those which follow, was written to the only child of
the five to remain in England, Henrietta who had married the Reverend
T.W. Boyce,

The *Calcutta* was what some contemporary seamen would have called
'a barque-rigged screw', that is, a vessel rigged with square-sails on her
fore and main masts and a gaff and boom sail on her mizzen, equipped

also with a steam engine driving a propeller in place of the then still common paddle wheels. More is known about the *Calcutta* than about most of her contemporaries because a log, beautifully kept by her first master, Captain John Vine Hall, and recording her maiden voyage to Calcutta and back to England is preserved in the National Maritime Museum. Of nearly 1300 tons, a large ship for her period, she was built at West Ham in 1852. She was equipped with steam engines of 300 nominal horse power in an engine room amidships which occupied 53 of the vessel's 244 feet length. The highest speed of the *Calcutta* on her maiden voyage was 12 knots, achieved with a moderately fresh breeze and a smooth sea, all working canvas except the mainsail set and both engines at full steam and the maximum revolutions of 68 per minute.

The two-bladed feathering propeller had a pitch of 17 feet and a diameter of 15½ feet. The engines were of simple design and consumed vast quantities of coal, so the sails were used almost continuously and at times the vessel was put on courses designed to make the maximum use of the prevailing wind like a purely sailing ship. When faced with a strong contrary wind it was a matter of some professional skill to determine when to steam and when to sail and if to steam how much power to use. On her maiden voyage the *Calcutta* steamed with varying degrees of power nearly all the time, using the sails and engines together and only very rarely sailing without power. On her second voyage, when she carried Rachel Henning to Australia, because the distances were much greater between coaling stations it was necessary to conserve fuel, and so when the wind was strong and favourable, as Rachel notes 'they took up the screw and the ship went on under canvas. I thought it a much pleasanter motion, but we rolled about a great deal more.' There was good reason for Rachel's preference, since the cabin she shared with two other women was immediately over the propeller and the vibration, given the sort of bearings in use at the time, was probably considerable. It would not have been improved by the device for raising the propeller which was a collar and screw jack arrangement with a clutch. Various mechanisms of this kind were tried in the early days of the steamship in order to eliminate or reduce the drag of the propeller on the vessel when she was sailing. The *Calcutta's* machinery for this purpose gave some trouble on her maiden voyage.

On this maiden voyage the *Calcutta* carried a crew of 110, including 6 mates, 20 stewards and servants, 2 butchers, 4 engineers, 18 firemen, and 43 seamen and boys. The ratio of stewards and servants to passengers was almost 1 to 4, it was a great improvement on the *Blenheim* and

Rachel Henning travelled under conditions which, for all the discomfort and boredom, involved none of the hardships of the sail only era which had recently begun the very slow process of coming to an end. The food was excellent and the passengers, who were well served, with special meals for the children, knew that they were, short of accident, faced with a voyage of predictable duration even if it took three months to reach Australia.

The *Argo* from which the master of the *Calcutta* on Rachel's voyage had been promoted was owned by the same company - the General Screw Steam Shipping Co. The vessels of this fleet were pioneer steamers on the round the world voyages which were the Australian trade and they attracted much contemporary attention.

Rachel is no less of a snob then some of the other ladies whose accounts of passages have already been given. She was twenty-seven, strong-minded, physically fit, an individualist, securely conscious of her position in British society as the daughter of a well-connected clergyman and related on her mother's side to a titled family. She never really got to know any of her fellow passengers and she could do perfectly well without their close acquaintance.

It is not surprising that Rachel Henning found colonial Australia not to her liking. Though her brother loved the new country she could not accept colonial life and homesick for England she returned there in 1856 in the full-rigged sailing ship *Star of Peace,* built at Aberdeen in 1855 and commanded in 1856 by Captain H. Sproat. Rachel corresponded regularly with her brother and sister in Australia and after nearly five years the pull of this close-knit family became too great and she determined to return to her brother's adopted country to see if the second time she could make a go of it.

This time she travelled in the vessel her brother and sister had used in 1853, the *Great Britain,* (sailing bill at Plate 20) one of the most important landmarks in the history of the development of the ship. The *Great Britain,* like the *Calcutta,* was a steam-and-sail vessel, but at first not a full-rigged ship. Technically speaking she was the world's first six-masted schooner, anticipating the pioneer American six-master, the *George W. Wells,* of Camden, Maine, by more than fifty years.

Much more important, the *Great Britain* was the first large iron vessel and the first really large screw-driven vessel ever to be built. She was 274 feet long and about 3000 tons gross. Initially she had accommodation for 360 passengers, 28 of them in single-berthed staterooms and 226 in rooms with two berths in each. She was built in 1843 in

Bristol in a dry dock especially constructed for the purpose which still exists, her design inspired by no less a man than Isambard Kingdom Brunel, creator of the Great Western Railway, the Clifton Suspension Bridge and the Saltash railway bridge as well as the fabulous steamship *Great Eastern*, by far the largest vessel to be built for nearly half a century, which was to follow the *Great Britain* in 1858.

The early career of the *Great Britain* in the North Atlantic trade to New York was somewhat unfortunate and in 1851 after spending the winter aground on the Irish coast, she was sold to Gibbs Bright and Company of Liverpool for the Australian trade. She was equipped with new engines and with new passenger accommodation providing space for 730 passengers, of whom 50 travelled first class. (Plate 21) On her third Australian voyage, Captain John Gray, who had previously been her second mate, was given command. This 'most jolly and genial-looking sailor, speaking broad Lancashire' of whom Rachel Henning formed such a very high opinion, was said to be the run-away son of a peer. He was an extremely popular and successful master of the *Great Britain* and indeed her very considerable success in the Australian trade was probably quite largely due to him. He remained in charge of her until he disappeared at sea in 1872. He was clearly a good man with passengers. When Rachel met him at Liverpool before her passage to Australia in 1861 he remembered that her sister Annie had learned some navigation on her passage in 1853 — a sixty-seven day run which was only the second the *Great Britain* had made to Australia. By the time of Rachel's passage in 1861 the *Great Britain* was a household word and one of the best known ships in the world.

The *Great Britain* made thirty-two Australian voyages. In 1886 she became a hulk in the Falkland Islands. In 1970 this ship, one of the most interesting vessels in the history of merchant shipping, was salved from the shoal on which she lay aground in a corner of Port Stanley harbour and was towed back to her birthplace, Bristol, for restoration.

Rachel Henning's passage in the *Great Britain* began inauspiciously, for she experienced an exceptionally severe gale on leaving Liverpool and had to put into Queenstown for repairs. Rachel compares the weather with the *Royal Charter* gale of 1859. This gale, in October, is thought by some historians to have been the worst to strike western England in the last century and a half. Not only was the *Royal Charter* a sister steamship of the *Great Britain,* disastrously lost on the coast of Anglesey, but many other vessels were wrecked, at least six in the immediate neighbourhood of Newquay in Cornwall alone. But the rest of the passage was prosperous and Rachel noted the advantages of steam and sail, 'Some days the thermometer was up to 90 in the saloon, but we were fortunate enough to steam through it, while the unhappy sailing ships we passed were flapping their sails helplessly in the calms of the Line, while their inhabitants must have been nearly roasted alive.' There were also disadvantages — 'You cannot think how dirty everything gets; hands, clothes, everything is black. The white in my dress is in a most disastrous state. I never saw such a dirty ship'. But in spite of this comment Rachel formed a justly high opinion of the *Great Britain*.

Rachel remained in Australia and somewhat surprisingly in March 1866 when she was forty she married Deighton Taylor, her successful brother Biddulph's sheep overseer. The couple lived happily, at first near Stroud in New South Wales and later for twenty-four years at Springfield in the same state. She died in 1914 when she was eighty-eight. She had no children but descendants of her family are living in Australia today and it is by courtesy of one of them, Mrs N.B. Gill her great-niece, and of Messrs Angus & Robertson Ltd of Sydney, New South Wales, that we have been able to reproduce those of Rachel's letters which concern her sea passages.

Letters written by Rachel Henning aboard the Calcutta *in 1854 and the* Great Britain *in 1861 describing two passages to Australia*

My Dearest Etta,

I begin to write to you today, as we hope to reach St Vincent's on Sunday or Monday and shall be able to send home letters from there. Amy, Tregenna and I watched you from the deck of the steamer on that rainy morning till we were so far from the shore that we could not see you any longer, and then returned to the corner of the cabin where you left us, and whence we did not move again till we arrived along-side the *Calcutta.*

We three betook ourselves to the saloon, where we sat and talked about you on your way homeward, and got rid of the time as well as we could till we were called to dinner.

Amy and I had been looking about and speculating upon the passengers, and had pitched upon a pretty-looking girl of about eighteen, dressed in mourning, as the only one we should like for a cabin companion, and when we went down to look at our berths after dinner, there she was.

She is very pleasant and good-tempered, and, I think, a lady, so we are very well off in that respect. She is going to Melbourne with her uncle and brother, the former a queer old gentleman who patronises us and objects to shaving; the latter, a good-tempered boy of fourteen. Both these are in Tregenna's cabin, together with a man of the name of Trench, who looks like a West India planter and whom Tregenna pronounces 'jolly'.

We found our berths more comfortable than we expected. Miss Maunder has the one under the porthole, and Amy the upper one on the opposite side, and I have the lower one. We put away all our things after dinner and found plenty of room for them. The two boxes which Mr Arnold conveyed on board were safe in the empty berth, and as soon as the ship was fairly off, I nailed up the moreen bags and put up some brass-headed nails, besides, and no one said anything to me.

Our cabin is directly over the screw, so that I dare say they did not hear.

It poured the whole day on Friday, so that we could not go on deck and see the last of old England. The last I did see was the Needles from the stern windows. We have had very fine weather since, with wind directly in our favour, and hitherto we have come very fast. Yesterday the wind freshened so that they took up the screw and the ship went on under canvas. I thought it a much pleasanter motion, but we rolled about a good deal more, and there were several alarming smashes of crockery, and some of the passengers having, contrary to orders, opened their portholes, the lower deck was streaming with water, so the first-officer had all the handles taken off the portholes, and now they cannot be opened at all.

Some of the passengers have been dreadfully ill, and Mr Arnold would have lost his bet, for I was seasick all Saturday afternoon, which I spent in my berth. I got better in the evening and came up to tea and went on deck, and have been perfectly well ever since; although yesterday and today the ship has rolled and pitched a great deal. I thought myself very well off to get off with half a day of it as, if people are ill at all, they generally are so for a week.

It did me a great deal of good. Tregenna and Amy have felt nothing of it. I believe Amy would be better for it, for she has a constant headache and always complains of being 'dreadfully tired', and spends half her time lying on the sofa, with her hands over her eyes. I read to her sometimes, but she does not care about it, nor is she fond of being on deck. She finds the voyage very dull, as might be expected, and I believe that what she feels now is her old complaint of want of excitement rather than any bodily malady, and I have no doubt she will get better as we go on.

The voyage is exactly what I expected: very tiresome, but bearable, like the other wearinesses of life. I do not venture to think how we shall live out three months of it, but I suppose day after day will pass away imperceptibly.

We breakfast at 9 am and then stay in the saloon and write journals, etc, or go on deck and sit and read. They give us no end of a breakfast, hot meat and potatoes and fish, etc. We lunch at 12 pm and dine at 4 pm. This is the great event of the day with most of the people, and they certainly feed the menagerie very well, giving us soup and fish, all sorts of meat and poultry, pudding and dessert. After dinner we generally read till tea-time, which is at 7 pm, and after tea we stay on deck till it is dark. This is the only pleasant part of the day. The sea was most beautiful last night in the light of a full moon, but they put out the lights at 10 pm, so we are obliged to go down at a quarter past nine, unless we like going to bed in the dark.

We already see the difference of climate and of time. The evenings are much shorter than at home and it is getting very hot. I do not feel the heat much, but I am afraid Amy does rather.

I have not said anything to you about the passengers because we do not know anything of them. There are very few of whom I can remember the names, though Tregenna sometimes tries to enlighten me about his friends. He has found a set, some of them Oxford men, with whom he smokes and drinks beer, but in general all the passengers keep to themselves, which I think much the pleasantest way. I do not think there are fifty first-class, but I do not know the exact number. There are very few ladies among them at all, and hardly any in the real sense of the word.

The captain is the only one of the officers of the ship whom I know, as I sit by him at dinner. He is quite a gentleman, but I have hardly exchanged ten words with him. This is his first voyage as captain; he came home last time as first officer of the *Argo*.

One of our passengers is a dumpy little German lady (?) who plays very well, but has most remarkable manners. She was screaming with laughter just now at some compliments which we paid to her music, and then she asked Amy if she could play, and on her answer, whatever it was, she took her round the waist and gave her something between a shake and a hug, to Amy's extreme astonishment. I shall take special care to avoid a similar salute, though I have never yet spoken to her.

Mr and Mrs Donaldson* are in their own eyes the great people on board, he being actually a member of the Australian Parliament (I did not know they had one). He is very stout, very bumptious and a great eater. She is handsome and affected and has not been married long. She has been dreadfully seasick, and today, for the first time, appeared at breakfast.

There are also a Mr and Mrs Westgarth. He has written a book about Australia, which is handed about on board, but I do not feel inclined to read it. She looks like a lady, but I never heard her speak. Then there is a dismal-looking Mrs Macdonald, who is going to Melbourne to look for her husband, that worthy not having been heard of for two years; a very hopeful expedition, I should think. She also is awfully ill even now, and retires in the middle of every meal.

We rather like a Mrs Hake, who is handsome and speaks like a lady.

* Stuart Donaldson, later Premier & Chief Secretary of New South Wales.

But her husband, Tregenna says, is a linen-draper in Sydney, of whom we shall probably purchase future gowns.

I have been writing this in little bits at a time and hardly know what I have told you.

Of course we do not know any of the fore-saloon passengers, but one of them has attracted considerable attention. She is a German girl, who is going out, quite alone, to open concert-rooms in Melbourne. She dresses and wears her hair in the most extraordinary style, and last Sunday she walked for nearly an hour by herself up and down the lower deck, just in front of the quarter-deck, while the officers and passengers were leaning over the rails looking at her and betting as to whether she was painted or not. She certainly has a most beautiful complexion if she is not. She has a piano on board, which she was foolish enough to have unpacked and taken into the fore-saloon. They say she does not play very well.

Some of the second-class passengers are very troublesome. The first day one of them with his wife took their seats at the captain's table, and refused to show their tickets, alleging that they were first-class passengers. However the purser enforced the appearance of the ticket and the steward expelled them.

Saturday, August 12

I have not written yesterday, as I have had a sort of feverish attack from a cold, but I am well again to day.

Yesterday year, Annie and Biddulph sailed. What a little while ago it seems, and yet, though we have only been on board a week, it seems about a year. If we ever survive to reach Australia, I am sure we shall stay there for life, for I do not think I could undertake another voyage even to get home again. It is most wearisome. The noise is wearisome, the people are wearisome and life is wearisome. It is too hot to work, and I am getting quite tired of novels, and there is nothing else on board.

I do not even think that a voyage is so good for people's health as it is said to be. Amy has never been well since she came on board, and I, besides the attack of fever, which was not pleasant, am continually getting sore throats owing to sitting in draughts. The saloon is a sort of Temple of Aeolus, and yet if the windows are closed we could not live. Most of the people live on deck, but we generally betake ourselves to the saloon. We like the sofas, and the glare of the sea makes Amy's eyes bad.

We have a band on board, but they do not play particularly well. Some of their instruments are out of tune. They play at dinner-time and

19 A sailing bill advertising the steamer *Calcutta*

20 A sailing bill advertising the *Great Britain*

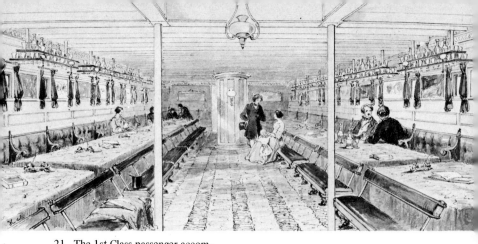

21 The 1st Class passenger accommodation of the *Great Britain* as seen
by an artist shortly after her launch

22 Rachel Henning

23 '– she is still afloat as a training ship
in German waters'

most of the evening and wash the dishes of the establishment at intervals.

The waiters must have a life of it, for they are continually at work. First, the children's breakfast, then ours; then luncheon, then the children's dinner, then ours; then the children's tea, then ours. One waiter is so like Lindon that we generally call him so. Another, who is likewise the bedroom steward, Tregenna took the precaution of feeing when he first came on board, and he accordingly stands behind our chairs at dinner and waits on us most assiduously. We like the stewardess. She is very kind and attentive, and tells us long stories at night, which we do not believe, but which are just as amusing as if we did.

There are eight or ten children on board, but they do not bother us much, as they live chiefly on deck. One baby screams dreadfully at night.

August 14, Monday

I must finish my letter today, as they expect to reach St Vincent's at five this afternoon. We shall not be able to write to you again till we get to Melbourne, as the mail-steamers are not allowed to send letters on board a ship even if they meet one. They must not stop. I have written a journal up to the day I began these letters and shall go on again now, but it will never be worth sending home, for there is nothing to tell. Nothing ever happens except an extra amount of rolling about, or a downfall of crockery.

We stay two days at St Vincent's and I suppose we shall go on shore to see it, but they say it is a bare rock with only a few houses and a heap of coal, and not a tree on it. The real trial of the voyage will begin after we leave it. I wish they would stop at the Cape.

St Vincent's is in sight now, and they close the mailbag this evening, so if we visit it, which I rather doubt – the sea is running so high for a boat – we must give you an account of it in the journal. We have had a most prosperous voyage hitherto, and I believe that the same Providence which has watched over us hitherto will keep us to the end. I dare say we shall both like the voyage better when we are got more used to the confinement of the ship and have forgotten England a little more.

How pretty Danehill must be looking now; those green woods quite haunt me! I wonder how the flowers are getting on in your garden and how the ducks are and if you often walk to Sheffield wood. [Sheffield Park wood, Sussex].

Goodbye, my dearest Etta. Kind love to Mr Boyce and with very, very much love to yourself; Believe me,

Your ever affectionate sister,   RACHEL HENNING

My Dearest Etta,

I hope you received this morning the little note I scribbled in the railway carriage on hearing from one of the passengers that we should be just in time to post it as we drove to the hotel. We got through the journey very well and comfortably and without at all feeling the cold. It turned out a much better day than we expected.

The 'black country' between Dudley and Wolverhampton was most curious. The whole country ploughed up for miles by mines and covered with furnaces and tall chimneys and wretched brick houses. We got all the luggage safe, and drove to the Waterloo Hotel, which was full, so we went on to the Angel in Dale Street, which is very comfortable and clean. We had tea and poached eggs, settled accounts and went to bed. Mr Boyce said he was hardly at all tired. I was rather.

This morning Mr Boyce went out to Baines's office, where he met with Captain Gray, and on his mentioning my name to him he remembered me perfectly at Melbourne and said he would call on me, which he did, and very kind it was, considering all he must have to do on the eve of his ship sailing. He is a most jolly and genial-looking sailor, speaking broad Lancashire. He talked much of Annie and Biddulph, and seemed to be greatly struck with the wonderful cleverness of the former in learning navigation; said she could calculate the latitude from an observation much faster than he could.

We went to the wharf at three, only Mr Boyce and I, took all my luggage on board, except the carpet-bags, and saw my cabin. It is a comfortable little place enough, the berths look very much so, and my cabin companion has been so ill-advised as to take the upper one, which I am very glad of.

I heard at Baines's office who my cabin companion was – a Mrs Bronchordt. They said she was a nice lady-like person, but I shall have to find out about that.

The last steamer, which is only for the first-class passengers, goes off at 5 o'clock tomorrow evening. I do not suppose Mr Boyce will be allowed to go on board with me, as it is against the rules.

February 15

Since writing the above we have been on board the ship again. Neither Mrs Bronchordt, my cabin companion, nor her luggage had arrived, so we took possession of the cabin and I unpacked and I put some things in order, while Mr Boyce screwed-up the little cupboard in a convenient corner and made things look quite comfortable.

Captain Gray was on board and was very kind to me. We came back in the 'tug' about 3 o'clock, with him, and he then informed us that I need not go on board till 9 o'clock tomorrow morning, a reprieve for which I was very thankful. The evening is a dismal time to go among strangers, especially with the knowledge that the ship is lying near shore and that I might as well be there. She will probably sail about noon, but nobody seems to know exactly. My Boyce will see me off, and then start for Kirby Lonsdale at 11.30.

The Angel Hotel is very comfortable. We dined at four today, after returning from the boat, and since that Mr Boyce has been taking a nap and is now reading *Punch* while I write.

I do not like to end; it seems like saying goodbye again, but I cannot write for ever. Everything is well, and I am going out under the best circumstances. Captain Gray is most kind, and I am sure I shall be taken care of.

Kiss those darling children for me, and farewell, my own dearest sister.

Ever your most affectionate sister,

RACHEL HENNING

My Dearest Etta,

You will be surprised to hear from me again, as no doubt you are thinking today that I am half-way down the Irish Channel; but, although we seemed to start yesterday, the ship only went a short distance down the river and then anchored again. There was some hitch about her papers, the captain said.

I am very much afraid we shall not put in at St Vincent's. I have not had an opportunity of asking the captain, but the passengers say that she never stops anywhere now, so do not be uneasy, dear, if you do not hear, as I am afraid there will be no opportunity of writing till I reach Melbourne. Of course, if there is the smallest chance, as a passing ship, etc, I shall write.

After I sent off my letter yesterday, we were called to dinner. By the steward's advice Mrs Bronchordt and I sat down at the top of the captain's table next to him, but I do not think that otherwise we have got among a very interesting set of people. There are several commercial gentlemen, or rather not gentlemen, and a little Scotchman, who looks more polished, also a pretty German, wife to one of the commercials, and who cannot speak a word of English. They are all very civil and un-offending, however.

The first evening was sure to be rather dull and dismal. However, we got books and sat round a candle in the saloon (where they have candles in dishes instead of lamps. I should think, in rough weather, the con-sequences would be disastrous), till nine o'clock, when Mrs Bronchordt and myself betook ourselves to bed.

I had been busy all day arranging my goods, so everything came to hand very easily, and Mrs Bronchordt is very civil and accommodating. I think we shall get on very nicely.

The cabin is so light that I can read well in bed, and the lamp shines into my berth, so, that being the case, I have nailed up a moreen bag just within reach of my hand, and put a little store of books into it; also my lantern matches, camphor, etc.

It was not to be expected that we should sleep very soundly the first night, especially as a baby cried in the next cabin considerably. What a life its poor mother will have when we get to sea and she and the children are all seasick! Of course the ship is now as steady as possible, but that will not last long. The stewardess called us at 8 and brought a jug of hot water, an unexpected luxury, and we managed about dressing very well, as I got up first.

I am so well provided with everything I want that there never seems any difficulty; my dress and jacket are warm and comfortable and everything just right. How nicely you helped me in all that shopping. The bag of tools is worth its weight in gold. I have driven innumerable nails for Mrs Bronchordt and myself, and though the steward did come and inquire if the carpenter was in our cabin yesterday, as he was particularly wanted, no one has found fault with the nails, and the cupboard which Mr Boyce screwed up behind the funnel has never been seen and is most useful.

They do not feed you so well on board this ship as they did in the *Calcutta.* There is a quantity of food, but it is coarse; great joints of pork and underdone mutton and chiefly cold. However, the first day out is not a fair sample, and when the captain is on board and we are fairly off, no doubt all will go smoother. I have not seen Captain Gray since I came on board yesterday. They say he is to come off at 12, and that we shall sail with the top of the tide at 3 today.

Some of the gentlemen went on shore again last night, to return this morning. The people are very impatient to be off now; it must be very tantalising for those who have friends in Liverpool.

I am very well content, dear, though a little lonely. There is nothing to complain of in the ship or passengers so far, though I do not see many who *look* as if I should care about them. Mrs Bronchordt is very kind and pleasant, but I do not think there is much in her.

I am writing in the saloon, after breakfast, with a great many people writing round me, for the last mail. The doctor appeared at breakfast today, a droll little man, extremely like Vincent Macey, when we *first* knew him, and covered with yellow buttons to express his being a officer. I hope I shall never want him, and it is most unlikely.

There is no clergyman on board, which I am sorry for; there is a Scotch minister in the second class, who will hold a service, I believe, in the saloon this morning and preach, but I like our prayers and shall presently read them and the psalms and lessons to myself, while you are in your corner at St Werbey's reading the same. How I should like to be there with you!

The captain sits at the top of the dining table, next the mast. Mrs Bronchordt sits next him at his right, and next her I sit; then a Mr Brand, a Scotchman; the pretty German and her husband sit opposite, and the 'commercials' down the same side. I can tell you nothing about the inhabitants of the different cabins, as, of course, I know none of them. I rather like a stout, good-natured women, who inhabits, with her husband, the one opposite to ours; but she is not a lady.

The 'ladies' boudoir' which they talk about is a nice little room enough, but rather dark and chiefly used by the children. I shall probably sit in the saloon, most likely where I am sitting now by the table just opposite the entrance to my cabin. I shall begin the pinafores tomorrow. I am so glad to have them to do.

I know you will think of the *Great Britain* when you pray for 'all that travel by land or by water.' Oh, how I should like to see your dear face once more before going! But all is right, and I am going hopefully and cheerfully. This letter seems all about myself, but you will like to hear all I can tell you about my new abode.

Ever your most affectionate sister,

RACHEL HENNING

My Dearest Etta,

Unless you have heard by the papers that the *Great Britain* has put into Queenstown, you will be nearly as much astonished at the sight of writing as you would be if I myself were to walk in. How I wish I could. It seems so tantalising to be detained, perhaps for days, within a few days' sail of Bristol. Still, the *Great Britain* might set forth again without me if I paid you a visit, perhaps.

I must tell you our adventures in due order, and most thankful I am to be able to tell them you, for when we lost a boat overboard yesterday I was quite miserable to think of the state of anxiety in which you might be kept for months as to the fate of this ship, for the boat and oars had the name of *Great Britain* on them, and, if washed ashore, might at least have given rise to great apprehensions as to what had become of us in the awful gales we have met with since leaving Liverpool.

We sailed, as you know, on Sunday 17th, had a quiet night enough, and Monday was tolerably calm till the evening, when it began to blow; and during the night we had such a gale as is seldom met with. It *did* blow with a vengeance. The captain and all the officers were on deck all night; indeed the former has not been in bed since we left Liverpool, such has been the weather. I saw him to speak to in the morning, and he said he had never had the *Great Britain* out in such weather before. However, there was no great damage done beyond making everyone, nearly, extremely ill and sorely frightened, and the wind went down in the course of the next day.

We had very rough weather during Tuesday and Wednesday, but still nothing remarkable, but yesterday morning it began to blow again, and for about six hours we had such a hurricane as no one on board ever saw before. To say that I never knew anything like it is nothing, but all the oldest sailors say a West Indian tornado was the only thing it was like. Providentially it came by daylight; began about 9, and the worst was over by 3. I could never give you the least idea of the force or roar of the wind, and some of the passengers who ventured on deck said the *Great Britain,* big as she is looked like a cockle-shell among the waves, and that it seemed impossible but she must be buried in them.

She behaved admirably, took in very little water, and came up as stiff as possible after every roll. Several seas came on board, however; one broke into the saloon and thence into the cabins, one of which was three feet deep in water. The steward mopped and dipped it out in buckets. Some water got into our cabin, and, on going in to investigate, I found that one of my boxes was standing in a puddle; and remembering that the children's likeness was at the bottom of that very box, I determined, gale or no gale, to unpack it and get the picture out, which I did.

It was not the least hurt, but it was so strange and sad to see their little smiling faces in such a scene. I was glad enough to think they were safe at home, and probably just going out for their walk, for the sun was shining, notwithstanding the fearful wind and sea. Nothing in the box got wet, so it was all right.

When I came back to the saloon I found all the passengers grouped about, looking grave and somewhat frightened, except one group of young men, who pretended to laugh over a game of cards, but who looked more alarmed than anyone when a harder squall than usual came on. I betook myself to a sofa at the end of the saloon to try and console some girls who were crying with terror, when the door opened and Captain Gray's cheerful face appeared. I asked him if the gale was abating, and he said, yes, the worst was over and that he had never seen such a one before; and from then the wind went gradually down, leaving only a heavy swell, which has tumbled us about all night and is now making this writing almost illegible.

There was considerable damage done to repair, which we are now running into Queenstown as fast as steam can carry us. The foreyard was sprung and a sprit-sail hook broken; the bulwarks smashed in in one place and a boat stove in and half-knocked away by a wave, and they had to cut her away as she was beating in the ship's side. This boat was a great affliction to me as the name of the ship was on her, but it will be all right now you can hear we are safe.

They report that one of the masts is sprung, but I cannot make out if it is true. How they ever stood at all I cannot imagine. The captain expected some of them to go, for he had axes laid all ready to cut away the wreck if they went overboard.

We have had a great escape, for which we are not half thankful enough. We hope to be in Queenstown tonight, and this letter will go tomorrow morning. I do not know how long it will take to repair the ship, probably some days; so if you write by return of post the letter will probably reach me, and it will be such a pleasure to hear from home again. Put your full address, and if we are gone, the dead letter office will return it to you.

We have made so little way that we have not been more than a day's sail from Liverpool all this time. I do not suppose they will leave Queenstown till a fair wind comes; it is no use beating about like this. We shall hardly be in Australia till the middle of May. It is very wearying prolonging the parting from England like this, but it is sure to be all right. It is such an inexpressible blessing to feel that it is all in better hands than ours; in a gale such as yesterday's it makes one not fear anything that may happen.

Although the voyage cannot be considered a very prosperous one so far, I have had more than my usual good fortune as to seasickness. I have generally been unwell for a few hours, but now I have not for a single hour of it, notwithstanding the bad weather. Mrs. Bronchordt, too, has never been seasick at all, which is fortunate for me as well as herself, but she is headachey and poorly and seldom gets up to breakfast. I am rather glad she does not, as dressing with the ship at an angle of forty-five degrees is quite difficult enough for one person. We get on very comfortably together, as she is pleasant and accommodating, but there is no one on board of whom I know much as yet.

I rather like an old widow lady – a Mrs Ranken – she is Scotch and the coolest, quietest person I ever saw. She is going for a fifth time, and minds gales no more than nothing. Curiously enough, she is aunt to that Miss Ranken with whom I came home in the *Star of Peace,* knows Bathurst and Mr Sloman and has seen Annie and Amy there. She is very good and kind to the sick people, nurses roaring babies whose mothers and nurses arc ill.

I have also made acquaintance with a rather dismal young lady, who is going out by herself and is sorely frightened, and a Scotch lady with two children and a sort of turban headdress, who is more frightened; besides a speaking acquaintance with a great many people.

The commercials I mentioned before have resolved themselves into rather a gentlemanly little German, with whom I play cribbage, a large and radiant squatter, whom may Biddulph never grow like, though he is the picture of good nature; and an intelligent sort of man, who really is a merchant, I believe, and comes from Bristol, besides the Melbourne merchant with the pretty German wife.

These are the people among whom Mrs Bronchordt and I sit at dinner. They are not a very aristocratic set, but they might be worse, and it doesn't matter for two months.

Most of the people have been frightfully ill and some have not yet appeared. The old Scotch lady and myself were the only ladies that appeared for a long time. I think we fraternised because we neither of us mind anything much. I believe she is a good woman, too, though stiff and silent and 'Scotchy'.

The cabin is wet just now, but all my things are in pretty good order, thanks to my exertions that first day. Mrs Bronchordt's are rolling about in sore confusion. She is not very tidy. The berths are very comfortable and I sleep well, when the ship does not roll beyonc measure.

I am at the end of my paper, and the difficulty of writing is extreme and of reading it probably greater. I shall be able to write again from Queenstown, perhaps more than once.

My kindest love to yourself, Mr Boyce and the children and Sophy, if still with you.

Ever, dearest Etta, your most affectionate sister,

RACHEL HENNING

My Dearest Etta,

It was quite pleasant to wake yesterday morning and find the ship quiet, and then to look out and see that we were steaming up the beautiful harbor of Queenstown. The sun was shining, the sea quite smooth and numbers of white-sailed ships dancing about and getting out of our way.

We were soon surrounded by shore boats, and the whole *Great Britain* population seemed to turn out upon Ireland. I went on shore with Mrs Bronchordt and a party of gentlemen to see what was to be seen. We had a pleasant row across the harbor and soon got to Queenstown, which is built on a sort of precipice, the white houses rising, tier upon tier, all up the hill and looking very well from a distance; but we soon got into a narrow, filthy street, swarming with children and pigs. Some parts of the town were much better, but we had soon seen all there was to see, and then we set off in a steamer for Cork.

The sail was most beautiful between low green hills covered with woods and gentlemen's houses peeping out, or sometimes wild heathy hills and downs. We were about an hour going to Cork, which, though rather dirty, was a better town than I expected. The population generally despise bonnets and go bare-headed, or put up hoods when it rains – not that they seem to have much to do.

We went to the Imperial Hotel and dined, and then set off in a real car to visit the ruin of Blarney Castle. The country round Cork is beautiful, something like Devonshire. We had a real specimen of an Irishman in the driver, who would have blarneyed the head off your shoulders, to say nothing of the money out of your purse.

We walked up a hill and I saw the furze in blossom, and the hedges budding as I did not expect to see them again in England for a long time.

Blarney Castle is a most picturesque ruin, and we went to the top and saw the famous Blarney stone.

We drove back to Cork intending to return to Queenstown by train, but were too late, and so had to get back by a most circuitous route, by train to Passaje, then a mile in cars to Monkstown, then we crossed a long ferry, then performed a night-march of two miles over some very dirty roads, to Mrs Bronchordt's great horror, and at last got to Queenstown about 8, when we took a boat for the *Great Britain.*

The moonlight row across the harbor was lovely and sea like glass, the Queenstown lights reflected in the water and the ships dotted about and all showing different lights. It was a pretty scene. I thought as we came along that Mr Boyce was probably about then arrived at home, and was telling you about his adventures and our Liverpool experiences. I will not say I wished myself back in your drawing-room, but I thought very lovingly of it.

We got on board the *Great Britain* about 9 after a pleasant day's excursion. The weather was beautiful and quite mild.

This morning we had service on deck. There is a Presbyterian minister on board; he read a chapter, prayed and preached very nicely and to a most attentive audience. Perhaps it was more suited to them than our long morning's service, though I did not like it so well.

A great number of the passengers are on shore staying at hotels. Perhaps I shall get on shore again tomorrow, but there is some report of the ship sailing at noon, though I hardly believe the repairs can be done by that time.

We have not seen much of the captain till today, when he appeared at breakfast. He has had a terrible life of anxiety since we sailed. Now I hope we may make a fresh start under better auspices. Do not be uneasy that we have met with such weather; such a gale is quite an exceptional thing, and there has been none such since the *Royal Charter* was lost, nor did it blow so hard then, only she was in-shore, while, providentially, we were in open sea.

We may make a good passage after all. I have no fears myself. No ship could have stood a gale better. There are some in the harbor sorely battered with bulwarks gone, masts down, etc; far worse than we are. Of course we cannot arrive in Australia till May, so you will not hear of us till July.

The saloon is full of visitors come off to see the ship, and I was surprised to hear my name called just now, and on looking up, to see Mr Humphries, one of our *Calcutta* passengers. I could not remember his name at first, and cannot imagine how he knew me, for I have not seen him these five years. He is living near Cork, and came to see some friends he has on board. He has sorely hindered my writing, and this has to go ashore by 5 o'clock.

Some of the passengers have talked of giving up the voyage, so dismayed were they at the weather, but I do not think any of them have done such a foolish thing. We have nothing to complain of on the whole, in the ship, though we amuse ourselves by grumbling a little at the table, which is not over-good for what we pay. The provisions are plentiful enough, but rather coarse in quality. Still, we have good appetites.

I have not made any great acquaintance with anybody except Mrs Bronchordt. I do not think we have a very eligible set on the whole, but perhaps they will improve as we go on, and it is only for two months, I hope, at all events.

You cannot think how dirty everything gets; hands, clothes, everything is black. The white in my dress is in a most disastrous state. I never saw such a dirty ship. We are well supplied with water, however, and as yet no animalculæ have made their appearance.

Ever yours very affectionately,

RACHEL HENNING

My dearest Etta,

I suppose the newspaper telegrams will have told you that the *Great Britain* has safely reached Australia before you receive this. We landed in Melbourne on 2nd May after a very good run from Cork of sixty-two days. I wrote to you from Queenstown the day we sailed, so you know my adventures up to that point. After that we had a calm passage on the whole; of course there were rolling days and stormy nights, but nothing that could be called a heavy gale. The passage was a pleasant one, take it all together.

After leaving Ireland we soon got into warm weather, and very warm weather it was. Some days the thermometer was up to 90 in the saloon, but we were fortunate enough to steam through it, while the unhappy sailing-ships we passed were flapping their sails helplessly in the calms on the Line, while their inhabitants must have been nearly roasted alive.

We crossed the line March 17th and rounded the Cape on April 6th. After that we had some cold weather, of course, but nothing very intense, as we did not go very far south. We never had very favorable winds. Once we made a run of 315 miles in the 24 hours, but only once, and it was chiefly owing to the screw that we made such a good passage as we did.

I liked some of my fellow-passengers very much, but not my cabin companion, Mrs Bronchordt. At least I did not dislike her, for she was good-natured enough, but a more helpless, childish, complaining mortal it was never my misfortune to come across. She could not do her hair fit to be seen, nor mend her clothes, nor keep her things in any sort of order. However, as she spent most of her time in bed, I gave up the cabin to her and followed my own devices elsewhere.

I think I told you about Mrs Ranken. I found her most pleasant all through the voyage, and now I am going to travel up to Bathurst with her tomorrow, and she has asked me to come and stay with her there.

Of the young ladies, the one I knew best was a Miss Shering. She was going out under the captain's care to be married, as were two other young ladies on board. She was a gentle, dark-eyed girl from Bristol, of some tradesman's family, I rather imagine, not very clever, but very kind and good. The young ladies, in general, were a very dull set. We had some pleasant people at our table. My next neighbor, Mr Brandt, was a German Jew, but who spoke English very well, and we kept up an incessant skirmish on the relative merits of England and Germany; below him were the Friend family, some Sydney people; opposite me were Mr and Mrs Feldheim – he was another German and rather a well-informed man. Then there was Mr Gifford, a flourishing-looking Adelaide squatter, who told the most amusing stories about the bush; Mr Uphill, a merchant, but *not* from Bristol, as I first thought, but he knew the place very well; Mr Payne, a young lawyer, clever and amusing and a thorough Englishman; who used to join in the battles with the Germans; and a Mr Compton, who, I think, was a little cracked – he used to come out with such extraordinary statements. We had far more fun going on at our table always than at any of the others, and the captain used to say it was the only one he liked taking the head of. He took them all in turn.

Somehow there was a good deal of stiffness and party feeling on board the ship. I hardly know how it arose, but half the people were not friendly with the other half. I enjoyed the voyage myself. I was always so wonderfully well; I never had a day's seasickness nor illness of any kind, and never was absent from a meal from the time I left Liverpool till I reached Sydney. It was a thing to be very thankful for; so many people were unwell at various times. I was more often than not the only lady at the table, except old Mrs Friend.

I will not say more about the voyage, however, as you will find plenty about it in my journal if you have patience to read that document. I am going to send it, together with the pinafores, to England by Captain Gray, and as he sails on 29th of this month, it will probably be in England at the end of July, a short time after this reaches you.
...

I rather enjoyed my stay at Melbourne. About twelve of the passengers were going on to Sydney, and of these six besides myself had taken their passage through and were therefore entitled to stay on board the *Great Britain* if they liked. (There was no steamer on until 7th May). We were quite a pleasant little party there; Mr and Mrs Paul, Miss Parkins, the latter's sister, Miss Dyson, Mr Golding, Mr Osborne and myself, besides the captain, the doctor and Mr Turner, the first-officer. We used to go ashore in the captain's boat every morning after breakfast, spend the day on shore and return to the ship to dinner at 5; and in the evenings amuse ourselves with music or whist or chess afterwards.

We spent one day in seeing Melbourne, its shops and streets and grand buildings, and a very fine town it is, far better than Sydney. Another day we went up the river to the Botanic Garden and Zoological Gardens, and another we made a picnic to a place called Gardener's Creek, about seven miles up the Yarra Yarra.

You cannot think how kind the captain was to me during the voyage and especially during my stay in Melbourne. He always took me under his especial care in all the boating and railway travelling backwards and forwards, for we had to go up by rail to the town; the ship was lying about a quarter of an hour's pull from Sandridge pier; and then there was about a quarter of an hour's journey by rail to Melbourne.

I was very sorry to say good-bye to the *Great Britain* and her captain when we sailed from Melbourne. She is a splendid ship, and I am sure we all have reason to speak well of her.

...

Ever your most affectionate sister,

RACHEL HENNING

The following information is given on the reverse of the handbill advertising the *Great Britain* (Plate 20). The provisions appear to meet with the requirements of the Passenger Act of 1855, the latest passed before the voyage on which Rachel Henning travelled in the *Great Britain*.

...

'DIETARY. – SALOON, First Class, will be found with a first-rate Table. SECOND CLASS Passengers will have to supply themselves with Bed, Bedding, Linen, Soap, but are found with Crockery, Glass, &c, by the Ship, divided into messes, and provided with stewards; the passengers are, however, expected to promote their own and each other's comfort by giving every assistance in their power. The table is supplied as follows, – each article being of the best quality.

Weekly Scale of Provisions for Second and Third Class Passengers.

ARTICLES	SECOND CLASS	THIRD CLASS
BISCUITS..............................	3 Lbs.	3½ Lbs.
BEEF....................................	1½ Lbs.	1¼ Lbs.
PORK...................................	1½ Lbs.	1¼ Lbs.
PRESERVED MEATS AND SOUPS....	2 Lbs.	1 Lbs.
FLOUR.................................	3½ Lbs.	3 Lbs.
RAISINS...............................	8 Oz.	8 Oz.
SUET...................................	6 Oz.	6 Oz.
PEAS...................................	1 Pint	1 Pint
RICE....................................	12 Oz.	12 Oz.
PRESERVED POTATOES..............	1 Lb.	1 Lb.
TEA.....................................	2½ Oz.	2 Oz.
COFFEE................................	2½ Oz.	2 Oz.
SUGAR, ½ RAW AND ½ REFINED....	1 Lb.	15 Oz.
TREACLE...............................	————	½ Lb.
BUTTER................................	12 Oz.	6 Oz.
WATER.................................	21 Qts.	21 Qts.
VINEGAR...............................	¼ Pint	½ Pint
MUSTARD..............................	½ Oz.	½ Oz.
SALT....................................	2 Oz.	2 Oz.
PEPPER................................	½ Oz.	¼ Oz.
OATMEAL..............................	1 Lb.	1 Lb.
CHEESE................................	½ Lb.	————
FISH....................................	½ Lb.	¼ Lb.
PICKLES...............................	¼ Pint	————
JAM.....................................	¼ Lb.	————
MILK....................................	½ Pint	————
TRIPE..................................	½ Lb.	————
LIME JUICE............................	6 Oz.	6 Oz.

Rice is served out as a substitute for potatoes when they are expended, (1 lb. of rice or oatmeal being equal to 3 lbs. of raw potatoes and 1 lb. of preserved potatoes equal to 3 lbs. of raw potatoes.) Coffee or cocoa may be substituted for tea. When fresh beef is issued, 1 lb. per day will be allowed to each adult; but there will be no flour, rice, raisins, peas, suet or vinegar. Salt fish will be substituted on Fridays, if required.

Passengers are expected to pay for any Crockery or Glass they may break from want of proper care.

THIRD CLASS AND STEERAGE. – In these Cabins passengers must provide their own Utensils and Bedding. The Articles required are Beds, Bedding, Towels, Knife and Fork each, Tea and Table spoons, a Tin or Wooden Plate, a Drinking Can, a Coffee or Tea Cup, Tin Quart Pot and Keg to hold 3 Gallons of Water. Small stores such as Ham, Bacon, Pickles, Sauces, can be purchased from the Purser at moderate prices. Price Lists are placed in various parts of the Vessel.

Weekly Scale of Provisions for Steerage Passengers.

ARTICLES	STEERAGE
BISCUITS	3½ Lbs.
BEEF	1¼ Lbs.
PORK	1 Lbs.
PRESERVED MEATS AND SOUPS	1 Lbs.
FLOUR	2 Lbs
PEAS	1½ Pints
RICE	½ Lb.
FRESH OR PRESERVED POTATOES	½ Lb.
OATMEAL	1 Lb.
SALT FISH	—
RAISINS	8 Oz.
SUET	6 Oz.
TEA	1 Oz.
COFFEE	1¾ Oz.
SUGAR	¾ Lb.
BUTTER	4 Oz.
VINEGAR	1 Gill
MUSTARD	½ Oz.
TREACLE	⅓ Lb.
WATER	21 Qts.
LIME JUICE	6 Oz.
SALT	2 Oz.
PEPPER	¼ Oz.

PROVISIONS ARE COOKED FOR ALL CLASSES OF PASSENGERS, And Will be served out according to the above Dietary Scales, and not by that in Contract Tickets.

BERTHS

The Saloon state rooms contain two and three berths, except the family rooms. In the Second, two and three and four berths; but rooms to suit applicants will be made, if specially arranged for. Persons engaging accommodation for themselves or others, will be held responsible for one-half the passage money, and be required to pay the same, whether they have made a deposit or not. Gunpowder, Lucifer Matches, and Combustibles of every description, strictly prohibited.

P.S.– The quoted rates of passage are not binding, unless the berths be engaged by return of post.

PART 7

The Last Woman under Sail

Commentary

Gwynneth Anne Stanley was born in Maidenhead in 1925. After working in an aircraft factory during the second world war she embarked on a degree course in engineering at Queen Mary College, London University. But she soon became restless and after two years she abandoned her studies and looked for a more active occupation. She held a number of jobs until, in the autumn of 1948, she visited the steel four-masted barque *Passat* then lying in Avonmouth docks, Bristol, awaiting orders after discharging a cargo of grain from Australia. Anne decided at once that when the *Passat* sailed she would be a working member of the crew if it was humanly possible for her to become one. She describes how she succeeded in her wish in her journal of the subsequent passage to Australia where the vessel was to load another grain cargo.

On arrival in Australia she left the *Passat* and after working as a nurse and on sheep stations she married Bob Moss, he of the 'Southern Cross fever', who had worked his way out to Australia on the same passage in the *Passat*. The couple eventually settled in Queensland where they brought up a family on a sea-going barge. Anne Moss now lives with her four children on a sun drenched peninsula north of Cairns.

The circumstances which led to this purely commercial passage by a four-masted square-rigged sailing ship around the world as late as the middle of the twentieth century merit some explanation. Generally speaking the nations of the western world abandoned the use of the cargo-carrying sailing ship as a commercial proposition after the first world war, but there were a number of exceptions, pockets of economic activity where the use of sailing vessels continued. These were almost always associated with old vessels bought cheaply and operated with the minimum of overheads from home ports in areas where the combination of a sailing tradition and lack of alternative employment ensured them crews. Sailing vessels continued to operate, among other places, in the North American coasting trade, in the British home trade, in the North Atlantic cod fishery, in the Baltic Sea and in the Mediterranean. Canadian and Danish schooners, some of them built after the first world war, conducted a busy trade across the North Atlantic carrying salted cod fish from Newfoundland and Nova Scotia to European ports. Very fine steel four-masted barques, owned in Hamburg, carried nitrate from Chile to Europe. These latter vessels were as well maintained and run as sailing ships have ever been in their days of economic prosperity.

Apart from these German barques, the most spectacular of the survivors were two very different groups of sailing vessels of the largest class. These were some big wooden four- and five-masted schooners which operated on the Atlantic coast of North America and a group of square-rigged vessels, steel and wood, barques and four-masted barques, which were owned and manned in the Åland Islands at the mouth of the Gulf of Bothnia. The area suffered from poor communications and lack of industry. The agriculture was crude and small scale. During the nineteenth century its people had taken to investing in small wooden sailing vessels carrying other people's cargoes, first in the Baltic and then in the North Sea and further afield. There is a parallel with the development of Norwegian merchant shipping, but in Åland the process was a generation at least behind. In consequence there remained after the first world war a very strong tradition of professional sailing. An enterprising and outstanding able local shipmaster, Gustaf Erikson, operated from this ideal base a fleet of large square-rigged vessels and schooners in the Baltic trade, the trade from the Baltic to Britain and in the grain trade from Australia to Europe which for a number of reasons still offered paying freights to sailing vessels operated in an economical fashion until the second world war. The history of this maritime economic anachronism and the reason for its existence has been brilliantly analysed by W.L.A. Derby in *The Tall Ships Pass,* one of the best books on merchant shipping history ever written.

The Erikson sailing fleet was at its greatest in the 1930s and though all the vessels were old and some very old, it was a well run concern

whose highly professional masters, mates and crews took a pride in
their ships and maintained high standards. Natural process of age and
the losses of war, coupled with a rising standard of living in the Åland
islands and the opportunities for alternative employment which went
with it, together with the consequences of the Finnish-Soviet war, had
finished the fleet by 1945, but one or two vessels were operated in a
run-down fashion until the beginning of the 1950s. *Passat,* a steel four-
masted barque built at Hamburg in 1911 for the trade with nitrates
from Chile for European ports, was one of these. Anne Stanley's passage
was part of her last voyage but at the time of writing she is still afloat
as a moored training ship in German waters. (Plate 23)

Viking, mentioned at the beginning of this narrative has also survived.
She lies in Gothenburg, fully rigged and provides accommodation for
the training of artificers and engineers.

Passat, with steel hull, with parts of her masts and most of her yards
of steel, with much of her rigging of iron wire, was a completely different kind of vessel from any of the others in this book. Many of the
major maintenance jobs on board her could be done only in a dockyard.
Her huge size made handling her a very different problem from sailing
the *Lady Holland* or the *Joseph Cunard.* At the same time, expertly
handled she could maintain higher average speeds in worse weather
with a cargo many times the size of that of the *Joseph Cunard* and she
needed few men per ton carried to sail her. The steel four-masted
barque was an efficient vehicle for sea transport by the standards of her
times, which were the 1880s and 90s.

But the handling of such vessels, like the handling of their predecessors,
was dependent on the existence of crews with highly professional skills
to whom this kind of seafaring was a way of life from childhood, if not
from infancy. Even in the 1930s there were only just enough men in
each maritime community which maintained sailing ships to keep the
vessels at sea. After the second world war there were no more. The sailing of *Passat* on this last voyage with an almost entirely amateur crew
was on the edge of danger. Although Anne Stanley refers to the vessel
tacking, this difficult manoeuvre was in fact carried out only once on
the voyage to Australia. On other occasions when it was necessary to
put the vessel on the opposite tack, instead of going round they wore
ship. The handling of all types and sizes of merchant sailing vessels was
a highly professional matter, not a romantic adventure or an escape.
After this voyage there could be no more. Anne Stanley and Miss
Northmore were the last women under sail.

*Journal kept by Anne Moss during the last passage to
Australia of the* Passat *1948-9*

SV PASSAT
26 October - Tuesday - 9.45 pm For a week I've been dreaming and
unable to believe that dreams can come true. I was keyed up, ready at
any instant for the vision to fade, but it hasn't done so. As I trudged
along the dockside the beauty of the afternoon and my wonderful good
fortune made me feel in an ecstatic mood and this was heightened by a
ship's siren sounding over the water.

Captain Hagerstrand received me cordially but he's worried about
obtaining men to work on the ship while she's in port. A vessel is a free
identity, as soon as she touches land she becomes tangled in meshes, she
is under regulations and authorities which are unnatural to her.

Miss Northmore, the Australian passenger, is still on board. I feel she
is a decent person and will help when I find it difficult to understand
the captain's Finnish accent. Tonight they have gone out to some
friends and I am left to my correspondence.

During supper Erik-John, the steward's baby came into the saloon,
banged everything within reach and then gave vent to its disapproval
when restrained.

I have a small cabin amidships; I believe it is officially the third
mate's.

28 October - Thursday - 7.45 pm Trouble has been brewing in the past
two days. Apparently the steward was successful in fermenting a row
with the captain this morning and was told he could go if he wished. I
suppose he will do so.

We did little yesterday except pack a few food parcels for Finland.
Today we despatched them and I wrote some letters for the skipper.

Gradually the vessel is getting a hold on me, I find myself wanting to
clear an untidy corner and do other similar things. She is a lovely ship,
but dirty and disorganised at present. British regulations are perplexing

to her Finnish master.

29 October - Friday - 8.30 pm   Mr Hodder came over with a friend this morning which delayed our visit to Bristol. When we did go it was one long trapse to find the appropriate forms for despatching parcels to Finland.

Mr. Reece came this morning. He despatched a telegram to Erikson's to the effect that the captain required news - whether the *Passat* will sail, or no, for if she does she must go into dry dock first. Later captain received a letter saying that should the *Viking* be sold her crew and master would take over this ship. I suppose we are still where we were before.

The steward is being paid off tomorrow. Until his place is filled, Miss Northmore and I will do his duties.

30 October - Saturday - 8. pm   Steward was paid off this morning; Miss Northmore and I have performed his duties today, this has been fun. The boys consider I am sufficiently qualified as one of the crew to receive a share of their collection made from the public today. As a result I am 7s better off.

Two tugs moved us down this morning, even in that short time the vessel began to live again. She seems to be waiting at her moorings to put back to sea. Already she is beginning to have an uncanny hold on me.

31 October - Sunday - 10.30 pm   I wasn't able to complete my entry last night for the local chief of police came in and we all went out to the fair. I had fun tracking an eccentric female who is well known on the streets of Bristol. She came on board and made a dive at Billy, the Australian member of the crew, he disappeared into the hold and stayed there. Having lost out she rushed into the saloon and began abusing, then hugging the captain. The chief of police escorted her on deck and I followed her to the dock gates.

I've been accepted as stewardess until and if we go to Falmouth for dry dock. Should I make the grade, all will be well for foreign waters. My duties begin in earnest tomorrow.

1 November - Monday   Today I have located the stores and tomorrow I intend to start on the job of sorting and listing them. I shall detail Eileen, the new mess-girl, to clean one room per day until all cabins and living rooms are fit to be locked up.

The former steward is still here. He has been less of a nuisance today and has even done some cleaning in the pantry. The zest for clearing the chaos seems to be spreading. Anyway, I think the Matsons will leave on Wednesday: I wonder how the chief mate will accept the new situation? The Finnish cook gave in his notice tonight, I'm afraid he dislikes the bar on the pantry and stores. One of the English boys in the foc'sle will probably take over.

The dockers continue to discharge grain and load sand ballast into the main hold.

2 November - Tuesday I had intended to begin the task of sorting stores but everything has happened to prevent this. Breakfast was held up by a visit from Mr Reece, then the laundry and the chandler arrived. I spent most of the day checking and issuing linen. Apparently the captain is pleased with the improvements. If one doesn't examine the more frequented parts too closely the ship might pass muster. The Finnish cook was paid off and an English boy took over. He is willing and with a few instructions may make the grade.

Thank goodness the former steward leaves tomorrow; this will make guarding the stores an easier job.

3 November - Wednesday Today has been the most hectic yet. Eileen and I have cleaned and tidied the pantry and sorted the provision room. This was a filthy job, it's disgusting to think that food ever came out of such places. Ernie, the cook, thought that the galley was becoming too much for him. After wavering he's decided to stick it. I think we shall make quite a good team. Steward and the Finnish cook left today.

After I'd written last night I decided to turn in, however this was not to be. Captain had been to a cocktail party that had been non-stop all evening under different roofs. He returned at 10.30 pm with three friends, only one of whom was sober and he was a test pilot. The others rambled on, speaking utter jibberish. For the first hour they were really amusing, after that they started to become abusive. I made them strong coffee as soon as they arrived and this gradually became effective on Captain 'Gus because he was the only one who really drank it. This enabled him to take the youngest member home. This is my first experience of tackling the tiddly.

4 November - Thursday My department is gradually sorting itself out, although meals are not always on time and the cook doesn't quite achieve what he aims at.

I went ashore this afternoon to see several people on business; the weather has been lovely. I hitched a lift up to Avonmouth on one of the goods engines. This is the first time I've hitched on a train.

6 November - Saturday The past two days have been the busiest yet. Our department was striving to finish the cleaning before the men came to fumigate. We did manage it though it was a terrible scramble, especially as they arrived nearly an hour early. Eileen went home during the afternoon, so I was left to cope almost by myself. I must say Ernie pulled his weight. At 7 o'clock we all abandoned ship and left the cockroaches to their fate. The captain, Miss Northmore, her friend Mrs Taylor and I went to Shirehampton and saw a poor picture called *Dark Passage*. When we returned there was a grey dust everywhere; I've only just cleared it by this evening.

Today I sent Ernie off at 2 o'clock and was left with everything; we had a cold meal which simplified matters.

The chief mate brought three friends instead of the one he had mentioned. I am waiting for them to finish their second round. Anyway, chief will have to pay for this by supervising the removal of rotting vegetables from the stern.

7 November - Sunday Although Eileen is still away, this has been the least hectic day since I took over. Miss Northmore helped with the washing up. The Bristol Ship Lovers came to view the ship; they were as impressed as all our visitors are.

Mrs Taylor and I walked to Avonmouth and back to post some letters.

8 November - Monday I rolled out of my bunk and slipped across to call Eileen this morning. She wasn't there. Ernie and I had to carry on alone. The men came at midday to remove the chimney in the galley; we had a cold meal and I sent cook ashore for a few hours' leave, he didn't get much of a weekend.

Thank goodness the weather has improved; it has allowed me to get some of the mattresses and cushions aired. Taking into account that Eileen was not here, the system worked very smoothly.

Captain said tonight, 'What you done to chief? For two years I try for to make him work — in one week you make him work and do overtime'.

10 November - Wednesday I went out on Mike's bike yesterday afternoon. I meant to confine myself to business. However, I missed the turning to the dry dock and came out on a road that runs for about a mile north along the shores of the estuary. It was there that I realised once more that all work and no play makes Jack a dull boy. It was misty and the water looked peaceful, I could just make out the coast of Wales and the forest of Dean. I decided to go ashore that evening and I did so again tonight. A crowd of us gathered at the Seamen's Mission and saw *The Barrets of Wimpole Street.* The sound track was poor and the focus as bad; nevertheless we enjoyed it. I do hope I shall be able to get home for the weekend, I need to get away.

Began checking the stores in the cellar today; found six foul cheeses amongst other things, captain says keep them to feed the rats!

11 November - Thursday Again it has been non-stop work all day, but there is a break ahead. Mr Reece brought news that we cannot get further ballast until next week; this is good news for me because it means I can get home for the weekend. Jim will be coming down for part of the time.

I completed checking the stores in the main part of the cellar today, quite a job. I forgot to mention yesterday that the jibsails and staysails were hoisted to dry; I managed to get two pictures, one of the entire ship and the other of the bows.

12 November - Friday I've finished checking the stores and have given captain a list in detail and in total.

This evening I received more wages for one week's work than ever before. I've been at it for twelve days without a stop.

15 November - Monday I hitched home on Saturday morning in four hours and took about the same time to return today.

Jim arrived on Saturday evening; it was lovely to see him again and I think he thought the same. Mother worked hard for us throughout the weekend and gave us wonderful food. I fear she had not much of our company in return. We walked by a round-about route to Swindlesham where Jim bathed in the Lodder despite the season. In the afternoon we also went for a stroll. Unfortunately, he had to return about 10 o'clock.

Things seemed to be running fairly smoothly when I returned here.

I left my oil-skins in the last lorry I had a lift in, tearing up to retrieve them I parted company with Mike's bike and made myself in rather a bloody and muddy mess.

16 November - Tuesday I have taken life easily today, with the stores sorted the domestic system aboard is beginning to run smoothly. I even had time for a few extras such as cleaning the captain's inkstand.

Mrs Wingfield Digby turned up again. Once more she brought her excellent collection of photographs; these consist mainly of pictures of the tall ships. I shall put her in touch with Basil Greenhill for Maritime Museum purposes.

A gentleman from the Port of Bristol Authority said today that there's no reason why the *Passat* shouldn't lie at this berth until the New Year if Eriksons so desire.

17 November - Wednesday It was a lovely midday as I cycled up to Shirehampton. I went by the high road and returned by the lower. As the sun was shining I took a few shots of the crew at work; this has allowed me to send off one set of exposures. They are all taken on or near the *Passat.*

Captain wants an inventory of china, glass and cutlery. I completed a list of the last this afternoon — surprisingly little.

Don bet Bill £1 that he wouldn't dive into the dock; of course that was too much for our Australian friend, Don is worse off than he was this morning.

I began polishing the woodwork in the saloon during the skipper's absence this afternoon, quite an improvement.

20 November - Saturday This evening cook left, he didn't approve of his wages but I suppose there must have been more to it than that. I shot off on Eileen's bike and went to several houses before tracking Boxall down. He came over here a fortnight ago and seems a good type. During my chase for the cook I got involved in chasing burglars too and ran a couple of messages for the police.

When I returned from a very pleasant evening at the Greenhills, their son had sent a post card asking if he might stay here tonight. I booked a room at the Miles Arms in Avonmouth and sent him a telegram saying so.

Captain, Miss Northmore and I went to *Daybreak* at the bug-house in Shirehampton on Thursday. I had hoped that there would be some decent shots of Thames barges, but I was disappointed and the film was poor too.

Until this evening's upheaval my department was beginning to run very smoothly. Eileen had Thursday afternoon off and I had yesterday afternoon.

21 November - Sunday Basil Greenhill turned up about 9 o'clock last night. After a fairly long session with the skipper, with whom he sailed in the *Viking* ten years ago, captain suggested that he might stay on board for the night. Basil left after tea today. As I had no cook my time with him was limited but it was pleasant to see him again. The new cook arrived this evening and is cleaning out his cabin – a good sign I feel. I am pretty tired so I'll turn in early.

22 November - Monday I was woken this morning by the cheerful news that there is no cook. I left a perfectly hail and hearty one in his cabin last night but he must have changed his mind; wish the wretch had told me. I enquired at his digs and found he had slept there and gone out to his old job this morning. Seeing what he is like, I gave up my search. Bill took over temporarily but I think will probably make a job of it. He has cleaned up the galley and himself beyond recognition.

I had a pleasant cycle round this afternoon, paying visits to James & Hodder, and Bell Brothers *en route*.

A real old scoundrel of a sea dog came on board today. The captain signed him on as sail-maker and then thought better of it before it was too late; goodness only knows what might have happened. Later he brought along another doubtful type who wished to be cook; I despatched him pretty rapidly.

23 November - Tuesday Little has happened today, life has been pretty calm on the whole. I had a dash round this afternoon, up to Avonmouth and back via the pier head where I paid a visit to Bell Brothers.

25 November - Thursday This will be the last time that I write from Avonmouth docks. We leave at 2 pm tomorrow for Port Talbot near Swansea where we are to go into dry dock.

The captain started the ball rolling yesterday when he rang the owners. The orders were to go into dry dock as I've already stated; wait for sails and part crew from *Viking;* and then sail to Port Victoria, Australia in ballast to collect a cargo of grain there.

It appears that I cannot go on the voyage as stewardess but if we have passengers I can go as mess girl. Eileen looks as though she's out of the running; I don't think that she'd stand up to the trip physically.

Tomorrow will be my first day and night afloat and doing a job at the same time.

26 November - Friday We have been proceeding down the Severn estuary for the past four hours; we shall reach Nash Point (near Cardiff) in about an hour's time. I went up on deck just now and could see lights on the coast of Wales; we also passed the Breaksea lightship which Basil mentioned so often.

The ship's cat nearly got left behind at Avonmouth, she was found on the wharf by the cook, who received the prize offered by captain, a packet of cigarettes.

I went for'd to the galley just now and found that there's quite a swell.

27 November - Saturday When I woke this morning I looked out of the porthole and could see nothing but sea. On further investigation I found we were lying in Swansea Bay about five miles from shore. It was a lovely morning and the Welsh coast and hills looked serene in the early sunshine. The wind gradually increased until there was a fairly heavy swell running. It has decreased slightly this evening but I am now getting my sea legs and don't notice the heaving so much, in fact I find it quite pleasant. At about midday the pilot came aboard and the tug *Queensgarth,* which brought us down from Avonmouth last night, spent several hours trying to catch a line to take the hauling cable. After many fruitless attempts because they were swept away by the heavy swell they eventually got our manilla rope aboard their tug. Then they got it caught on their rudder, after retrieving it the entire rope gave and so postponed our trip to Port Talbot. There was another reason why we couldn't leave today; the donkey engine that hauls the anchor up wouldn't work. For an hour the men turned the capstan by hand, at the end of that time they'd only taken in three out of the sixty fathoms.

Captain, chief and Mike are working on the for'd well deck at present, by the light of a hurricane lamp they are splicing the broken tow-rope.

Two members of the crew have succumbed to the swaying of the ship, Eileen and Don.

Bill, the cook, showed me how to hoist the ensign this morning, I'll see if I can do it tomorrow.

I have got cook to bake some bread tonight as we still have ten riggers aboard who are fast consuming our supplies.

28 November - Sunday As a contrast to yesterday's efforts all went well with the cables and the donkey engine. We weighed anchor soon after 2.30 pm. It took only about an hour to reach the dock. It appears to be fairly expansive and not nearly so dirty as Avonmouth. Pinnochio and I have been rowing around for the last hour in the dark, it was so peaceful, only the sound of gentle splashing and the rowlocks crunching. The chandler came aboard at the lock and took an order for tomorrow.

30 November - Tuesday I had a hectic day yesterday and went into the town for a rest, both mental and physical. I saw *Fanny by Gaslight.* Of course the producers have altered the book but as I read it a number of years ago the changes did not jar and I quite enjoyed myself.

The press have been down here taking photographs and asking questions. They are putting in short articles which are full of inaccuracies.

Miss Northmore went off today. She is visiting her English friends before returning in the *Passat.*

We have been in dry dock two days. The ship isn't quite such a pleasant shape below the water-line as I would have imagined. We find it most inconvenient having to go ashore for the lavatory and not having the usual freedom of chucking liquid waste through the scuppers.

I have rarely enjoyed a bath more than I did this afternoon. A small man from the Seaman's Mission invited us to go down there. It's a pleasant thought that we can have baths while at Port Talbot.

1 December - Wednesday Captain showed me some letters from passengers applying for berths; if they come I am safe for the passage too.

Mike left today, he was the best of the bunch. I'm glad to think that Pinnochio will get a week's leave with him. Eileen and Mike·bought her engagement ring yesterday. She will stay here until the new steward arrives, which is very good of her.

I walked up to the small post office beyond the dock. Port Talbot is rather a dirty little town but has outstanding scenery around, hills on one side and sand-dunes and sea on the other.

2 December - Thursday With one thing and another I've hardly stopped all day. During the afternoon captain mentioned quite casually that seven of the *Viking* crew arrive this evening. So far they haven't but it is a wretched night for them; I expect they're drowning their sorrows en route. Eileen went ashore for a couple of hours and that left me with more to do.

It has been dark enough for lamps all day; unfortunately we haven't enough oil to burn for that number of hours so we've been groping around in semi-darkness, a type of atmosphere sufficient to get anyone down. Cook found life extremely grim this morning; having softened the harshness at the local at lunch time, he made a poor show of cooking the tea; he was finding it difficult to keep his balance but he was more docile than this morning when he was chucking ladles around the galley.

Seven new members of the crew have arrived. Eileen and I had contemplated a visit to the pictures this evening but we had to set to and cook them some bacon and eggs. They include the chief mate, steward, 1st cook and boatswain. From tomorrow I take over Eileen's duties and become mess-girl.

3 December - Friday   The new arrivals have altered the usual routine of daily life aboard. The chief difference for me is that I am now down-rated to mess-girl as the chief steward came with the others. I couldn't make him out at first but during the course of the day I've come to the conclusion that he's an honest-to-goodness hard-worker with the disadvantage of having had his face smashed in many years ago. He has a good sense of humour. So also has the chief mate. The latter speaks English quite well, and the steward sufficiently to make himself understood. Although I couldn't comprehend a word of their conversation at tea, I enjoyed the meal as they were so jocular and cheerful. Eileen left by launch today.

Tonight, after correcting and writing some letters for captain I transferred all my tackle to the mess-girl's cabin which is aft, off the passenger's dining room. I have now settled in and feel quite fond of my new quarters even if they aren't as grand as the third's which I occupied amidships. I have enjoyed my five weeks as chief steward, but I must say I feel relieved now the burden of responsibility has been lifted from my shoulders.

The best news of the day was that Jim is coming tomorrow.

6 December - Monday   I have worked hard today but it hasn't seemed so because I have had the events of the past weekend on which to reflect.

I had just finished my main duties for the day on Saturday, when a shout attracted my attention to Jim standing on the after well deck. Steward gave me Sunday free. Jim and I spent the day together in the open, on the hills above the shore. Jim bathed in the morning; today the

24 *18th December, 1948* '– the mates were picking the watches'

25 *11th January, 1949* 'Steward decided to wash all the soiled linen and I rose half an hour early to assist him.'

26 *12th January* 'The port watch bent another fair weather mainsail'

27 *13th January* 'Each man was led blindfold up a gang plank onto the hatch. The black cloth was removed and they were questioned by the clerk'

28 *17th January* 'The new fore-stay is in position and will be completed tomorrow'

news seems to be half way round Port Talbot. It was good to be free and breathing the fresh sea air. The wind was strong on the beach, but when we were over 800 feet above on the curving hills, it was blowing half a gale. One day's break has made all the difference. I was getting stale, and although it isn't a thing I often admit, a little lonely. I enjoy being with Jim — one of the main reasons is his friendly approach to everyone we meet.

The skipper went to Newcastle last night to collect canvas and other gear from the *Archibald Russell.* When he returns on Wednesday I shall know my fate. I intend to pack off to Berkshire travelling by night, for I shall have precious little time at home.

6 December is Finland's Independence Day — the crew had a holiday. I didn't because there was much to be done and I shall be taking leave from Thursday.

7 December - Tuesday I got up at a reasonable hour this morning which meant I finished my duties by 4 pm. I took the ferry and went into town. Although I was pretty wet on my return I'd had a breather and managed to buy some things which have been on my shopping list for some time.

Tomorrow I shall know my fate.

9 December - Thursday I know my fate all right. Captain could think of no further excuses, I am permanent mess-girl for the *Passat.* Six days' embarkation leave doesn't give me much time.

Before Captain gave his verdict I'd arranged for a lorry to give me a lift. We travelled from 7 pm last evening till 5 this morning when we arrived in High Wycombe. I called Zoe at 6.30 and had breakfast with her and Mrs. Collins. I hitched into Reading in less time than the bus. My shopping occupied the rest of the morning; it consisted mainly of warm clothing for the trip and a framed rucksack. This afternoon Ma and I bought accessories like toothpaste and hand-jelly, etc. We are both too tired to do much else so are turning in before 10 o'clock.

13 December - Monday I'm sitting in the snack bar at Aust Ferry. I rushed down the ramp but the boat had just pulled away. It'll be back in about an hour.

I spent a hectic twenty-four hours in town kitting up and saying my good-byes. Jim and I returned to Wokingham on Saturday afternoon. There was a letter from Evans, the agent at Port Talbot. Captain says there's a mess-boy coming from Finland and he won't be able to take

me with him. I am now on my way to the ship to discover the real
reason for this change of plans.

I arrived in Port Talbot eight hours after leaving Wokingham, not
bad going. I rang Mr Evans who came down to the station and had a
fatherly chat with me over a cup of tea.

The outcome of my evening with captain is that he has composed a
telegram for me to send off to Eriksons. 'Have served in *Passat* in port.
Can I sign on as mess-girl or deck-hand for five pounds per month. Captain agrees'. I shall get a reply tomorrow.

14 December - Tuesday   The train for Paddington is just drawing out
of Port Talbot. I wired Jim to meet me in town at 9 o'clock.

Half an hour ago I signed on board the *Passat* as mess-girl at £5 per
month. There's no going back now, either by captain or me. She should
sail at high water on Friday morning. I propose to travel back by night
on Thursday. My other plans are that I should spend this evening with
Jim; persuade Chamberlains of Maidenhead to cut my hair without a
previous appointment tomorrow morning; then return to Wokingham
for the remainder of my leave. Maybe it's as well that I haven't got a
book with me because after supper at 6.15 I think I'd better sleep and
make up for the time I intend to lose later. Really and truly with the
thousands of varying thoughts revolving through my head, I shall be
lucky if I feel sufficiently composed to sleep.

Grälan gave birth to four kittens during the night. Mother and children are progressing well.

15 December - Wednesday   Again I write as my train leaves Paddington
for Maidenhead – Jim met me last evening. We spent a couple of hours
with Basil and it was 2.30 before Jim and I got back to Streatham. He
left me at Hyde Park Corner this morning; buses and trams are not
convenient places for good-byes.

16 December - Thursday   I succeeded in getting my hair cut at Chamber-
lain's, although it looks rather peculiar because it is so short.

It is marvellous to be selfish for once and know that it doesn't matter.
I'm disorganising everything and everybody. Good job that this state of
affairs can't last for long.

17 December - Friday   Once more I write on board a GWR train bound
this time for Port Talbot. Mummy and Vera came down to Reading to

see me off. She was very brave, she couldn't have been a better mother.

Vera and Bertie came to my farewell dinner last night, hearts and minds are at sixes and sevens so naturally it was not too relaxed. I love those two dearly, if it wasn't for Vera I shouldn't go off into the blue, she will look after mother. I paid the Bettles a visit at Bracknell, some more true friends. God is truly very good to me.

10.45 pm Just turning in because I must rise at 4.30 am. The tugs arrive at 6 o'clock to tow us out into the Bay. This is the last night in dock. Captain treated us to dinner at the Walnut Tree Hotel, excellent.

18 December - Saturday - 11. am We are out in Swansea Bay swinging the compasses. We left Port Talbot at 7.30 this morning. Mr Evans and Mrs Taylor were amongst others on the dockside to bid us farewell. A most undramatic leave taking; if the mist remains we've probably lost sight of the coast for good. The tug should take us down to Lundy Isle.

I've been trying to make friends with the livestock. The oldest pig is feeling the effects of the gentle roll and is not very sociable. However, its younger brethren welcomed my visit, covering my hands with their somewhat repulsive breakfast. The geese don't know what to make of me or the *Passat,* still they needn't worry, the shadow of the knife approaches with Christmas.

I have taken several photographs today, the conditions are poor, unfortunately. I am lucky in having high-speed film from the National Maritime Museum. Took two photographs when the mates were picking the watches. (Plate 24)

7.45 pm I've been checking the lighthouses on the English coast by their flashes. We passed Ilfracombe and Bull Point before tea, we are practically abreast of Lundy. I picked out the island some hours ago. As the mist cleared the darkness came upon us so the last we saw of the British coast were the smooth curves of the hills behind Swansea Bay. The crew number thirty-four now. Two members never joined at Port Talbot.

I was expecting two parcels that never arrived, one was my ICS stationery and the other manuals for the course, also other reading matter. This leaves only a few strangely assorted books in the ship's book locker. The moon pokes its head at intervals from behind the massive black clouds, hope they will clear as that will give the raw crew setting sail for the first time a better chance.

10.15 pm At 8 o'clock the tug sang out, 'let go the tow-rope'. We have been setting sail ever since. While in tow we had our jibs, fore-lower topsail and topgallant stay-sails set. Now we have both fore topsails, the lower topgallant and the main topsails and the same on the mizzen mast in addition to those originally set. I had wanted to see the mainsail set but this may happen any time tonight and I am rather tired after the lack of sleep for over a week. Miss Northmore has a rotten cold, poor soul.

Gralan and babes continue very healthy although she only has two now, the others were destroyed.

19 December - Sunday - 11.30 am - Lat 50° 57' N, Long 7° 27' W
Apparently the mainsail was set at 11 last night, the rats have been at it and at some of the others, so they won't remain bent long before being replaced. The royal sails haven't been bent at all yet. Apart from the latter all the sails on the fore and mainmasts are set, the topsails and topgallant sails on the mizzen and in the last hour the lower spanker. The sun has been out making a very pleasant shadow of the ship on the pale blue sea. The wind is fair, blowing from the east so that we are running well at eight or nine knots an hour; although she is proceeding steadily there is no apparent straining by men or canvas. The starboard watch are on deck at present. Some of them are moving our coal supply and dumping it in No 1 hold. At present the watches are 8 am to 1 pm to 7 pm to 12 pm to 4 am.

The dust from captain's carpet was too much for me and I was sick at breakfast. This was soon cured by a breather on deck.
8 pm This is the end of our second day at sea and our first under sail. We shan't benefit from the moon this evening as the weather isn't so good; I must forego these landlubber's expressions and say that the weather, or at least the wind, is very fair. We continue on a WSW course, the sails remain the same.

Miss Northmore stayed in her bunk until lunch time. She is now busily engaged in cutting up strips of silver paper for the Christmas trees.

There was a shout for all hands on deck this afternoon. Normally this wouldn't include me but this time it did. Captain was giving out comforts, Christmas presents from the Seamen's Mission at Port Talbot. I got a pair of grey mits, a scarf and balaclava; each man had two or three gifts. Plenty of joking!

The roll and pitch got the better of me again this afternoon.

Some fishing trawlers were sighted by the lookout this evening. At first we imagined the bells to denote steamers. One bell denotes light to port, two to starboard and three immediately fore or aft.

10.20 pm Just had a game of knock-out whist with the first cook and mess-boy, the former won. I'll turn in now and try to sleep despite the roll and sound of swirling waters.

20 December - Monday - Lat 48° 52' N, Long 11° 39' W Today has not been of any particular interest as the old roll got the better of me after breakfast. When I'd finished my main duties for the day I retired to my bunk. Here I find I am unaffected. Miss Northmore has been very kind, giving me a helping hand, dosing me with brandy and soda water and providing me with a hot water bottle.

The carpets in the saloon, captain's cabin and the midship alleyway have been removed until we make port in three month's time.

I feel much better this evening. Had a stroll round the deck just now; the watch were hauling in the spanker, the steering was becoming stiff. The wind changed from the port to starboard bow about four o'clock this afternoon and a cargo steamer passed to port about four or five miles away.

There hasn't been much sun today, tonight it is very dark. Already one can feel the air becoming slightly warmer. We've covered some two hundred miles in the past twenty-four hours, at an average of nine knots.

21 December - Tuesday - Lat 46° 43' N, Long 15° 55' W Except for a few minutes this evening due to spending too long aft, I have been free from sea-sickness. It's been a blessing, especially as the roll has given me something else to cope with.

Today the watches have bent the fore and main royals, I have taken two photographs of the men on the main royal yard. It was nearly dark before they'd finished aloft on the fore-mast; all I could see were their silhouettes, one of these upside down with foot on the lift fixing something underneath the end of the yard arm. They set the royals and the mizzen course. The wind is increasing so the latter has been hauled in again and I should imagine some of the other canvas as well. The entire crew including myself were hauling on the royal main halyard this afternoon. I'm now beginning to find some fascination in watching the large waves collecting, heaving us skyward, rushing beneath and then dispersing as rapidly as they've come.

Tom, the mess-boy, finds understanding anyone a difficult task, but when it comes to speaking with the Finns life becomes too complicated for words.

22 December - Wednesday - Lat 43° 35' N, Long 19° 28' W I haven't been feeling so good again today but I think it's probably due to a cold I'm striving to stave off. Miss N has turned up trumps again and has made many suggestions for my recovery.

The wind is dying away tonight, we can't grumble because its been blowing constantly for four days. During that period we've covered over 200 miles a day (236 yesterday).

The crew had the *Archibald Russell's* sails on the for'd well deck to dry, of course it had to rain and they were swapped to the 'tween decks; then the sun came out again.

Captain has been livery and rather peeved with life. Chief helped me when I was shelling almonds this afternoon; he has a kind heart even if his drinking habits tend to cover up this quality at times. Of course, he doesn't drink at sea — nor does anyone else.

Retiring very early.

24 December - Friday - Lat 39° 7' N, Long 19° 56' W Yesterday was squally, main and mizzen staysails blew out, the first before anything could be done, the second while all hands were endeavouring to take it in. Today the weather has been fine, the one drawback is the wind, it is ahead, so we are now making towards Gibraltar, much to captain's annoyance. These reports are second-hand because I've been lying low for two days.

I suppose I must have got 'flu. Miss N. has been truly good. Steward and his men have been working like beavers for several days now. The Finns have their Christmas dinner on the Eve; officers, Miss N and sailmaker, etc are in the passengers' dining room at the moment, enjoying a spread and no doubt washing it down well.

I am very touched. Two men who have done more than anyone else to prepare for Christmas have remembered me. Steward made me a little man and a pig out of biscuit mixture, he is a dear. The second cook came in with nuts, he stayed for a chat which was somewhat slow, neither of us knowing the other's language. Everyone is very kind, Tom blows in at intervals to see how the world is treating me.

25 December - Saturday - Lat 37° 13' N, Long 16° 47' W Got up for a few hours today. Sat up on the seat beside the wheel on the poop deck. The weather has quite changed; to one who has always put warm breezes out of mind towards the end of September, this mildness seems extraordinary. The deck-log was just turning, progress is slow. It appears that we first tacked on Friday morning in the early hours; we are now running once more. The German carpenter came and chatted with me while I was on deck, cheery fellow. Miss N woke me this morning with two parcels. One had in it some gifts from herself including a hand-woven Czechoslovakian scarf. The other was a tam-o'-shanter of dogs' combings crocheted by Mrs Wingfield Digby; I did appreciate that she should remember me.

The crew have a holiday all today and tomorrow, the minimum of deck-work are the only jobs. After their Christmas fare last night it's probably a good thing. They began with a type of smorgasbord then haddock and white sauce and potatoes, followed by ham and potatoes, held down firmly by somewhat stodgy rice porridge. The captain issued a fair supply of spirits to wash the whole lot down. They finished with biscuits, cakes and coffee; and had nuts and fruit afterwards.

26 December - Sunday - Lat 35° 51' N, Long 14° 16' W   I got up today just before lunch, which I had in the saloon for the first time for several days. Miss N and I sat on deck all afternoon, she sewing and I writing.

It was entirely peaceful. We are just plodding gently through the water on a southerly course. Only the mate of the watch and the boy at the wheel have been occupied and they seemed to be taking things fairly leisurely. Much washing has been done and the for'd well-deck is filled with drying clothes.

A Constellation air liner flew over this afternoon, I don't suppose it saw us because of a low cloud. Another airborne visitor, a sea-gull, flew over, the first bird we've seen since Wednesday. We are somewhere west of Morocco and north of the Madeira Islands.

27 December - Monday - Lat. 33° 54' N, Long 14° 34' W   I got up in the middle of the morning and resumed my duties. It appears that this was just as well — captain often contemplates moves which in reality he would never carry out; the last was yesterday evening when he was discussing with the chief whether or not to put me ashore on the Madeira Islands so that I could return in a banana boat. He was getting fed up with the time I took to recover. Anyway, no more has been said and we must be well south-east of the islands by now.

If the wind continues without a radical change we shall sail right through the Canary Islands, probably in about two day's time. The wind did veer a little this evening and the yards have been squared up.

Cory has been bending the gaff topsail, it is the one from *Archibald Russell*. The other sails have been drying all over the decks, a proper Monday washing day scene.

Before I got up this morning a steamer was sighted to port heading straight for us. She came fairly close, dipped her ensign in reply to ours and then went her way. I think she might have come closer having come so far. She was an American liberty ship, *Blue Grass State*. Everyone got quite excited and gathered on the poop as she steamed well astern of us. I had a look through a telescope but couldn't pick out any figures on deck.

I saw a fairly small bird of the snipe type fishing low over the water this morning.

I noticed a peculiar white ribbon running just to starboard and appearing to dissolve when worked upon by other eddies. Miss N and I wondered what it could be for sometime before chief enlightened us. Apparently it's the air from the keel as she cuts through the water.

28 December - Tuesday - Lat 31° 22' N, Long 16° 1' W My first full day since I crocked up, am feeling much better.

The weather has been superb. We had a following wind which blew us along between nine and ten knots. The blue sky was reflected in the sea which had numerous small white horses on it, in the sky were large fleecy clouds. All the sails were out drying again; one made a pleasant back rest and shelter as I lay on the poop for an hour or so this morning.

The port watch dismantled the anchor derrick and lashed it up for its three month's rest. The second does seem unlucky; when his watch were changing the old main lower topsail for that of the *Archibald Russell*, everything that could went wrong. He knows what is to be done but cannot explain it to men of several nationalities. To cap all, the Frenchy at the wheel became interested in these mishaps and went off his course, nearly sending the ship aback.

One of my duties is to issue the clean and collect the soiled linen every ten days. I did this for the first time, it doesn't involve much as only seven of us have ship's linen.

Apparently all captains get liverish and bad tempered. I imagined Hagerstrand would be an exception but he's not. Tonight he pretended not to see the supper on the table and returned some half hour later complaining that no one had told him; he despatched me to collect some hot food. He was pretty teasey all the time.

29 December - Wednesday - Lat 28° 40' N, Long 18° 56' W Another lovely day, just a few showers but they soon blew away. The wind has veered slightly tonight and our yards have been braced almost against the backstays.

I did my first washing this afternoon. Blowing in the wind above No 4 hatch, it was dry in three hours.

A steamer was sighted to starboard this evening. She came very close right across our bows, no attempt at signals was made by either vessel. Captain lit a white flare — must have given the other ship a surprise to find a square-rigger on top of her!

30 December - Thursday - Lat 24° 43' N, Long 20° 53' W When I awoke this morning there was quite a list to starboard, it varied between 10° and 15°, sometimes becoming as great as 20°. This is ideal sailing weather; we covered 270 miles between noon yesterday and today.

Our speed puts all the crew in good spirits; there has been joking and jovial behaviour wherever work was being done. The engineers have been fixing an aerial on the main mast for captain's wireless. Other members of the watches have been greasing the cables aloft, some of them have been swinging about in bosun's chairs.

I had a chat to our Welsh donkeyman this morning while he over-hauled one of the lifeboat winches. He was at sea before 1935 but then went into the Army till he was discharged a few months ago. He told me that all Tom's grand stories about being in a tanker are pure bluff; I gather this must be his first long trip.

Captain seemed sorry for the harsh words he spoke to me the other evening and gave me a bar of chocolate. He is quite himself while the fair wind follows. His benevolent attitude prompted him to give Moss an old wireless; we shall probably hear the news occasionally.

This list has made me very tired and I'm retiring early.

Steward killed and drew the geese for the New Year dinner which will take place tomorrow evening.

31 December - Friday - Lat 29° 50' N, Long 22° 52' W We've just eaten the largest spread I've seen for many a long year. It was our New Year dinner. We started with the Swedish Smorgasbord, then goose with fruit stuffing, followed by rice porridge, then Christmas pud and we ended up with a wide selection for dessert. I've been writing in my bunk, I doubt whether I could have sat up at a table.

At midday captain worked out our position as usual and found we'd run 290 miles since yesterday. As this was more than he'd anticipated we were heading straight for Cape Verde Islands. The order was given at once to alter course as we have to go west of these islands. The yards which had been practically against the backstays are now nearly squared and we have lost our tiresome list.

A small sea swallow has been following, skimming above the pale water in our wake.

1 January 1949 - Saturday - Lat 16° 53 N, Long 25° 59′ W We altered course again this morning heading further south. Once more we have to put up with a list to starboard. There was a sudden squall this afternoon and the flying jib was carried away. All the royals and upper topgallants are furled this evening. The cable which forms the sheet of the foresail got stuck between the wheel and the block on the foc'sle head. The starboard watch ended by smashing up the block to free the cable, they then replaced the broken part.

Today is an official holiday although due to the strong wind and uncertainty of the weather it hasn't been as peaceful as Christmas.

Some of the crew have seen flying fish. I put on shorts and left off my vest.

2 January - Sunday - Lat 13° 14′ N, Long 25° 8′ W Another holiday and I've taken things very easily. The sky has been grey and where yesterday the decks were crowded with sun bathers, today they are deserted.

I sat on the poop this morning and took a mental trip to the Lake District — I was reading Wordsworth's *Prelude.* While I sat there, flying fish were driving from the sea in shoals and then dropping quietly back after soaring for ten or twenty feet. They have white bodies about six inches long and black wings. One can hear the gentle little splashing above the continual swish of water.

Captain has developed *Passat* 'flu. He's a wretched patient, refuses meals, won't go to bed and then when really sweating, he climbs up on deck. Tom is our other patient, the poor fellow has chronic toothache.

The second cook and I gave the pigs their supper tonight. The small ones were so obstreperous that they lost half their meal in the scuppers.

3 January - Monday - Lat 9° 31′ N, Long 23° 58′ W The tooth got the better of Tom and he remained in his bunk all day. Captain is most peculiar; he is persuading himself that Tom isn't suffering much so that he won't have the unpleasant job of extracting the tooth. In port he told stories about his various surgical operations and how he enjoyed performing them. In the mess-boy's absence I have had his duties to do; I only did the most important of these because I still had my own jobs. The wind is much gentler and we are sailing at about eight knots. We sport two B.Sc Engineering degrees on board. Jack Braithwaite is one of these. He was with Wimpeys on the steel works at Port Talbot, when the *Passat* turned up there he told the Labour Exchange to find a genuine excuse for retaining him. Today he began to sketch the details of the ship, starting with the decks.

The watches have bent old sails for the trade winds. Today they've completed the foresail and mizzen course, the flying jib, mizzen staysail and main lower topgallant. I went aloft for the first time at sea to take a photograph of Charlie on the fore lower yard arm as they were bending the sail.

4 January - Tuesday - Lat 6° 27' N, Long 22° 50' W· We are in the doldrums and practically becalmed, the gentle breeze has been dying away all day. It seems so quiet, only the lapping of water against the hull, (a sign that we are still moving).

Chief has excelled himself as a fisherman. This morning quite a large shoal of bonitos were catching flying fish around our bows. Chief went up on the bowsprit net with a line and piece of rag attached to a hook, he jumped the bait about for a few minutes and soon he was struggling with an eighteen inch fish in his arms. They are very thick and powerful, he knifed the wretch but to little effect. Between them, he and the carpenter killed it after they'd both been spattered all over with blood. The light catches on the scales on their backs and they gleam in a multitude of colours. Just as it was getting dark a small shark was sighted astern. This time a rope with a large iron hook attached was baited with bacon and slung over the poop rail. Quick as lightening the shark was on the bait, the first time the hook slipped. However, the foolish animal made sure the next time and so did chief. They let him hang for a few minutes so that he might lose his strength; even then when they brought him on deck he was pretty lively. He must have swallowed his pilot fish because that came up too and was thrown back. The crew dragged the shark all along the deck and down onto the for'd well deck. There Cory, who is a fisherman by trade, cut up the beast who was still struggling, the different parts palpitated considerably even when filleted — from sea to galley the whole operation took twenty minutes.

My one regret was that it wasn't light enough for a photograph. We had bonito for supper and we shall eat shark for breakfast.

It rained quite a bit this evening; we are nearly in the rain belt. Tom has turned to again; his tooth isn't quite so bad.

5 January - Wednesday, Lat 5° 5' N, Long 22° 53 W Today has been hotter than ever, the atmosphere seems heavy and weighs on top of one's head. After I'd been sweating with my hands in hot water while washing up this evening, I took a turn round the deck in the moon-light. It is the first bright night we've had since the one when we set sail near Lundy Isle. I strolled over the flying bridge, below on the hatch lay men asleep or smoking, on the foc'sle head were a small collection of figures. Lalu, the Frenchman, was playing German airs on his mouth organ and Heinz was humming quietly. Some men already lay in the bowsprit net on mattresses. There is a haze in the west from where the moon is shining, but the remainder of the sky is starlit with just an occasional small cloud. A slight breeze has risen and the temperature is just right on deck. I cannot picture a scene more peaceful than that on the foc'sle head just now. The sails were just filling as they towered above us, greyish in the moonlight; the water was lapping gently against the bows.

The sunsets have been disappointing so far. Tonight there was an unusual one; a bank of thick cloud formed a range like mountains, the sun sank behind these sending golden rays upwards and touching the peaks with bright light; below the range was a narrow strip of clear sky and a soft crimson sun sank into the grey ocean.

6 January - Thursday, Lat 3° 20' N, Long 22° 48' W A perfect day for a holiday, as peaceful as could be, the only excitement was when a shark was sighted and chief tried for about an hour to catch him. All in vain, we wait for him tomorrow.

7 January - Friday, Lat 2° 51 N, Long 22° 57' W We waited and he turned up late this morning. This time I managed to get several photo-graphs of the shark that the third had hooked. There was quite a bit of excitement because there were four sharks of varyihg sizes and one albacore. It was this last fish that chief wanted to harpoon, he tried several times but missed, (we are too high out of the water). Meanwhile, the shark fisherman was having some fun, for he wished to catch the large fish but the smaller ones would come for the bait. Eventually he caught the large one which was about six feet long and between them the crew landed it. The carpenter chopped off its tail with an axe and it was returned dead to its native element. The tails of these fish are supposed to be lucky and bring good winds; the one we caught the other day had its tail nailed on the end of the super-spanker-boom. Just before dusk a really huge one was caught. This time it was about eight feet long and stout. When it was cut up, five baby sharks were born as Caesarian offspring, they are now in a tub on the for'd well deck. Chief never got his albacore because the remainder of the fish took fright at the corpse hurled overboard.

During the afternoon I sighted a dolphin and another shark. Again chief tried in vain for this beautiful creature, which I must admit I had no wish to see killed. In the water dolphins appear blue with apple-green tails. A school of them swam across our stern during one of the fishing operations, with them were a few albacore who are various shades of olive; they were a lovely sight.

My short entry yesterday was due to my sudden exodus on deck. It was a wonderful tropical night and it would have been a crime to sleep inside. I lay down on my mattress on the poop and for a time the beauty of the scene kept me awake. The moon was half hidden by small white clouds so that the sails stood out like silhouettes. The sea shimmered and around the hull were large pieces of phosphorous dancing on the ripples. I slept peacefully till 4.30, then I became conscious of thunder and saw lightening on the horizon. I decided to go below, threw my mattress through the smoke room skylight, shut it and Miss N's, and put the covers on. I then fell asleep again in my own bunk.

Although the chart indicates that we are in the centre of the rain belt, until late this afternoon we'd only had one or two minor showers. When rain came, it was fairly heavy, men rushed about in all directions collecting water in buckets, barrels, jugs and basins. The catching of rain water became of more importance than the catching of sharks and lines were deserted until later. Just now there has been another heavy fall of rain. I'm afraid I'll probably have to sleep with my porthole shut tonight.

8 January - Saturday - Lat 3° 26' N, Long 22° 1' W At 7.30 am three weeks ago we left the small harbour at Port Talbot. At a stretch it feels like two, but certainly not three weeks. Life is very much the same day in and day out, so one doesn't notice the passing of time. It was about this hour (8 o'clock) in the evening that we set sail and left the lights of

Lundy Isle astern.

We tried to catch another shark this afternoon, he took one bait but was too clever to bite again. Porpoise were sighted astern this evening.

My attention was attracted this afternoon by laughter on the poop and the starboard yard arm of the mizzen lower yard. Tom was struggling between pride and cowardice. He was just below the cross-trees, trying to pluck up courage to go a little way along the footrope, so that Mossy on the other end could take a photograph. More laughter because Toni of all people tried to show him. In the end our poor mess-boy was defeated, much to the general amusement.

Toni is half Spanish and half English. The first we heard of him was that on being ordered aloft on a fairly windy night, he burst into tears and cried like a child. Since then he has been punished for this behaviour and his general laziness by the second, the mate of his watch. The other night he was asleep in the bowsprit net during his watch on deck. The mate came to hear of it and Toni was rapidly awakened by a bucket of salt-water being thrown over him. Sleeping out there with little between him and the ocean, it is easy to understand how he felt; he nearly screamed himself into hysterics. Another characteristic which doesn't tend to increase his popularity, is his dislike of soap and water.

There was another sharp shower this evening and I went on the poop in a bathing suit to cool down. My only other garment was a sou'wester.

9 January - Sunday - Lat 2° 58' N, Long 22° 7' W Today hasn't been like the holiday weather we've had so far. This morning there was a tropical downpour, men were scurrying left, right and centre collecting water. Chief and steward ended up by blocking the outlets in the starboard scuppers of the aft well deck and letting that side fill with rain water. There they washed suits, shoes, blankets and anything they could lay hands on. I can still hear the water swishing from one side to the other as the ship heaves slightly. The rain hardly stopped although by midday it had moderated somewhat.

I wrote a letter and later in the afternoon went through my photographs and stationery, mainly to check my meagre supply of the latter.

Mossy and I were chatting to the second this evening. He is aimiable enough to talk to but I gather he's getting everyone's back up. He was in both the German army and navy during the war. He and his father were at Stalingrad and his old man never returned. His mother lives in Hamburg. He gave us quite a list of the various land jobs he's had since 1945; is anything suitable turns up in Australia he will probably jump ship.

I am waiting for Len and Mossy who said they'd play a game of Lexicon.

10 January - Monday - Lat 1° 20' N, Long 22° 8' W I've been taking photographs on and off all day. My main object was to get a picture of the ship almost becalmed, as we've been for nearly a week. I took various aspects of the sails flapping; they move aimlessly backwards and forwards because of the slight swell. I went up on the end of the main lower yard arm to get a complete picture of the foresail looped up like draped curtains. I also began to take pictures of the deck from aloft by starting with the poop from the jigger-mast. It was easy clambering about in the rigging as there is only the slightest movement. The sun has been shining brilliantly all day and this made my work pretty hot (83½°).

Tonight the sky was clear and the stars twinkled in the moonlight. Just at present some large rain clouds are gathering; I didn't expect to see them after the clear sky of only an hour ago. I've been up on the foc'sle head talking to Lalu and latterly John, our youngest crew member.

Len and the second have been for rapid dips in the sea. There didn't appear to be any sharks around but you can never tell as they shelter under the hull.

11 January - Tuesday - Lat 0° 59' N, Long 23° 28' W We have been sailing slowly all day, at times we have been doing five knots; after floating about almost becalmed for a week this seemed quite a speed.

In calm weather extra work can be tackled by the crew. For some days they've been removing the footropes, testing, re-binding and tarring them before replacing. Other men are over the side chipping off the rust and painting with red-lead. Captain was a little worried today as we were moving; if a man falls from the rigging it is an accident, but if one was eaten by sharks through falling from a stage over the side it is unnecessary and therefore the skipper's responsibility!

We must be within fifty miles of the Line. As we approach preparations are being made for Neptune and his court; those who will perform the doctoring are getting excited and the others begin to wonder what will happen, (especially poor old Tom!)

Steward decided to wash all the soiled linen today. I rose half an hour early to assist him, (Plate 25) but pottered about doing practically nothing till breakfast. I did carry a few buckets of water from the dinghy, where the rain had been caught, to the galley for heating and then back again to the well-deck for steward and his wash tubs. That man has endless energy.

Whether or not it was the exertion in the heat this morning I don't know, but this afternoon my spirits were rather low and I felt most nostalgic for England.

Tonight I sat up overlooking the stern and watching the moonlight playing on the ripples that fanned out from the ship's eddies. I wished that one of my friends was here to share this entirely new experience. I found myself seeing and hearing familier sounds (we are progressing so slowly through the water that the lapping of the sea might be water on the side of any small craft on an English river). My desire to share was really a desire for companionship. Of course I could go up to the foc'sle head and chat with any of the boys or find the mate on watch, but these are people I don't know. In the end I decided that all was so un-familiar that I needed someone or something I could understand straight away. In England, wandering around the countryside, I knew the limits that the weather could reach, and I knew that I'd come across one old friend or another. Now I look at the sky and my surmises for the ensuing weather are invariably wrong; either we sail away from those particular conditions or they just don't come about.

12 January - Wednesday - Lat 0° 3' N, Long 25° 23' W   We crossed the Line about midday - tomorrow afternoon the celebrations!

The third gave me a lesson in serving cables this afternoon; we were doing one of the jib sheets.

The port watch bent another fair weather mainsail. (Plate 26) I managed to get several photographs of them at work; some I took from the foremast and its lower yard arms. I continued to make my selection of photographs of a lower yard this morning; I don't think there is much else I can take to any advantage at present.

I'm waiting for Charlie, Len and Mossy, we're going to have another game of Lexicon. Sunday night's effort was quite a success, the English beat the Aussies.

13 January - Thursday - Lat 2° 5' S, Long 26° 59' W   Everyone was teasey this morning including Captain. Steward roared at the cooks, mess-boy and myself in turn. He insisted on hanging sheets to dry with-out pegs and of course they dropped to the deck.

However, troubles were forgotten this afternoon when Neptune, (steward), rose out of the bowsprit net and came on board with his

29 *26th January* 'The watches have been hard at work bending the heavy-weather sails'

30 *1st March* 'It is difficult to believe that yesterday I was watching the largest waves I've ever seen'

31 *10th March* 'This afternoon the starboard watch furled the fore lower topgallant'

32 *29th March* 'We have had a pleasant surprise, about a mile astern lies *Pamir!*'

33 *31st March* 'Yesterday our first mail arrived'

Queen (Lindholm). Charlie was the doctor, Pinnochio chief astronomer and Bob Ryan clerk. The other Aussies who'd been across the Line were policemen and kept a close watch on the prisoners, who were shut up in the lamp-locker under the foc'sle head and were brought forward one by one. After the procession had greeted the Old Man, they returned to no 2 hatch where the royal pair were enthroned. Each man was led blindfold up a gang plank onto the hatch. (Plate 27) The black cloth was removed and they were questioned by the clerk; if any man was foolish enough to say he was a sailor he had extra doctoring. The chief astronomer asked the prisoner to look at the Line by peering into bottle which squirted sea water into their eyes. He then went spluttering to the foot of the throne and kneeling down kissed the Queen's toe. The doctor then weighed in looking very businesslike with a bag of carpenter's tools, a white coat and a stethescope made of a rubber tube and a funnel. Each patient was dosed with a spoonful of curry and mustard mixture, or a mouthful of Worcester sauce, or both. The donkeyman felt the need for alcohol to give him sufficient courage to act as barber. He was not sparking too efficiently by the time he came to shaving and tarring the unfortunate greenhorns. Simpson had a fair doing. But when Toni's turn came he refused his medicine and a fight began. In the end his bags were removed. The finale of the whole show was poor old Tom. The police began by removing his trousers, so Miss N and I had to retire. Apparently they tarred him from head to foot and cut off quite a number of his yellow curls. In spite of all his fuss earlier, he took his punishment much better than the Spaniard. The final act was to hurl the dirty prisoners into a sail full of salt-water which became somewhat discoloured by its unwilling bathers.

Apart from Toni's behaviour, they took their punishment extremely well. I must say the executors were most reserved and never allowed the fun to get out of hand. (Simpson succeeded in dragging Cory, one of the police, into the bath with him; otherwise all went according to plan).

Orders were given that I shouldn't go through the ceremony. This seemed most unfair; these folk don't know what to make of women on board.

14 January - Friday - Lat 4° 46 S, Long 29° 10' W The south-east trades which began gently on Wednesday increased yesterday and again today; once more we have a list to starboard. At present, due to the wind and current, we are less than 400 miles from Brazil and still heading WSW. We have done an average of ten knots per hour today.

The men began to paint the backstays. They do this with a mixture of white lead and tallow which makes them quite smart.

I've noted before that steward is a tireless worker. When there doesn't appear to be any work he goes round looking for some. Having completed the washing, boiling and airing of all soiled linen this week, he took the mats and carpets from the saloon and cabin and proceeded to scrub them this morning. They were dry-cleaned in Port Talbot. From eight till nine o'clock this evening we folded the clean linen. After that he transferred the carpets from the rail of the flying bridge to another line.

15 January - Saturday - Lat 7° 36' S, Long 31° 18' W We are now within 150 miles of the Brazilian coast. Either the wind will have to shift or we'll be forced to alter course. Captain is fed up with the wind this evening and hopes it will change to the west as we come closer to land. If it doesn't we shall find ourselves heading north east again. The Old Man's temper is usually indicative of the presence or absence of a fair wind. The third mate has been preparing a new forestay. This morning I took some photographs of him and the Finnish apprentice working on the fore cross-trees. It was lovely up there, the sea was bright blue with small white horses, and the white sails were bulging with the steady breeze.

16 January - Sunday - Lat 10° 10' S, Long 32° 28' W The wind veered round to the north east during the night so we are now running due south about parallel with the coast. The wind is fair and so is the Old Man's temper.

17 January - Monday - Lat 13° 32' S, Long 32° 59' W The weather has been really oppressive. There has been a good breeze blowing, yet a weight seemed to be pressing on one's temples and eye balls. Maybe we're too close to the Brazilian jungle.

The new fore-stay is in position and will be completed tomorrow; (Plate 28) I took some further photographs of work in progress.

I had a chat with chief this evening in the navigation house. He showed me the chart as he usually does if I ask him. Then he produced a number of others and discussed the various places and islands. Most of these have just been names to me but had very little other significance. We also talked about his wife and children; he softened down considerably, becoming quite different from his usual rough and tough self. He is the strongest man on board, the other members of the crew will follow him anywhere. 'Must come!', Chief's own expression has become part of our language, and the obstacle does come, however heavy the yard or uncontrollable a flapping sail.

Mossy pointed out some of the chief stars tonight and then we checked them on his star chart.

The kittens have been on deck for the first time. They found the world outside intriguing but somewhat overpowering. Their mother had them playing among the sails on no 3 hatch.

18 January - Tuesday - Lat 17° 19' S, Long 32° 23' W I've been using the captain's typewriter for some hours during the day. I wrote to mother and also typed out a copy of Donne's *Song* — 'Sweetest love I do not go'. I think I'll stick it up in my cabin and learn a few poems by heart.

The wind has been dying away all afternoon but there is still a heavy swell running. Although we've lost the permanent list to starboard the ship is rolling, flinging the sails to and fro and making an awful row, almost as if someone was turning hundreds of tools out of a large box.

If the skipper's temper is once more indicative, he thinks the wind is dying away too soon; we should lose the SE trades in three or four days but not before.

19 January - Wednesday - Lat 19° 56' S, Long 32° 23' W The forestay is now in position; the delay was due to the thread on the bottle screws being buried. We did an average speed of six knots today; the wind is lighter than ever tonight.

I washed my hair this morning. It dried faster than ever before, whether at home by the fire or under a dryer in the haridressers.

This evening there was a good sunset, the first we've had in the tropics, which is unusual.

20 January - Thursday - Lat 22° 00' S, Long 32° 8' W This afternoon I took photographs of the mainmast starting from the base and working up to the royals. I did this by climbing the mizzen and going onto each yard arm in turn until I reached the top. At Avonmouth I went right aloft, but hadn't done this before at sea. It was a beautiful afternoon and I found it most exhilarating.

We had some fun disposing of old rye-bread that was infested with weevils. Tom and I carried armfuls of packets Covent Garden style and flung them overboard.

21 January - Friday - Lat 24° 30' S, Long 30° 52' W The starboard watch braced this evening and we are now squared up. It was the first time since we left the doldrums eleven days ago that this has been necessary, apart from the slightest trimming once or twice.

We are nearly out of the tropics now, the weather is altogether fresher which is a relief.

A group of Welshmen and Australians had a short sing-song on the foc'sle head when I was up there this evening. I had a chat to Don who was on the look-out; he has toughened up considerably since the Avonmouth days.

22 January - Saturday - Lat 26 1' S, Long 29 48' W For the past few days steward has been searching for further soiled linen, carpets or anything else he could lay his hands on in order to launder them. As his search has been unsuccessful, he decided to check all the rye-bread and remove weevils.

Of course every biscuit harbours its colony of these insects. There were about 200 packets and we had to knock and brush every single biscuit. Steward and I began at 10 o'clock and finished at 5. I shall dream about weevily biscuits.

The wind has practically died out this evening. The crew painted the hull black from gunwhale downwards.

Tom has been in a foul temper, at first this was somewhat amusing but later became tiresome.

23 January - Sunday - Lat 26° 55' S, Long 28° 59' W It was raining when I got up this morning and continued steadily until mid afternoon. I sat in the navigation house for several hours doing a jig-saw puzzle. I beat chief by completing it fifteen minutes quicker than he.

I climbed up to the mizzen royal when the weather cleared; soon after I'd perched myself astride the yard a voice said, 'what are you doing up here?' Mossy was close behind me. We sat up there for some time and watched activity on deck, such as it is on a dull Sunday afternoon with little or no wind.

Captain has been in good spirits; he even went as far as confessing that his behaviour is somewhat eccentric at times. He soon relents and forgives me when things go wrong. Bet he was a tough master once upon a time; he must have been to round the Horn 39 times. He soon lays down the law, even now, when he sees weather, ship or crew getting out of hand. Mossy gave Tom a pipe last night; since then he appears to have smoked away many of his sorrows.

24 January - Monday - Lat 28° 13' S, Long 27° 46' W During supper the wind rose, had it been fair we should be travelling along about eight knots. As it is the royals have been furled and the lower sails remain looped up, because the head wind is rapidly driving us back towards the South American coast and we are trying to delay its efforts.

I timed myself when I went aloft today, six minutes to the royal yard — the record for this trip is one minute fifty seconds, so obviously I've got far to go. I was sitting astride the royals when I sighted a bird skimming the water, even from that height it appeared fairly large. I yelled down and got a reply that it was indeed an albatross. I was most impressed when it glided about fifty feet from the deck, the bird is aerodynamically perfect. The body viewed from the side is a genuine aerofoil section. I should think the wing span was about five feet, quite a small member of its species.

Mossy and I have been playing Chinese chequers this evening. All hands went back on watches tonight. Len and Mossy are on at 12 o'clock, so the latter won't get much sleep as it's 11 already.

25 January - Tuesday - Lat 28° 13' S, Long 27° 46' W The head wind has increased and although royals, upper topgallants and lower sails are furled we are still logging about 7 knots. We ought to head SE instead of SW.

Miss N fished out a small book of poems about the tall ships written by Isabella Kiernander. I copied one of these, since it is dedicated to the *Passat.* For an amateur her work was of a surprisingly high standard.

The starboard watch were bending another stiff weather lower top-sail this afternoon. As usual they made as many mistakes as possible, the second bawling at them continuously. This racket that goes on when he is on duty is becoming one of the ship's jokes, even the Old Man chuckles to himself.

I've just taught Tom to play Chinese chequers, he picked it up quite quickly, which shook me.

Mossy is on watch, there's not much doing so he came aft to have a chat. I gather the Southern Cross has an amorous effect on him.

For the first time for three and a half weeks I put on a vest this evening. This must be the longest period in my life that it has been possible to go without one, English summers being what they are.

26 January - Wednesday - Lat 31° 33' S, Long 31° 43' W The head
wind has died down considerably, we are managing to head further
south this evening.

The watches have been hard at work bending the heavy-weather
sails. (Plate 29) After I'd finished my duties I spent a couple of hours in
the rigging on the mainmast opposite the crew. I made a fair selection
of photographs as they were bending the mizzen upper topsail. I am
quickly gaining confidence clambering aloft.

We have four albatrosses flying around the ship today, the big one
that was with us on Monday is now accompanied by three smaller companions. One has a white body and dark grey wings which makes it even
more attractive. I don't think I shall ever tire of watching these birds
gliding.

The large pig was let out of her sty early this morning and was sniffing around the for'd well-deck. The small black kitten had its little paws
on the bulkhead looking out in amazement at this snorting giant. Both
kits are really attractive. I do hope they don't get hurt frolicking around
in the dark alleyways.

27 January - Thursday - Lat 33° 48' S, Long 32° 23' W At last we're
heading in a more easterly direction, about SSE, I think; the breeze is
very mild. The weather has been wonderful, warm enough to be comfortable and yet giving one plenty of energy.

When the Old Man gets rattled about something, he barks at the first
person within reach. I have unluckily been that person in the past two
days. He doesn't like anyone around him when he's taking the sun at
noon. Yesterday he was on the poop, which is not his wont, and so was
I, trying to feed the albatrosses with bacon. He grunted and mumbled
into his beard and said something about why didn't the steward find me
a job. At lunch but half an hour later it was all forgotten. I was foolish
enough to chat to Bill in the rigging and we both got a bark. This evening I just asked for it; I was feeling in a somewhat crazy mood and when
cook put one of the kits on the meat dish I marched into the saloon
with it. On another occasion all might have been well but I timed it
badly.

The second has a prejudice against Bill Castle, I really don't know
why, for he's a good type. Whether or not the Old Man believes all the
mate says about him, I don't know, but he also thinks he's unsatisfactory.

At any rate he was the only member of the foc'sle to bathe Toni when his hand was bad. The latter appears to have blood poisoning and is in pain. I suppose his Spanish temperament doesn't help but he's making an awful fuss, crying like a baby in the galley this evening. Mossy and Len came and had a chat before turning in. They both have an amusing sense of humour, especially Len who's so spontaneous. He has been splicing, rushing up and down the rigging, furling sails and threading buntlines all day – he yawns, stretches and as he departs says in a casual manner, 'H'm, I had a busy day at the office'. Had a little difficulty in getting rid of his friend; bout of 'Southern Cross fever' again.

29 January - Saturday - Lat 36° 25' S, Long 30° 2' W The fair wind has increased slightly this evening.

Last night, six weeks at sea seemed no time at all, this morning it appeared to be its full forty-two days. My thoughts turn homewards at the weekend and I begin imagining what the family are doing, I felt quite miserable this afternoon although the weather was once more superb.

I heard the six o'clock news from London at 3.30 pm (GMT). As reception had been so poor this was the first time since we sailed. Although it was good to hear a familiar voice the content was of small interest; it was like picking up a book and opening it in the middle.

30 January - Sunday - Lat 37° 28' S, Long 26° 47' W This morning the sun was sufficiently hot to give me quite a tan. During late afternoon the sky gradually clouded over and the wind increased. To my inexperienced eye it appears that a rough night should be expected. The watch on deck are furling the royals. We covered 180 miles yesterday, the current is favourable and took us 36 of those.

31 January - Monday - Lat 38° 38' S, Long 22° 8' W At midday we'd covered 230 miles in the past twenty four hours. It blew pretty hard last night and practically all day. The royals and upper topgallants and the mainsail have been furled, (the main and mizzen upper topgallants have just been set again). There have been no sails on the jigger mast for the past twenty four hours.

There are three men on board who don't waste water on their ablutions; they are captain, chief and, of course, Toni. The Old Man washes every other day when he remembers, in between nothing is done to his face which becomes grey all over, especially around the rough chin. Chief usually leaves his toilet until his clothes begin to fall off, when he changes a garment it reminds him to cleanse the skin beneath.

I dropped through the sky-light into the sail-locker this afternoon. Grälan has removed her young to this spot as she probably feels they are safer. It is ideal for their games, they climb on piles of sails, crawl into exciting passages amongst the cloth and stalk one another in the folds. I spent forty minutes down there thoroughly entertained by the fluffy kits.

Miss N is consistently amiable which is truly relieving after the varying moods one comes across on board. There are just a few things that aggravate her. One of these is leg-pulling by the third, who repeatedly tells her that it is unlucky to have women in a ship. She feels this is an aspersion against her many days in sail.

Someone in the foc'sle must have been teasing Tom once again; he has shaved off the hairs on his chest to prevent lice and last evening he went to captain for ointment to keep them away. 'De mess-boy he must be one of de simplest men in de ship' was the skipper's comment this morning.

1 February - Tuesday - Lat 37° 58' S, Long 18° 27' W Once more we begin a new month at sea.

The cloud rolled back from the sky early this morning, it's been a heavenly day again. The wind died down until we were only covering about five knots an hour; the swell remained giving us a slight roll. Photographically the weather was ideal, I took advantage of it this afternoon.

Chief called me into the mess-room this evening while I was washing-up. The cooks were catching cockroaches and he was sticking a needle into their abdomens, then giving the insects a little piece of stick. They held the wood, passed it upwards, turned it over and then passed it downwards again. This procedure went on continually until the poor little wretches lost their grip and were promptly squashed as a reward for their entertainment. At home I'd never condone such cruelty, but I know that to argue against it here would be useless. I am ashamed to admit that I was also amused by the antics.

The sunset was brilliant this evening: behind large grey clouds was a wide belt of bright green on top of which were bands of flame gradually becoming darker till they were crimson. These beautiful evening skies fade rapidly. This part of the world is noted for its superb sunsets; for some reason we have seen very few.

Tristan da Cunha is only about a hundred miles to the east, more or less in our course. I wonder whether we shall see it tomorrow.

2 February - Wednesday - Lat 37° 43' S, Long 15° 16' W We are almost becalmed once more, the lower sails are looped up as in the doldrums. This enabled me to take some more shots of the deck from aloft.

I was chatting to Len on the upper topsail yard this morning when he sighted a whale about 400 yards off the starboard bow. I saw it once only but was impressed by the mass of body heaving out of the water. It soon disappeared westwards. Len thought it was a sperm whale as the nose was blunt.

Chief, as our expert fisherman, tried his hand at trapping birds today. He wrapped bacon round a triangle of tin and succeeded in persuading an albatross to stick his bill into the triangle, so hauling him on board. Chief carried him struggling on to the well-deck where he paraded around in none too friendly a manner. We only kept him on board for a few minutes while the cameras were at work. He had a wing span of at least five feet and when standing reached a height of about two and a half feet. These birds have extremely tender webbed feet which bleed at the slightest provocation; they are also seasick; so for both reasons it is unfair to keep them on deck for long. They appear quite large as they circle the ship but still I was surprised how big they really are.

3 February - Thursday - Lat 37° 22' S, Long 14° 24' W There are about seventy miles between us and Tristan da Cunha; the question everyone is asking is if and when we shall see the islands. Another peaceful day with plenty of sun and very little breeze.

As I'd washed my hair I spent several hours on the poop drying it. This was best passed by reading. At present I am in the middle of Jane Austen's *Mansfield Park* – strange days when women never left home until they married and certainly they never thought of sailing round the world. These simple events, if described by another would be entirely commonplace. The atmosphere of eighteenth century England is a pleasant contrast to life in a square-rigger.

Mossy's 'Southern Cross fever' re-occurs with some regularity; three months at sea is a long time.

4 February - Friday - Lat 36° 32' S, Long 13° 19' W The large pig was slaughtered today: she was killed by stunning her with a mallet and then battering her brains in. Steward made a thorough job of the butchering as he does with everything else. We had blood pancakes for supper.

The second let the helmsmen get off course last night, instead of heading east we were going north. At 8 o'clock we tacked and are now heading south-west which is most unsatisfactory; instead of approaching the islands of Tristan da Cunha we are sailing away from them. Chief said tonight that we'd be lucky if we made Australia in forty days.

5 February - Saturday - Lat 37° 29' S, Long 3° 30' W During breakfast chief came to the saloon door to tell captain that one island of the Tristan de Cunha group had been sighted. At first it appeared fairly small and grey, gradually the mist cleared until its shape was quite plain.

Len, Mossy and I went to the royals with a telescope; this instrument didn't make much difference. However, from that vantage point, 220 feet above the sea, we could see more of Inaccessible Island. Further away was a long, low piece of land — later this was seen to be Tristan, for the clouds dispersed and we could see the 8,000 foot mountain. The cloud had been sufficiently dense to hide the higher ground. During the afternoon Nightingale Island and another large rock hove into sight, then we could look at all three together; by this time the mountain on Tristan had disappeared again in the clouds. It has been wonderful to look at land again even if we never approached nearer than fifteen miles. The sight has cheered everyone.

I finished *Mansfield Park* last night and went to sleep with my mind in eighteenth century England, far, far, away from the *Passat*.

6 February - Sunday - Lat 38° 12' S, Long 10° 32' W Another quiet Sunday has passed away. I've written a few letters and begun re-reading *Pilgrim's Progress.*

The islands had quite disappeared by this morning. The weather has been dull all day.

I cannot understand the reason, but Tom's rowdy behaviour towards me has changed for the better; it is a welcome change, his voice being far from harmonious at the best of times.

7 February - Monday - Lat 38° 41 S, Long 8° 42'. I wish yesterday's weather could have compared with today's clear sky and brilliant sunshine.

Captain is beginning to close all ports again. Although a deep sea man for so many years, he is definitely afraid of draughts. His apartment becomes almost unbearable to Miss N and myself; thank goodness I only have to eat in there. It is my intention to remove one of the four ports at regular intervals in order to clean them, but with the ulterior motive of airing the saloon.

Our ration of washing water is half a bucket per day. Some have been exceeding their quota and the pumps are now padlocked.

There has been very little wind for the past few days; the porpoise playing around the ship tonight are supposed to indicate that a breeze will soon spring up.

8 February - Tuesday - Lat 39° 15' S, Long 6° 20' W Captain called me to the navigation house this afternoon to look at a map of Mariehamn and the Aland Islands. There are about 6,500 of these isles, large and small. One day I must try to see them, they have a great attraction.

The map belongs to 'Sails'; in order to break the ice with that reserved old gentleman, I volunteered to return the map. There is peace in the sail-locker. To begin with it's comfortable because of the canvas, but more important is the influence of age, that is neither fighting for or against anything. For an hour I watched 'Sails' working while he chatted to me first of the islands and then of his days under English sail. He was putting cringles into the leech of a sail. As two bells struck he dropped his needle and prepared to leave the locker.

The carpenter has caulked the seams which cause leaks in Miss N's cabin and the saloon decks. First of all he chiselled out the old material, then refilled it with oakum packed very tight, and finally applied a thick layer of pitch.

The watches have been chipping and painting the inside of the hatches for the past two days.

9 February - Wednesday - Lat 40° 7' S, Long 4° 15' W This morning's sunshine soon disappeared, the breeze gradually increased and now a thick sea-mist has descended. The fog horn blows every second minute.

10 February - Thursday - Lat 40° 44' S, Long 0° 56' W The mist cleared around 5 o'clock this morning, however it hasn't been very bright all day. Towards evening a wide belt enveloped the ship, later gradually rolling away and disappearing eastwards. When I climbed aloft, as is my wont, the rigging had dew drops on it as after a Scotch mist.

The boys are baling out the bilges in the hold; there isn't much water in them. I took two time exposures down there. I wonder whether they will come out.

I've been making a menu for the saloon table. It's so made that I can insert the appropriate items as required.

11 February - Friday - Lat 41° 34' S, Long 1° 45' E The weather has been clear all day even if somewhat cloudy this morning. The mist returned tonight and with it the mournful sound of our foghorn. I looked up at the deathly white sails and thought we might be a 'ghost ship upon a ghostly ocean', every now and then a peculiar glimmer pierces the mist where the moon is still making a feeble effort.

Steward was amused by the menu I made yesterday; the small pieces fitting into the slots fascinated him. I have just completed a similar board for the galley — if it doesn't get covered in fat within two days it will be lost.

I paced out a distance of 120 yards in the 'tween decks this afternoon. I then walked and ran round and round the hatches until I covered one mile. After running a third of that way I was truly puffed; — too much food and too little exercise. Miss N and I played around with a small ring of rope for about an hour.

12 February - Saturday - Lat 42° 20' S, Long 4° 32' E The Scotch mist has persisted today, it is much damper than before. Tonight the sails are flapping aimlessly, a sign that there is no breeze.

Our crazy game of deck-tennis in the 'tween decks yesterday has gone one stage further. Mossy made a full size quoit with stout manilla rope; actually it was far too heavy and cumbersome and really it wasn't a severe loss when it went overboard, although we'd had quite a good game by then. While on watch tonight he's going to manufacture a lighter model.

Porpoise were playing joyfully around the bows this afternoon. This species have brown backs and are white underneath like the common dolphins. They really enjoy life, chasing one another at about twenty five knots, rolling over, diving and leaping from the water just for the sheer delight of living. Simpson cut an amusing figure as he came up on-to the foc'sle head in a maroon dressing-gown. No wonder they call him Gladys.

13 February - Sunday - Lat 42° 53' S, Long 6° 47' E While the mist is with us we cannot hope for wind. Although we travelled a hundred miles yesterday, this must have been in fits and starts, for it was practically calm last evening as it is again tonight. We are well into the Roaring Forties that don't roar and the Westerlies that don't blow.

Len and Mossy made a lighter ring. We set up a makeshift court and played quite a good game of deck tennis. Having rushed about for a couple of hours we than swarmed up to the royals to complete the morning's exercise. From there we could see porpoise round the bows. These were larger than those we saw yesterday, had no dorsal fin, their backs were black, their noses, undersides and fins were white and their tails grey. There is a dispute going on upon the difference between a porpoise and a dolphin. The only information that sounds reliable is to the effect that the first species range from five to seven feet long and the others from seven to nine. In that case the creatures that accompanied the ship for more than half a day were dolphin.

I have been trying to settle down to writing, but each time I have made an attempt something has happened to stop me. At last all is quiet.

14 February - Monday - Lat 42° 38' S, Long 8° 24' E I've been chatting to chief in the navigation house all evening. When I returned this note was sitting on top of my wet shorts which had been scrubbed in my absence.

'Clean Wash
for the stewardess
Adress s/v Passat
Lat 42° 58' 2
Long 0.8° 24' 1
time 12 14.2.49'

I think steward wrote it. The Finns are always washing their trousers and they considered my shorts required the same treatment. I guess they were a bit grubby.

Mossy and chief have been working on the motor boat for the past few days. I spent the afternoon helping Mossy tinker with the engine.

We sighted several whales this morning, they rose about a quarter of a mile from the ship. 'Espaniola' fished with a bucket until he caught two Portuguese men-o-war, these are small jelly-fish that have a tough vertical membrane which acts as a sail. Their bodies are Prussian blue, tinged with pink.

15 February - Tuesday - Lat 43° 16' S, Long 13° 47' E A fair wind sprang up last evening which blew us along at about 6 knots for twenty-four hours, it's now dying out again unfortunately.

Captain was sewing the motor boat sail on our deck tennis court this afternoon so we couldn't play.

16 February - Wednesday We sailed reasonably well this morning, sudden calm this afternoon followed by southerly wind.

Mossy, Len, Tony N and I played Chinese chequers this evening. Managed to do a little writing.

17 February - Thursday We have been dead becalmed all day. A slight breeze has arisen this evening but this is sending us south rather than east.

There have been twenty albatross sitting on the millpond around our ship; when there is little wind they require more energy to fly, at these times they spend the majority of their days upon the water and therefore get very hungry. We fed them with bacon and bread, they natter at one another growling like small dogs. Lindholm tied two rashers, one on either end of a piece of string; two birds made a grab and had a tug of war until one swallowed the whole lot, string included.

Len is scraping the inside of a life boat; I gave him a hand this afternoon. It reminded me of a similar operation on the *Puffin* first at Hammersmith and then Gillingham.

Captain fell off no 3 hatch this afternoon when he was cutting sails. He looked a bit shaken but seems all right.

18 February - Friday My first impressions on waking this morning were of swishing water and my slacks hanging at an angle over the bar; and as I washed and dressed I thought that now we should make a steady dash, driven to Australia by the force of the westerlies. On stepping outside I found the courses looped up and the royals and upper topgallants furled, the unfavourable wind was driving us further into the forties.

At 1 o'clock when the watches change and all hands are on deck, we tacked. The lower sails were already looped up. The spanker was taken in temporarily; first the mizzen then the main yards were squared; Captain gave the order, 'let go the staysails', which were made fast in the opposite position; the fore yards swung right over; then the mizzen and main completed their journey; the spanker was reset and all was well. The mad dash and the usual storm of abuse ceased. The *Passat* is now heading NW.

The mist has remained with us all day; it has been cold, damp and uncomfortable.

19 February - Saturday   Last night between eleven and twelve we tacked once more. By this morning the wind had veered sufficiently for us to remain more or less on course without going around. Our course has been ESE all day. The royals and mizzen course are furled and the yards are braced well over giving us a considerable list to starboard. Shifting boards at table again — bother!

It is amusing to find what childish and ridiculous trifles can entertain us after nine weeks at sea. Some of the port foc'sle have been reading wild west stories, they are dropping behind hatches and other shelters to fire their imaginary revolvers at one another, in much the same way as they did when they were small boys.

Thomas has been playing merry hell; I think the rougher seas worry him, at any rate he's been shouting and abusing me all day.

20 February - Sunday   We have been forced to head too far south by a stiff breeze which has now become a head wind. As we must be nearing $45°$ either the ship or the wind will have to alter its tactics. The mist cleared off this morning and hasn't returned since. Miss N and I, wrapped up warmly, were able to sit on the poop this morning.

The weather on the whole hasn't been inducive to work, so Sunday has passed with little to show. I read Lockhart's account of the *Mary Celeste* mystery, otherwise I've accomplished little. The temperature in these latitudes does not encourage writing in the cold, damp smoke-room. While I scribble this I am leaning on my dressing table because I've created a warm fug in my cabin which I don't wish to leave.

Tom continues his ludicrous railings; I've ignored the fool all day. He made an ass of himself by going to the captain about me. I gather he found little joy there for his loud mouth was somewhat silenced this evening.

'Espagnola' was chased howling into the rigging. When his pursuer had trapped him on the main top he was called off, because Toni was crying and shaking like a leaf, it appeared that he might fall at any minute. Slowly he clambered down the shrouds in a laboured fashion and went blubbering to the foc'sle. He is so very frightened of heights, and not much can be done about a situation which produces more work for the rest of his watch. He's quite a clever linguist, though.

21 February - Monday The wind has died down somewhat today, we've been averaging 5 knots and had it not been for the adverse current we might have added another 3. We are now about 13° east of the Cape and therefore that distance into the Indian Ocean. The temperature today is 51°, but last night it dropped a further 11°.

There are a few ice-birds around, small, grey and shaped like swallows. There is also a black bird the size of a crow but with a swallow's build. There were more whales blowing at a fair distance — we can see the spray when they are nearly as far away as the horizon.

Tom's behaviour was as bad as ever this morning but improved towards evening.

Captain has been in quite a jovial mood. He was relating some of his experiences, first in the Navigation School and then during world war 1.

22 February - Tuesday An excellent breeze has been driving us before it. This morning we were heeling over at an average of 12°. I snatched the opportunity of taking some photographs of the ship listing. Aloft I succeeded in photographing the starboard watch furling the royals — it was certainly good up there today! Captain decided to take in sail as the barometer was dropping regularly. At 4 o'clock the wind suddenly veered until it was immediately astern and the rain came down in torrents. It has been like that ever since. The second spent three hours roaring at his watch. He prevented the watch below from sleeping and thoroughly ruffled everybody's temper.

Len, Miss N and I played lexicon in the late afternoon.

23 February - Wednesday The superb wind which appeared yesterday has now died away, once more we are becalmed, the log is in board. Nobody expects to be stationary in the westerlies! The rain of yesterday gave way to sunshine this afternoon. I used this light for photography, taking shots of the brace and halyard winches. If I write I try to do it in the late afternoon as the smoke room is too cold and damp in the evenings. I then read tucked up in my bunk. The alteration in the weather also means that Mossy, Len and I see less of one another as the evenings used to be the time when we held our little gatherings.

24 February - Thursday We still lie becalmed. Apart from lack of wind the weather has been superb. I took advantage of the warm sunshine to wash my hair.

I had more exercise than usual today, not only did I run and walk one mile in the 'tween decks, but I also played quite a hectic game of deck tennis.

The Old Man has been in a more jovial mood than I've yet seen him in at sea. When he was sewing sails he was joking with chief and the old sailmaker.

A number of Cape swallows have been flying around almost dancing on the calm water when trying to catch a tit-bit.

Mossy and I have just had a long and interesting discussion upon our lives and where this unconventional path is taking us.

25 February - Friday We remain becalmed, with wonderful sunshine. Steward has retired to bed; I imagine nature has taken a firm hand and insisted that his body should have a rest. Tom was holding forth in the galley for over an hour this evening. He was in a pretty heated state by supper; instead of jumping into cold water he put his foot into a bucket of boiling water!

This is our seventieth day out and the end of the tenth week. I wrote to Jim this evening to say that I wasn't fed up as he'd prophesied.

26 February - Saturday No progress once more. Captain discussed the various things which might be delaying our passage. Although he admits that such superstitions are foolish, at the back of his mind he feels there must be some truth in them. He feels sure that working on the motor boat sails brings calm weather and adverse winds; he maintains that a captain should not work on deck.

Charlie, Cory and I were discussing the things that we miss most at sea – all agreed about the lack of fresh water.

The new foresail bent yesterday is far too large; this error is due to the unfortunate man who cut it out. Captain cannot roar at anyone this time, for he is the culprit.

27 February - Sunday Wind gradually increased today, unfortunately it is far from fair, the lower sails, royals and upper topgallants are all furled and there are no sails set on the jigger mast. It has been raining continuously. I gave the port watch a hand on the ropes when they hauled up the mainsail. Captain seems to think the wind may veer.

Mossy and I got a fug up in the smoke room this morning by lighting the blow lamp. After lunch it was too damp in there to play lexicon. Len and I retired to my cabin which is one of the driest places on board, thank goodness. Water is even coming into the saloon.

The galley is full of drying clothes, as each watch comes off duty they try to dry their gear before returning on deck. Captain gave the officers and others who dine in the messroom a drink all round this evening; it livened up our dreary hearts.

We tacked at 8 am.

On wet and rough nights I rarely get back to my cabin before 8.30 because I have to wait for Tom to do the washing up. Those he waits upon stay on deck until after 7.

28 February - Monday In the past I've complained of a list; for twenty-four hours the ship has been rolling like a steamer and we've been flung from side to side until I longed for the steady list again. Tonight we are braced to starboard and so I shall not roll out of my bunk as I nearly did several times last night. The galley, pantry and alley-way amidships were like a skating rink this morning, I began to loathe the thought of a trip for'd.

This has been our roughest day so far; foresail was set and no other lower sails; the royals and upper topgallants were furled, the main upper topgallant being set this afternoon; no jigger sails again; lower staysails only.

1 March - Tuesday The wind died out after midnight and once more we are becalmed. It is difficult to believe that yesterday I was watching the largest waves I've ever seen. (Plate 30)

The chief cook appears to have a slight kink, he is far too rough with me and much against my real wishes I had to mention his behaviour to captain this evening.

2 March - Wednesday Yesterday's calm was followed by a fair breeze which has blown us along at about 7 or 8 knots all day. At first we were listing to starboard, but since this afternoon the yards have been squared up, a good sign. Now we are rolling once more, but never mind if we get to our destination soon. If the wind persists we ought to make it in about twenty-five days.

Whatever captain said to steward and the cooks has had a marked effect upon their behaviour, I have been treated with the utmost courtesy today.

For the past few weeks I've been considering the points for and against returning in *Passat*. It would be an experience to round the Horn and would provide further writing and photographic material. I should also have time to devote to my ICS course. However with these advantages come five months cooped up in a ship; in three months one has sufficient opportunity for observing the social life aboard; another prolonged period would provide little new. I am well aware that my name is down in the crew list as signed on for the round trip, but if my course home does not lead round Cape Horn this will not be an obstacle.

3 March - Thursday It really appears that we are at last running our easting down. Yesterday we covered 222 miles, it's a long while since we reached 200.

If the photograph I took on the lower foreyard arm comes out it ought to be quite impressive. I was sitting on the tip well over the sea and took the water swishing away as the bows cut through it.

The third allowed me to have a lesson at the wheel this afternoon; it is much harder work than I'd imagined. Tony Newton was instructing me.

A sudden roll developed during last night, it threw me backwards and forwards until I woke up. Apparently it lasted for about an hour. We've been exceptionally steady today when one considers the sea and wind.

4 March - Friday Last night there was a slight squall which rent the lower spanker, this is not a serious loss as it already looked like a patchwork quilt. Len and Mossy bent a new one and I gave them some assistance; it occupied my morning and gave an excuse for leaving my domestic duties, I'd much rather work on deck than below.

At 7.30 am tomorrow we shall have been at sea eleven weeks. The length of our trip is beginning to tell; at times I was slightly depressed but the mood soon disappeared, now there is an ever present desire to make our Australian landfall. Mossy played deck tennis with me this afternoon which brightened life a bit.

The small pig was slaughtered this afternoon; a case of ten little pigs and now there is one. There was very fresh pork for supper, but few would eat it, captain included.

5 March - Saturday The wind continues fair although we are braced to port this evening.

Last night I foolishly tried to wedge my lamp on the dressing table in order to read in bed. The ship heeled over suddenly, the lamp went skidding across the table and struck the bulkhead. I made an attempt to replace the glass but it rolled on to the deck and was smashed to smithereens. I now have a botched up arrangement which gives a poor light. There are only one or two spares in the whole ship.

6 March - Sunday   Another quiet and damp Sunday has passed. I wrote a bit this morning but have done very little else which could be called constructive.

7 March - Monday   The westerly breeze continues although it is more gentle than last week. The sea is also running in a favourable direction which makes the ship fairly steady, there are small white horses as the wind catches the tops of the larger waves.

Mossy has agreed to become my hitching companion to Melbourne. I am glad to have someone to accompany me on my first trip of this kind in Australia.

Tom's latest ambition is to become a barrow-boy selling fruit in Liverpool. This idea struck him with enthusiasm this afternoon, we've heard nothing else since, he imagines he is already a made man. I expect there'll be another idea in a couple of days.

8 March - Tuesday   The wind abated this morning until it veered, now we continue on our way at the steady pace of about 6 knots. Captain says that another seventeen days ought to see us lying off Port Victoria. The sun has been shining, first time for ages. After breakfast captain screwed up his face like a spoilt child and said, 'Ugh! Vash-day.' One of the few occasions when his ablutions occupy more than half a minute. Mossy and I took down our daily positions from the old log book which made them up to the middle of last month.

Steward suddenly decided to hunt for cockroaches in the pantry cupboards this evening; it didn't matter that the washing up was in progress or that he couldn't see at night, he'd found another task and would dash at it until the job was complete. I gather he must have broken the lamp-glass for he's just been to the drawer in the smoke room for another; I heard his usual puffing and blowing.

9 March - Wednesday   This is really sailing, the log is now registering 14 knots in the hour, and we haven't done less than 10 all day. Yesterday's mileage was 239. The ship is rolling from $15°$ to $25°$ to port. The weather has been ideal for photography; Len and I spent sometime this morning scrambling around obtaining good angles; at one stage in the proceedings I was made fast by a gasket to the shrouds and was leaning outboard. On the jibboom I managed to take several shots; there the water is sliced by the bows and hurled outwards in a translucent surge until the foaming crest turns under and can be seen rushing up like smoke in the clear water. I'm very glad that the trip did not end without some strong weather. I've enjoyed myself today. The royals were furled in the late afternoon.

10 March - Thursday   The seas have been even greater, some higher than houses. Below life has been difficult but on deck it is thrilling. Several minor waves have been shipped which is unusual for a vessel in ballast. Our roll has varied from 5° to starboard to 30° to port, at the latter position it is only just possible to keep one's balance on a dry portion of decking. This afternoon the starboard watch furled the fore lower topgallant (Plate 31) — I swarmed up the mainmast into the equivalent position to photograph them. It was glorious up there, from the crosstrees you could watch the massive waves gathering and spilling their foaming crests all around the ship; looking at the water was like gazing at an ever-changing landscape of hills and valleys. The man on the windward side of the wheel now wears a safety belt to prevent his being flung over the top. I am finding it increasingly difficult to write at this angle. A slight squall hit us this afternoon and the jigger staysail which was in the process of being set had to be cut down to prevent it blowing out.

Last night there was a squall which lasted for about half an hour, our outer jib blew out and I nearly fell out of bed. It is not particularly comfortable rolling about in my bunk. We covered 284 miles in the last twenty-four hours, 290 is our record so far this trip.

The sails set at the moment are:
fore: topsails and lower
main: lower topgallant and topsails
mizzen: topsails
jigger: none
fore topgallant: staysail
main topgallant: staysail
mizzen: top staysail

11 March - Friday   I hope two weeks today we shall at least be in sight of land.

The gale has abated somewhat and the sea in accordance; however, we are squared-up and rolling like a steamer. I believe the record is 25° to starboard and back 28° to port. The motion is affecting everyone's temper. Yesterday's mileage was 241. The mainsail is set but the royals and upper topgallants are not nor the jiggersails, the staysails are also furled. Upper topgallant and two topsails have been bent on the fore mast, the starboard doing one and the port watch two in the same time.

I took the opportunity of writing this afternoon as I don't know when we shall be sufficiently steady again. With the mattress pulled over the side of my bunk and a rug tucked under that I slept like a log and I hope to do the same tonight.

12 March - Saturday The strong wind continues. In four days we've covered 1140 miles. Today the log read 234 for the twentyfour hours. During a period between two and six o'clock this afternoon there were four squalls, none of them lasted for any length of time. The second squall cleared away rapidly and a yellow sun shone upon the sea making the waves appear bottle green; three quarters of an hour later the sky grew dark grey and the sunlight became a mock as it shone upon the stormy scene, the wind appeared to whirl because while the mainsails were bulging forward the mizzensails were blown back against the mast. Captain took over at the wheel for the duration of the squall; it is most unusual for a skipper to do this. A few more sails are set.

For the past two evenings captain has been picking up the news and times signal from Melbourne. Until yesterday he'd been getting London and Greenwich time, (more often nothing at all).

13 March - Sunday The gale is increasing this evening, the mainsail is in again. The weather has been too rough to encourage me to write or mend; I've read a little but nothing else; it's a full job keeping one's balance. Squalls have been beating upon the ship at an average of two an hour all day. During one of these Mossy was flung right over the wheel, luckily a large lump on his leg is the only damage. Captain had been telling us but half an hour before that men have broken their necks in this way!

If this wind holds we ought to reach our destination in about a week. Tonight we are in the longitude of Western Australia.

The donkeyman is a good type; at weekends he helps the cooks to clean up the galley in the evening so that they may have a few hours of leisure.

During a squall last night a chain sheet (for upper topsail) was rent apart. At three in the morning the unfortunate members of the port watch were repairing it. Hail has beaten upon the decks twice today; it has been freezing cold.

14 March - Monday At midday there were 1,100 miles between us and Port Victoria. We are about 600 miles south of Perth and the wind continues. This morning the royals and cro'jib were set but were furled again this afternoon; I took a rough weather photograph of two men on the main royal. If the wind could remain as it is now we would reach our destination in four days. However, this is unlikely and a week would be a nearer guess. Last night several waves hit our weatherside with such force that for a minute I thought we'd struck an iceberg or something equally solid. This was the first time that I'd been scared. The ship steadied up for a time and I began to imagine that she was settling in the water.

(Mileage 243)

15 March - Tuesday The wind has been dying down all day, I pray that it won't disappear for we are so near now. Yesterday we covered 257 miles.

16 March - Wednesday Today's mileage is a hundred less than yesterday's. However, the breeze is fair and continues steady, as this rate we ought to reach Port Vic about Monday. This pleasant thought is putting everybody in a good humour, *Passat* is a happy ship tonight. I've been collecting signatures to stick in the back of this diary. Everyone is most cheerfully disposed but chief says he never signs such things.

17 March - Thursday If the wind doesn't veer further we shall reach our destination in about three days. Is it exciting! Port Vic may be a dump but it's built on *terra firma*. Events of the next week ought to prove interesting after three and a half months. Five people including myself were working on the motor boat this afternoon in order that we may go ashore when we reach the anchorage. Although the jobs could have been done during the long months at sea, they have been left till the last few days.

18 March - Friday O woe betide! We have been becalmed all day, the wind died out just after I'd finished writing last night. Here we are so near — yet so far and no guarantee as to when we shall reach Port Vic. All the cheerful faces have become solemn and the crew depressed. However, the sunshine has been glorious, a week ago the gale was blowing and the atmosphere nearly freezing. It is difficult to imagine it now.

(Mileage 90)

19 March - Saturday   I've been helping Mossy and Holgar to paint the motor boat this afternoon. As I was working I felt a gentle breeze fanning my cheek, then I heard water lapping the hull and knew that we were just moving again.

Last night I tried on my few dresses, blouses, etc and to my dismay found they were all too tight. How I must have put on weight.

20 March - Sunday   The gentle breeze continues, we've averaged about 6 knots. The direction appears to be changing, it is coming from the SE and I hope it won't veer further.

It has been pleasant weather and sunny this morning. I collected most of the crew's signatures and took more photographs this afternoon. As a Sunday it has been more profitable than the last few.

I was reading in bed last night when three bells sounded from the foc'sle head. A steamer had been sighted on the starboard bow, it crossed our track and turned about 400 yards away; Mossy answered the signal querying our identity, I wonder if it reported us? The fact wasn't given on the news from Adelaide today. It was the first sign of life since we saw a steamer on 29 December.

21 March - Monday   O dear! Head wind again, by midnight we shall have tacked three times in twenty-four hours. At present we are only 100 miles from Neptune Island, but when we go around at twelve we shall be heading in the opposite direction. The wind is increasing and still coming more or less from the east. The masts are undressed and are only wearing topsails and lower topgallants, even the staysails are in tonight.

There is one advantage in this weather, my washing dried in a couple of hours. I was worried lest it blow away but all was retrieved safely.

Steward continues to work himself into a frenzy, he's been rushing around like a madman this evening, any minute one imagines that he may give a shrill squeak and disappear in a puff of smoke.

22 March - Tuesday   The entire ship's company has been on deck to view the Southern Lights *(Aurora Australis)*. They first shone as search lights radiating from the Pole, then the sky above became pink and later crimson, looking much like the aftermath of an incendiary raid. We are virtually hove-to, the topsails alone remain set and we are as it were pacing about outside the strait; we're about 130 miles from land with little hope of decreasing this distance until the wind veers.

Steward asked the Old Man to tell me to 'doby' my trousers, he really is fussy, but captain and I couldn't help being amused by his concern. The sunshine has been glorious and most suitable for drying the despised garment. Captain completed the sail for the motor boat this afternoon. He now imagines that we shall get a fair wind.

23 March - Wednesday We continue to pace up and down like an agitated beast, a few fore and aft sails have been set to make the ship point further up into the wind. The weather forecast from Adelaide hinted that the wind would change to the north which would be nearly as bad as it is now.

I washed the walls and deck over my cabin this morning, it doesn't look much better but from the dirty water that I poured overboard it must be.

Bill Loosemore amused us this evening by suddenly clucking in a frightened way that made us all imagine there was a hen in the galley — Steward answered by crowing.

24 March - Thursday Sailing prospects are a little more hopeful, lower sails and topgallants are set this evening.

Captain has been like a child with a new top; chief set the sails in the Old Man's motor boat, the owner has been admiring his handiwork all afternoon.

Another steamer came fairly close in the early hours of the morning. I heard about it when I got up.

25 March - Friday Today is Conception Day which is celebrated by Lutherans as a holiday; the number of British far exceed the Swedes, nevertheless no work has been done on board and the hours have passed away much like any Sunday.

Len showed me all the ropes around the jigger and mizzen masts this morning. I've started to make a diagram of the information which he gave me.

He and I had our first game of deck tennis for sometime, the rough weather interferred with this form of exercise. I must get into some sort of training before beginning to hitch once more.

I'm reading the third book of the *Forsyte Saga*. There was something sound and admirable about conservatism as pictured there; Galsworthy had a subtle way of describing human relationships and in this particular case he portrayed the awkward and ungraceful characteristics of youth.

Gladys was at the helm this afternoon wearing a black pin-stripe suit, collar and tie. It appears that he was airing his civvy clothes; not a bad idea but it did look amusing.

We continue to tack up and down waiting to enter the straits.

26 March - Saturday Fourteen weeks at sea and still a head wind blowing, not a cheerful outlook for those who are on board *Passat*. Yesterday evening I was very depressed, today Mossy has the same bug; everybody is longing for the shores of Australia.

'Sails' helped to raise my spirits by his cheerful manner of relating incidents in his long life. He took me into his cabin and illustrated his tales with photographs, many of them old, faded and battered. His family are of the professional class, disliking his stepmother he left home and went to sea. He appears to have no regrets that he has not had a distinguished academic career like his brothers.

I began letting out some of my civvy clothes this evening.

27 March - Sunday So endeth the 100th day of our voyage and the most perfect day we've had. This is Australian sun and Australian skies, blue as one sees them only on the rare occasion over Britain; the crew have taken advantage of the perfect weather by lazing on deck and I have been no exception.

The breeze improved a little, all sail is set, we continue to tack, Kangaroo Island can be but 100 miles to the east.

28 March - Monday At 9.30 am chief sighted Kangaroo Island. It goes without saying that everybody was excited but the Aussies nearly went mad with joy. Bill C has not seen home shores for nearly five years. The wind is northerly, forcing us to tack every three hours. At 6 o'clock we must have been within ten miles of land. Tonight we can see the lighthouses flashing, one is Cape Borda and I imagine the other to be Cape Redout.

Although I've only been scared once when the large wave hit us

during the gale, I must say I thanked God for the welcome sight.
I won't make any wild speculations this time about the date of our arrival. The anchors were heaved over the side today and remain suspended until we reach the ballast ground.

Little white seagulls like doves came out this morning as if to welcome us into Australian waters. Their cousins the albatross have nearly all left the ship, a few of the smaller variety remain.

29 March - Tuesday - 6.30 am An hour ago I watched the continent of Australia turn from grey into yellow and dark brown. It was no good watching this from the deck, the royals were the place for me. We are sailing towards Corny Point in Spencer Gulf with another three hours to go before we reach the ballast ground. The wind backed to the south west about 4 o'clock, we proceed steadily towards our destination with the yards squared-up.

11.30 am: Half an hour ago I stood on the foc'sle head while the anchor splashed into the sea dragging the great chain after it. Sails were gradually furled, first the royal, then topgallants, next the cro'jack and main, then the flying jib and staysails, followed by the fore and then the topsails, the spanker was last to come down. We lie about a mile off Wordang Island and five from Port Victoria. The latter place is really difficult to pick out due to its minute size. All this was expected. We have had a pleasant surprise, about a mile astern lies *Pamir!* (Plate 32)

8.0 pm: The SW wind increased this afternoon. The Adelaide radio reported that the Finnish barque *Passat* was sighted in the Gulf at 9 o'clock, that she was a beautiful picture sailing under full canvas in the sunshine, that she came to anchor at midday and began discharging ballast near *Pamir,* (of course this is pure imagination because we have done nothing of the kind), and that the harbour master, Mr Edwards, the doctor and customs are waiting for calmer seas before venturing out in a small boat. A small 'plane flew around this afternoon apparently taking photographs for the press. I do hope someone brings the mail out tomorrow.

I asked captain about going to Melbourne with Len and Mossy, at first he made a number of excuses and then told me it would be all right if the emigration officers have no objections. When I left him I went to tell Miss N. She feels that the Old Man is not bold enough to tell me that he'd rather not take me back. I shall have to leave that in the lap of the gods.

31 March - Thursday - 7.30 am   It was already after midnight when we returned from Port Vic, there was no point in writing at that hour, so I will recall yesterday's events now.

I have set foot in Australia at last. The events of the evening were trivial but wonderful after these long months at sea. I thought that to put foot on land once more would be a queer sensation but I might have left it a few hours before. I guess I must be a landlubber.

One thrill followed upon the heels of another yesterday, beginning when our first mail arrived (Plate 33) and ending when we returned to *Passat* early this morning. I had about a dozen letters, a welcome packet. All seems well and reasonably happy at home and I am profoundly relieved on that account. Mrs Irving sent a telegram and two letters inviting me to the station as soon as possible — this is a surprise. There was nothing from Maurita; however, when Mossy leaves I intend to hitch to Melbourne with him.

The press were on board all day, correspondents from the *Advertiser* early and later those from *Women's Weekly*. Peter, their photographer, proved to be amiable and will assist us when we stay in Adelaide and also supervise the development of my films. I heard my name on the air at lunch time yesterday. I must say I've done very little to deserve all this publicity.

Miss N treated us to dinner at the Wauraltee Hotel. It was excellent. Fresh food — goodness me! There was a calf lowing behind the Post Office when we went there for tea and cakes later in the evening, it was too glorious to be true listening to sounds on shore and sniffing the scents associated with growing things.

Captain wouldn't take me ashore this afternoon; as events turned the jetty; having previously expressed his love for Mrs Agar, the post mistress, he continued to sing at the top of his voice across the six miles of Gulf between Port Vic and *Passat*. He ended by trying to fight the steward, luckily Miss N averted this catastrophe. It was pretty choppy coming out by motor boat at that hour. Taffy and Peter were in the bows with no brains and one pair of eyes between them, Tom was too scared to go for'd as we came alongside; seeing that we should be crushed against the hull I grabbed for the rope hanging from the boom, (unfortunately I had to submerge my watch several times in an effort to get at it). We eventually made fast without further panic.

9.45 pm: Nothing of particular interest has happened on board. I've packed most of my gear for Len to take tomorrow.

Captain wouldn't take me ashore this afternoon; as events turned out it was just as well, for I was prepared for the emergency which occured when the motor boat returned in the dark. The sea was still very choppy, captain leapt on to the bottom of the gangway and Miss N tried to follow. Somehow or other she slipped and fell in the water between the platform and the small boat. The Old Man yelled at the top of his voice and fled up the gangway. Hearing the scuffle I rushed down the long flight of steps. By that time Frank had her arms and gradually drew her into the boat; he then passed her to me and I grabbed her fast round the waist and 2nd cook escorted her on deck; meanwhile chief who was roaring drunk was slipping around in the boat and yelling at everyone in turn. He had apparently been so busy abusing captain *en route* that they were off their course several times.

I dried and reclothed Miss N, gave her hot water bottles and sweet tea, followed by a delayed supper. Captain dressed the bash on her leg and generally fussed around. She is sleeping over in the saloon tonight and I think will weather the storm.

2 April - Saturday Miss N was much better but still rather shaken by yesterday. She wished me to telephone to her friends on the station, so captain allowed me to go ashore. I put on a skirt for the first time in fifteen weeks; Mossy told the crew who lined up along the gunwhale to cheer me as I went down the gangway!

I did my few commissions in the township and went for a stroll along the foreshore. There is little on the peninsula except sand and sparse scrub; it didn't matter because I was enjoying all the little things, smells and sounds and the very fact of walking on dry land. The bird life is more varied here, on the shore I watched small birds with dark grey backs, white bellies and no tails, they were trotting around in the shallow pools and on seaweed; there are a number of shags who look clumsy after the albatross; the white and pale grey seagulls are the most attractive, they have bright red beaks and legs. Wandering to the top of Port Vic I found a few miserable cows walking about on the scorched grass and there was one newly-born calf with its mother.

When we land at the jetty there is a ketch loading wheat for *Pamir,* as we walk up to the shore horse-drawn trucks are running on the single track line. We put foot on land and ask one another, 'where's Port Vic?' I think the best way to describe this place is to say it is a cross between an English holiday camp and a Mexican township where the cowboys come galloping in on horseback. The bungalows have verandas outside and a low iron rail just suitable for making fast your horse. However, I didn't see any cowboys, just a few carts careering up the only street and one or two cars which had left the factory in the early 1920s.

The second boat came in about 11 o'clock at night, by that time I had given up hope that it would ever come. When they did arrive, Len and Mossy decided to stay at the hotel for the night, I believe three of them slept in the same bed. Mrs Agar, the wife of the postmaster, put me up and gave me supper and breakfast. Captain Bjorkfeldt from *Pamir* stayed there too, he is a jolly little man, rather full of his own importance.

When we came back to the ship at 10 o'clock this morning, he followed and returned to Port Vic with captain. The boys left after lunch leaving Miss N, myself and about five others on board. We have lain at anchor in a calm sea and beneath clear, cloudless skies, the sun has been just hot enough. Miss N and I had all our meals on the bridge, laid out on the life-belt box.

3 April - Sunday   Last evening when I wrote this my intentions were to continue writing a letter and then retire early but I was foiled. At 8.30 a jolly little party gathered round the saloon table, they were Captains Hagerstrand and Bjorkfeldt, Miss N, *Pamir's* chief mate and his wife Molly, our chief and myself. One can hardly count Mr Kitchen as he was bowled over very early. At 3.30 this morning those who were still sober succeeded in breaking it up. At first all went well and drinks were followed by coffee and cakes. Our chief sang a little but was perfectly amiable; as he consumed more his hostile attitude towards the Old Man welled up, everything pointed to a fight which we had to avoid at all cost, chief is a very strong man. Over and over again we diverted them by one of three things — singing, dancing and, as a last hope, by Molly flirting with captain. As they wouldn't let him attack the Old Man, chief suddenly grabbed hold of me, his chair broke and we both fell over backwards, where he stayed for sometime. Luckily the two officers from *Pamir* were little affected by the alcohol and were able to help us cope with the situation. I locked my cabin door for the first time since we set sail. Chief was still drunk this morning and behaved in an obstreperous manner whenever he saw me.

The peaceful day we spent on *Pamir* has been a contrast indeed. An immaculately served lunch was prepared for us and an equally excellent tea. The officers' and stewards' department over there is heaven compared with the bedlam that reigns here. The crew are mainly sailors unlike our mixed bag, we should be called the home for unsuccessful students.

Their crew, and in fact all their living accommodation, is good; the remainder of the ship is not in such order. I took several pictures from aloft. I have now been to the royals on two square-riggers. I must not forget to add that we had our meals where but a few months ago Princess Elizabeth and the Duke of Edinburgh were entertained.

This afternoon *Pamir's* chief took Mr Kitchen, Molly, three of their crew and myself over to Wordang Islands. It was a perfect afternoon and dead calm. There was a well in the fishing boat moored at the jetty, in it were fishes of all colours; blue and bright yellow, pink, purple and green. There was also a squid, in fact here was an aquarium where we least expected to find one.

Pamir's officers were just cheerful enough last night to enjoy my company more than they would under normal circumstances and I have been long enough at sea to understand why a sailor has a wife in every port.

4 April - Monday The mess boy was amongst other members of the crew still ashore, they went on Saturday afternoon and returned today. Apparently he fell off the jetty while drunk and noone would rescue him until an American, seeing him rise for the third time, dived in and saved him. Both crews have been creating havoc in Port Vic, I don't know how the unfortunate inhabitants will survive for two months.

Captain and Miss N have been ashore most of the day. I had little to do in consequence and enjoyed quite a bit of sunbathing. As the men at lunch had reverted to peasoup and pancakes, I sat on the poop in the sunshine and feasted off fresh banana, peach, tomato and apples. It was just what the doctor ordered.

Unless events go against us, Mossy and I ought to leave on Wednesday morning; Miss N will leave at the same time.

I must now retire to my cabin as there is a hectic party amidships; chief has been carried to his cabin; donkeyman and Lindholm are roaring drunk and the majority are more than cheerful. I'll lock my door again tonight.

5 April - Tuesday It was just as well that I barred my door as I had two visitors. Heinz, the quietest man on board, came to invite me to promenade in the moonlight, I declined but he returned twice asking me to join him in a drink. Mossy came later and wanted to tuck me in, he was despatched in a similar manner and all was quiet. Chief was still tight this morning and threatened me with a carving fork on which was a large lump of pork. 'I'm still a man if you're not a woman', he said, nearly breaking my ribs as he put his arm round my waist. I'm glad to say he went ashore when *Pamir's* motor boat towed our's away.

For a few hours Miss N and I had some breathing space. I bid *Pamir's* chief goodbye this morning as I am leaving tomorrow. He and Captain Bjorkfeldt returned for tea and suggested another party as a farewell. Chief has gone over to fetch his wife. I wonder if another night like Saturday is in store for us?

7 April - Thursday - 6.30 am   Mossy and I are sitting on the side of the road waiting for the lorry which gave us a lift last night. We signed off yesterday afternoon and set out on our hitch first to Adelaide and then to Melbourne. The first lift was in the Royal Mail car from Port Vic.

At 12.30 yesterday afternoon I left *Passat* in her motor boat. Captain signed us off in the agent's office and added 'you are free'. Yes, I am and what exciting prospects. All the same as I looked back across the bay, there was considerable regret in my heart that I'd left the tall ships.

Index

INDEX 213